REALM OF THE DAMNED

TENEBRIS DEOS

ALEC WORLEY
Writer

PYE PARR
Art, colours & lettering

Additional colours by
Steven Denton and Luke Preece

WEREWOLF PRESS

Creative Director and CEO – Steve Beatty
Technical Director – Adrian Wear
Design – Adrian Wear, Matthew Harle

Published by Werewolf Press Ltd
Avtech House, Hithercroft Road
Wallingford, Oxon, OX10 9DA
United Kingdom

www.werewolfpress.co.uk

ISBN – 978-0-9934158-1-4
Printed in The EEC
First Printing April 2016

A CIP catalogue record for this book is available from the British Library.

For more information please visit:

www.werewolfpress.co.uk
www.facebook.com/werewolfpress

www.realmofthedamned.co.uk
www.facebook.com/realmofthedamned

REALM OF THE DAMNED

OF THE

®

DAMNED

TENEBRIS DEOS

PART I

HELL'S HUNGER

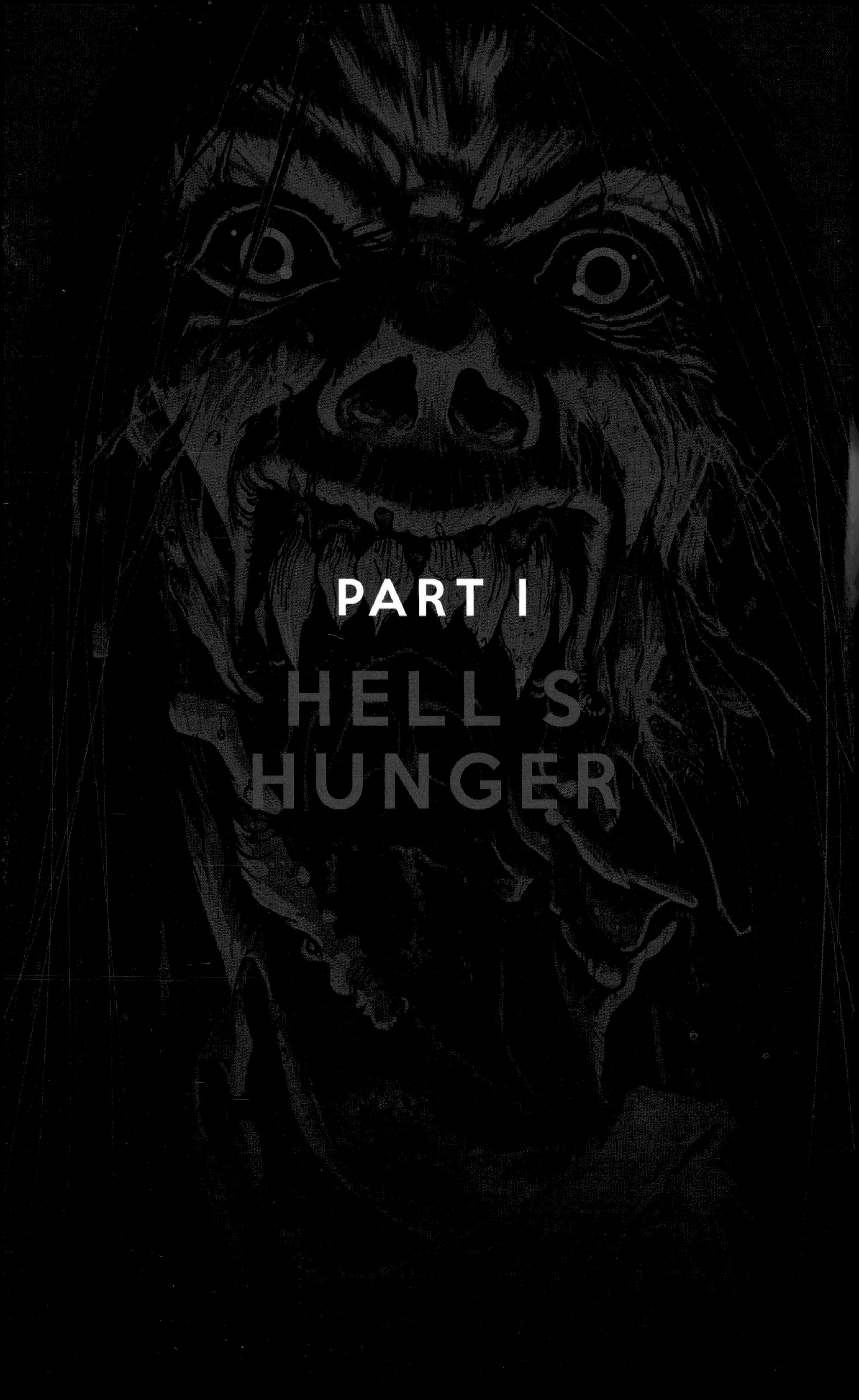

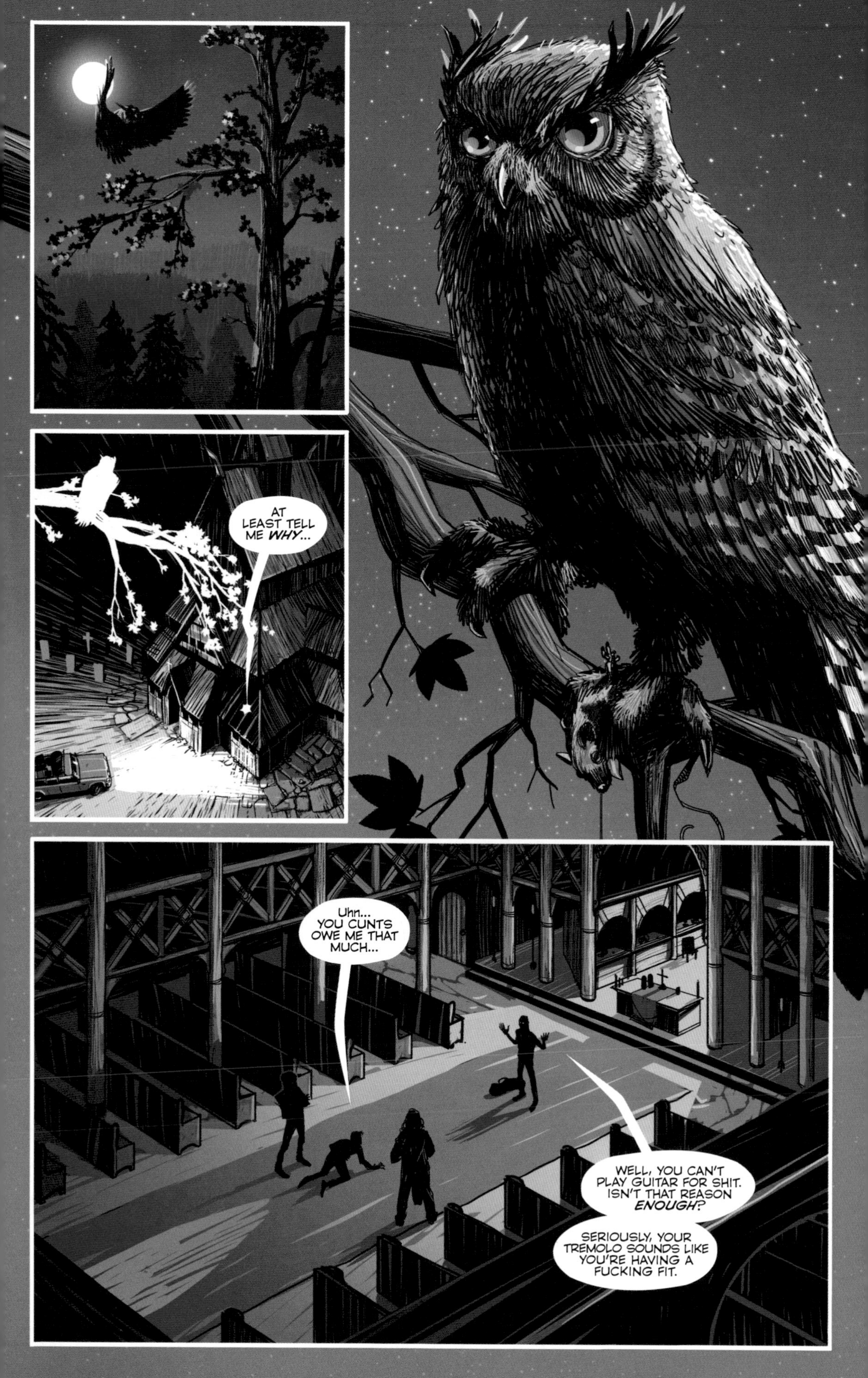
AT LEAST TELL ME *WHY*...
Uhn... YOU CUNTS OWE ME THAT MUCH...
WELL, YOU CAN'T PLAY GUITAR FOR SHIT. ISN'T THAT REASON *ENOUGH*?
SERIOUSLY, YOUR TREMOLO SOUNDS LIKE YOU'RE HAVING A FUCKING FIT.

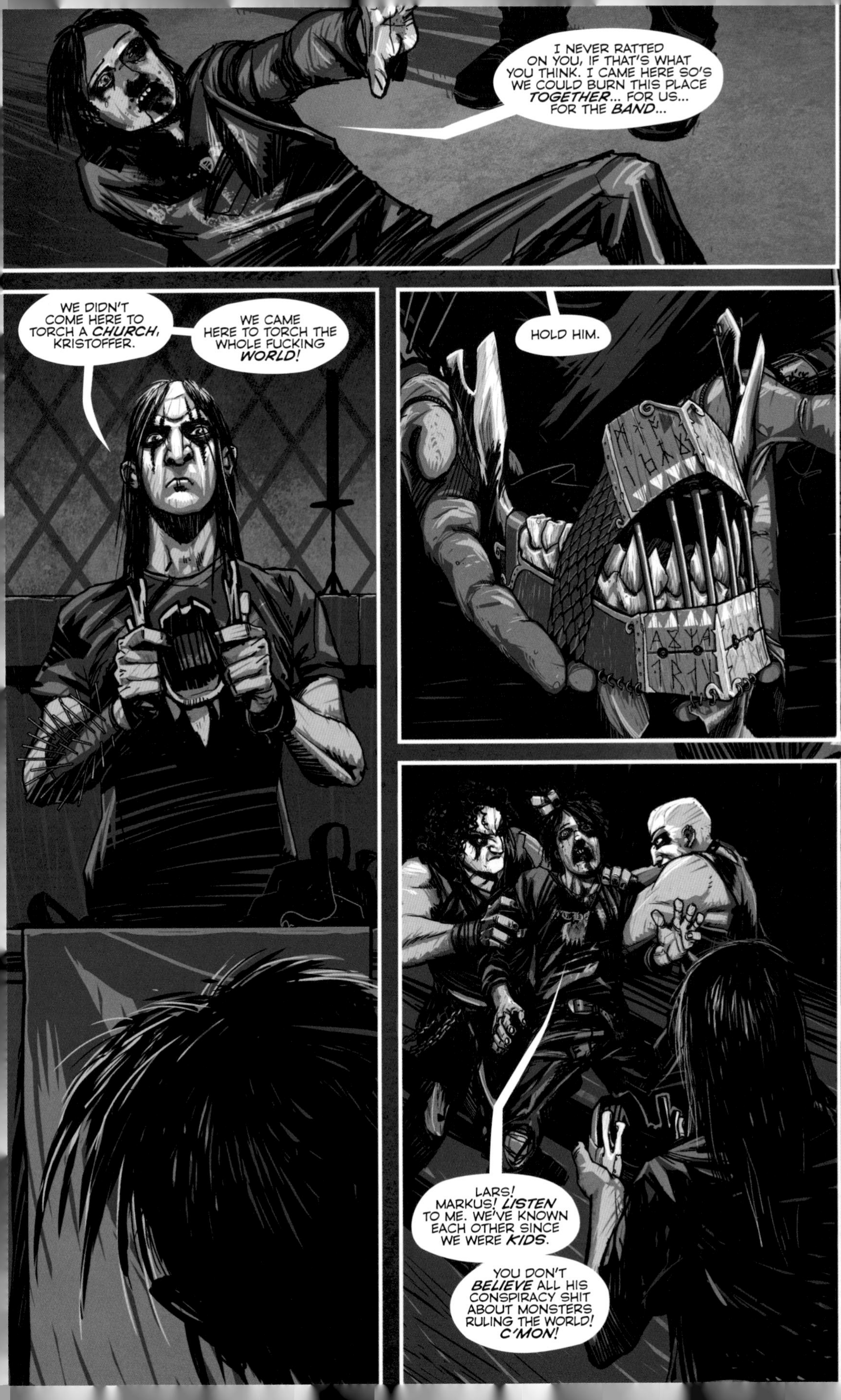
I NEVER RATTED ON YOU, IF THAT'S WHAT YOU THINK. I CAME HERE SO'S WE COULD BURN THIS PLACE TOGETHER... FOR US... FOR THE BAND...
WE DIDN'T COME HERE TO TORCH A CHURCH, KRISTOFFER.
WE CAME HERE TO TORCH THE WHOLE FUCKING WORLD!
HOLD HIM.
LARS! MARKUS! LISTEN TO ME. WE'VE KNOWN EACH OTHER SINCE WE WERE KIDS.
YOU DON'T BELIEVE ALL HIS CONSPIRACY SHIT ABOUT MONSTERS RULING THE WORLD! C'MON!

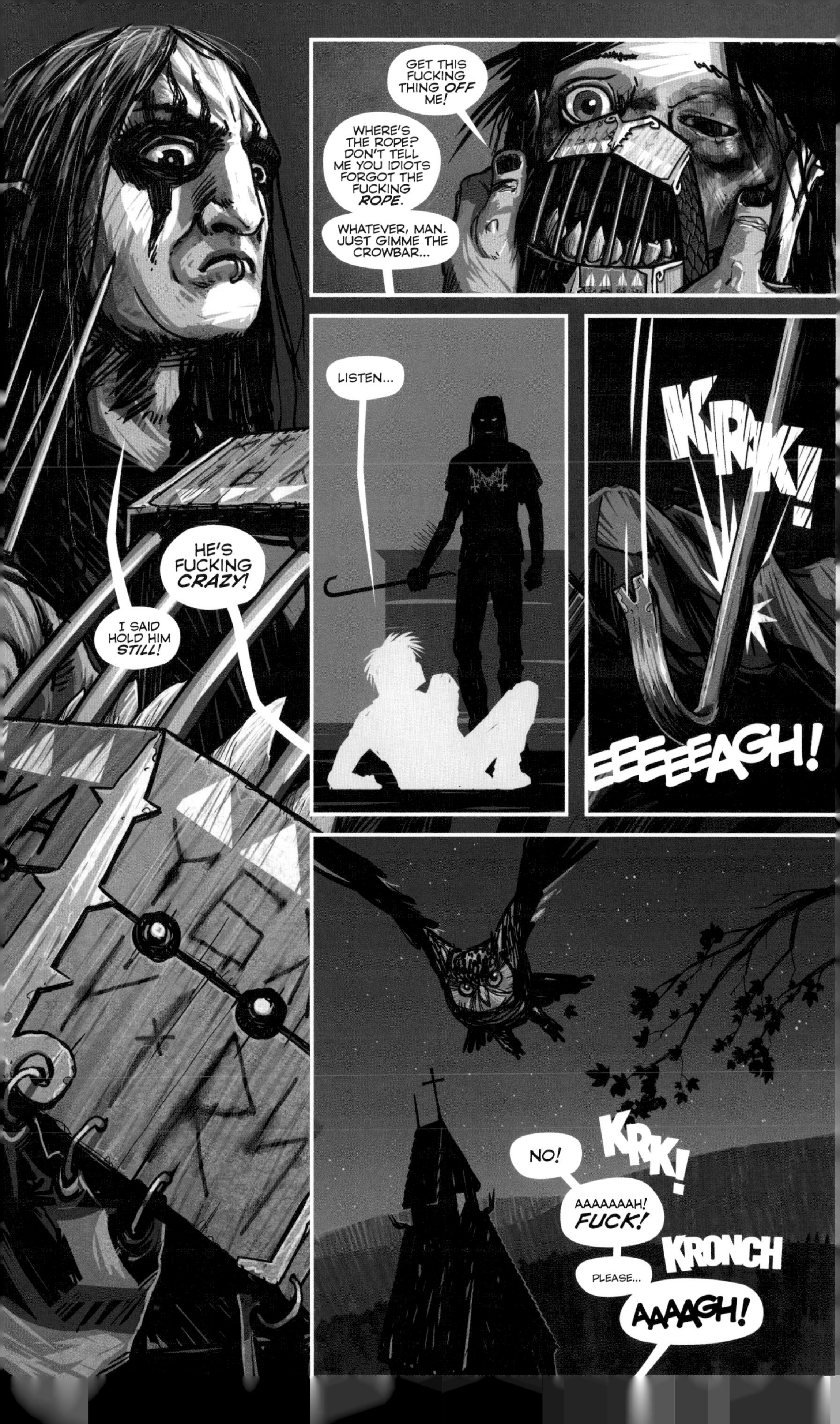
GET THIS FUCKING THING *OFF* ME!
WHERE'S THE ROPE? DON'T TELL ME YOU IDIOTS FORGOT THE FUCKING *ROPE*.
WHATEVER, MAN. JUST GIMME THE CROWBAR...
HE'S FUCKING *CRAZY*!
I SAID HOLD HIM *STILL*!
LISTEN...
KRRK!
EEEEEEAGH!
NO!
KRK!
AAAAAAAH! *FUCK!*
KRONCH
PLEASE...
AAAAGH!

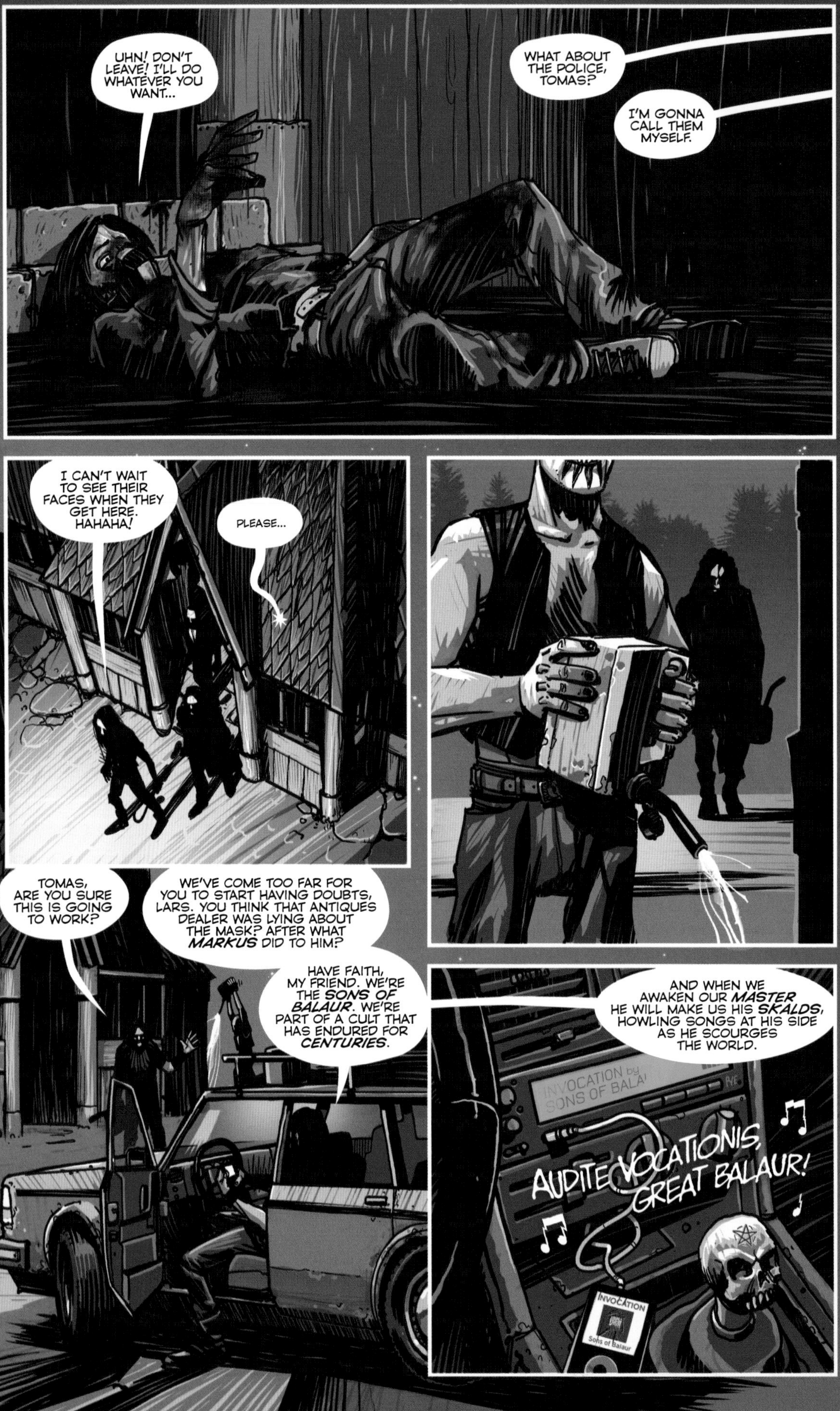
UHN! DON'T LEAVE! I'LL DO WHATEVER YOU WANT...
WHAT ABOUT THE POLICE, TOMAS?
I'M GONNA CALL THEM MYSELF.
I CAN'T WAIT TO SEE THEIR FACES WHEN THEY GET HERE. HAHAHA!
PLEASE...
TOMAS, ARE YOU SURE THIS IS GOING TO WORK?
WE'VE COME TOO FAR FOR YOU TO START HAVING DOUBTS, LARS. YOU THINK THAT ANTIQUES DEALER WAS LYING ABOUT THE MASK? AFTER WHAT *MARKUS* DID TO HIM?
HAVE FAITH, MY FRIEND. WE'RE THE *SONS OF BALAUR*. WE'RE PART OF A CULT THAT HAS ENDURED FOR *CENTURIES*.
AND WHEN WE AWAKEN OUR *MASTER* HE WILL MAKE US HIS *SKALDS*, HOWLING SONGS AT HIS SIDE AS HE SCOURGES THE WORLD.
AUDITE VOCATIONIS, GREAT BALAUR!
INVOCATION
Sons of Balaur

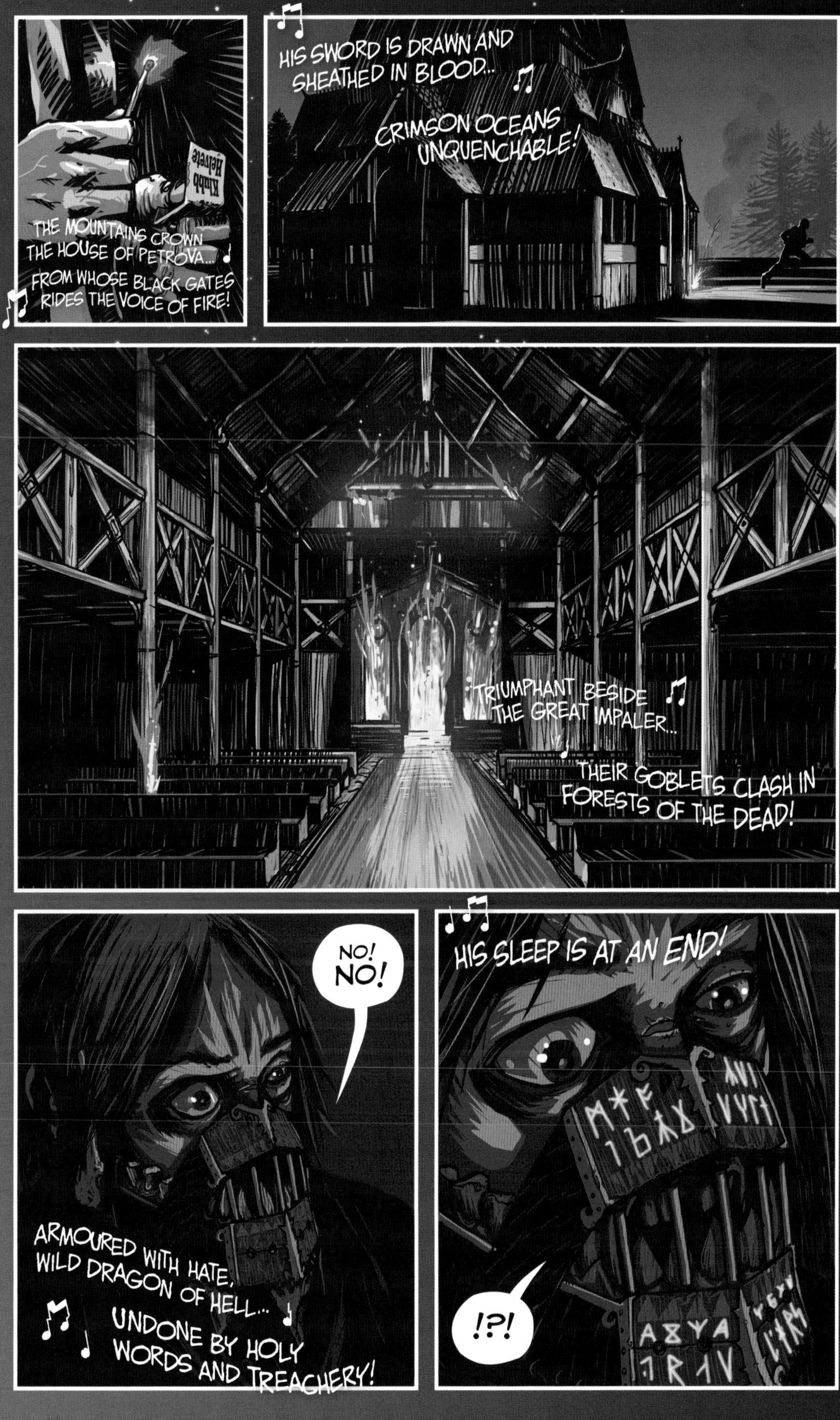
Klubb Helvete
THE MOUNTAINS CROWN THE HOUSE OF PETROVA...
FROM WHOSE BLACK GATES RIDES THE VOICE OF FIRE!
HIS SWORD IS DRAWN AND SHEATHED IN BLOOD...
CRIMSON OCEANS UNQUENCHABLE!
TRIUMPHANT BESIDE THE GREAT IMPALER...
THEIR GOBLETS CLASH IN FORESTS OF THE DEAD!
NO! NO!
ARMOURED WITH HATE, WILD DRAGON OF HELL...
UNDONE BY HOLY WORDS AND TREACHERY!
HIS SLEEP IS AT AN END!
!?!

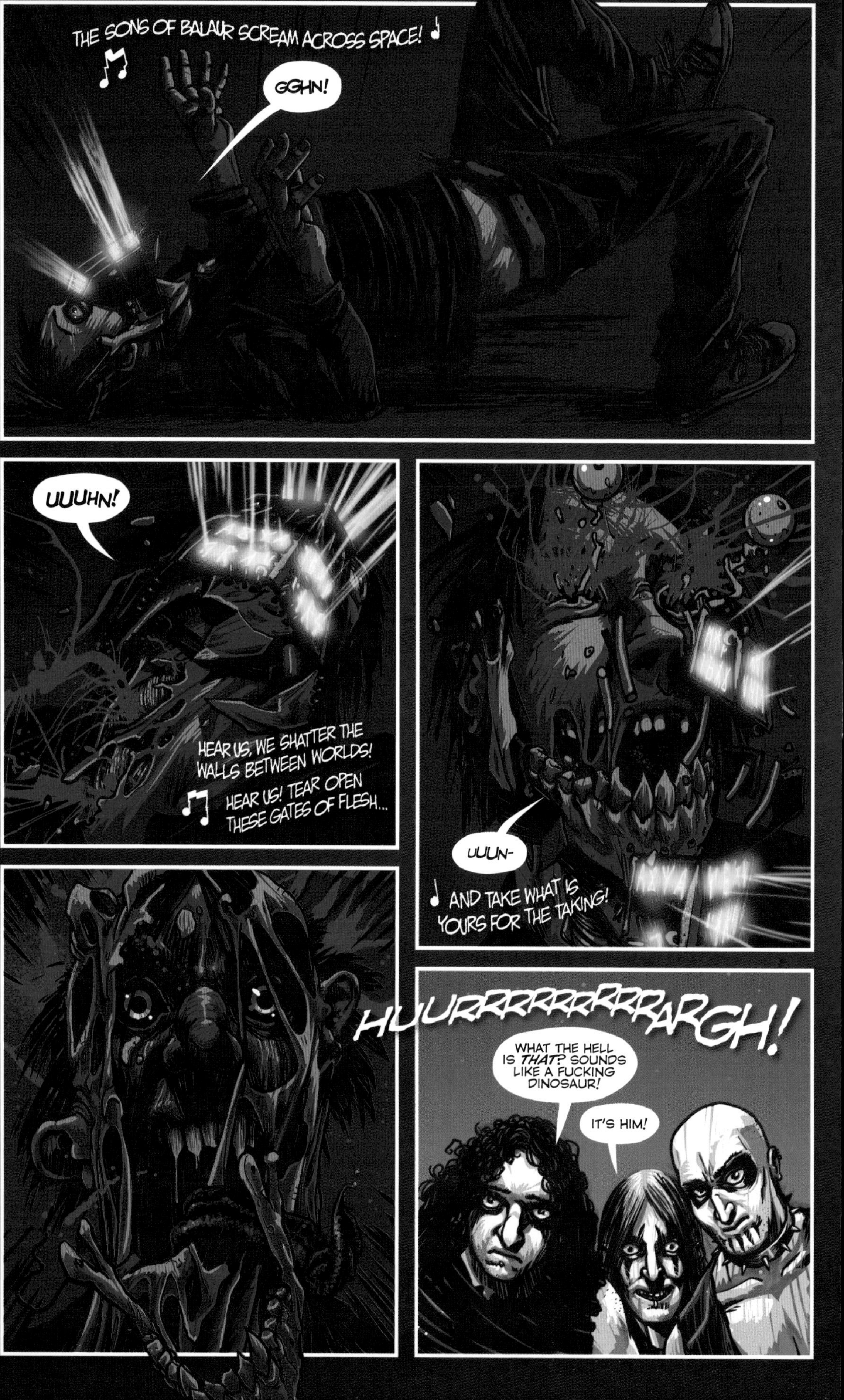
THE SONS OF BALAUR SCREAM ACROSS SPACE!
GGHN!
UUUHN!
HEAR US, WE SHATTER THE WALLS BETWEEN WORLDS!
HEAR US! TEAR OPEN THESE GATES OF FLESH...
UUUN-
AND TAKE WHAT IS YOURS FOR THE TAKING!
HUURRRRRRRRRRARGH!
WHAT THE HELL IS *THAT?* SOUNDS LIKE A FUCKING DINOSAUR!
IT'S HIM!

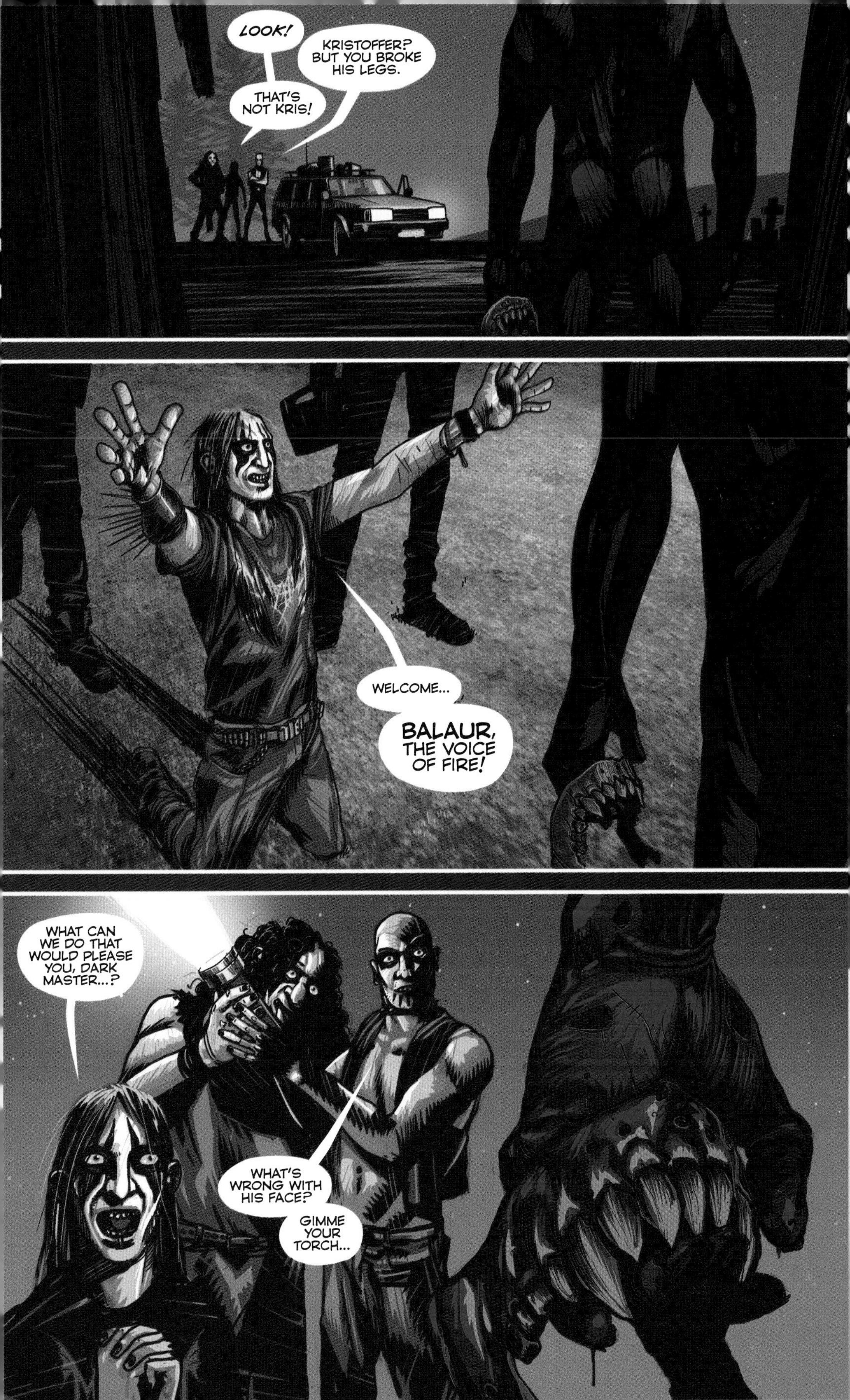
LOOK!
THAT'S NOT KRIS!
KRISTOFFER? BUT YOU BROKE HIS LEGS.
WELCOME...
BALAUR, THE VOICE OF FIRE!
WHAT CAN WE DO THAT WOULD PLEASE YOU, DARK MASTER...?
WHAT'S WRONG WITH HIS FACE?
GIMME YOUR TORCH...

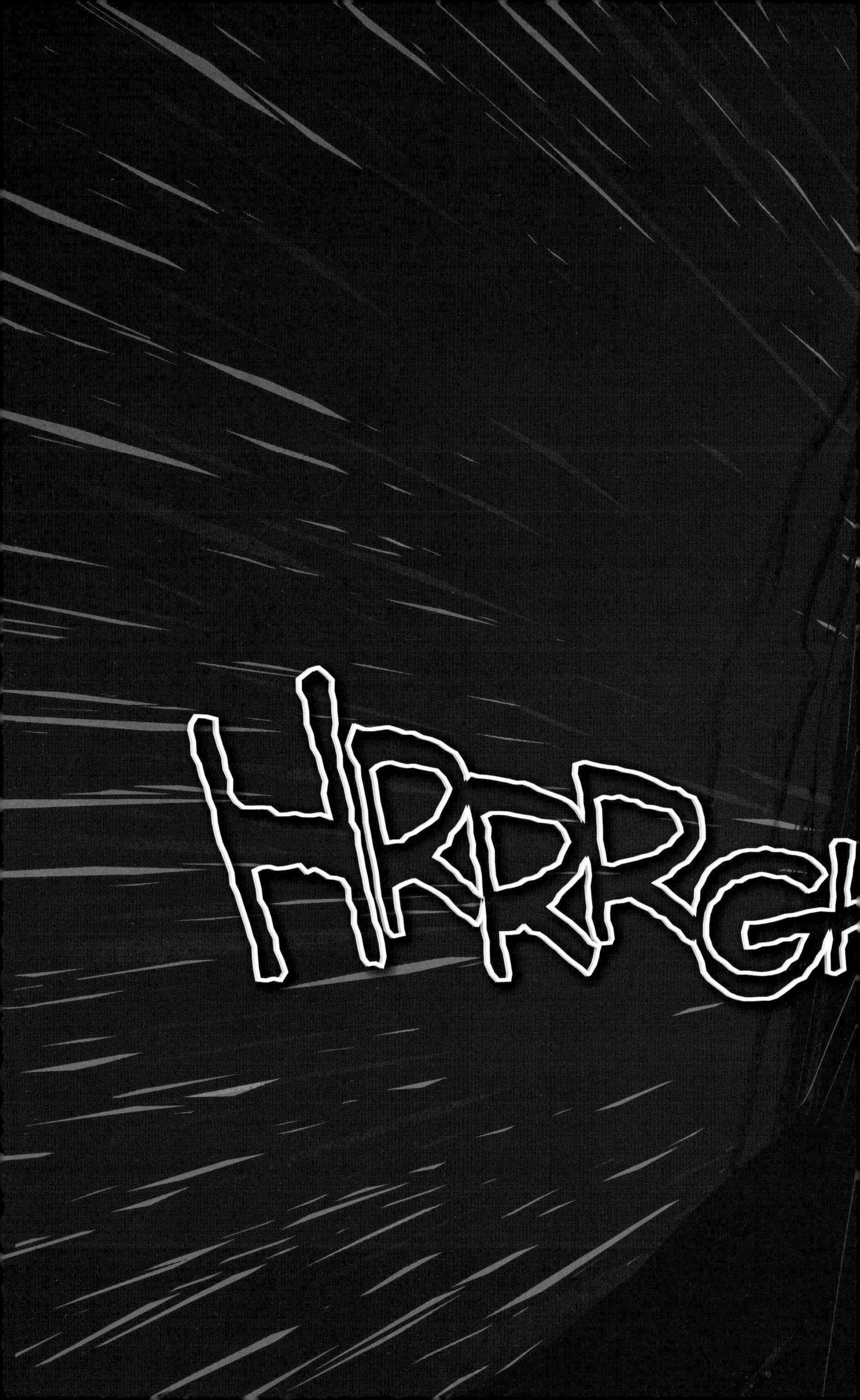
HRRRG

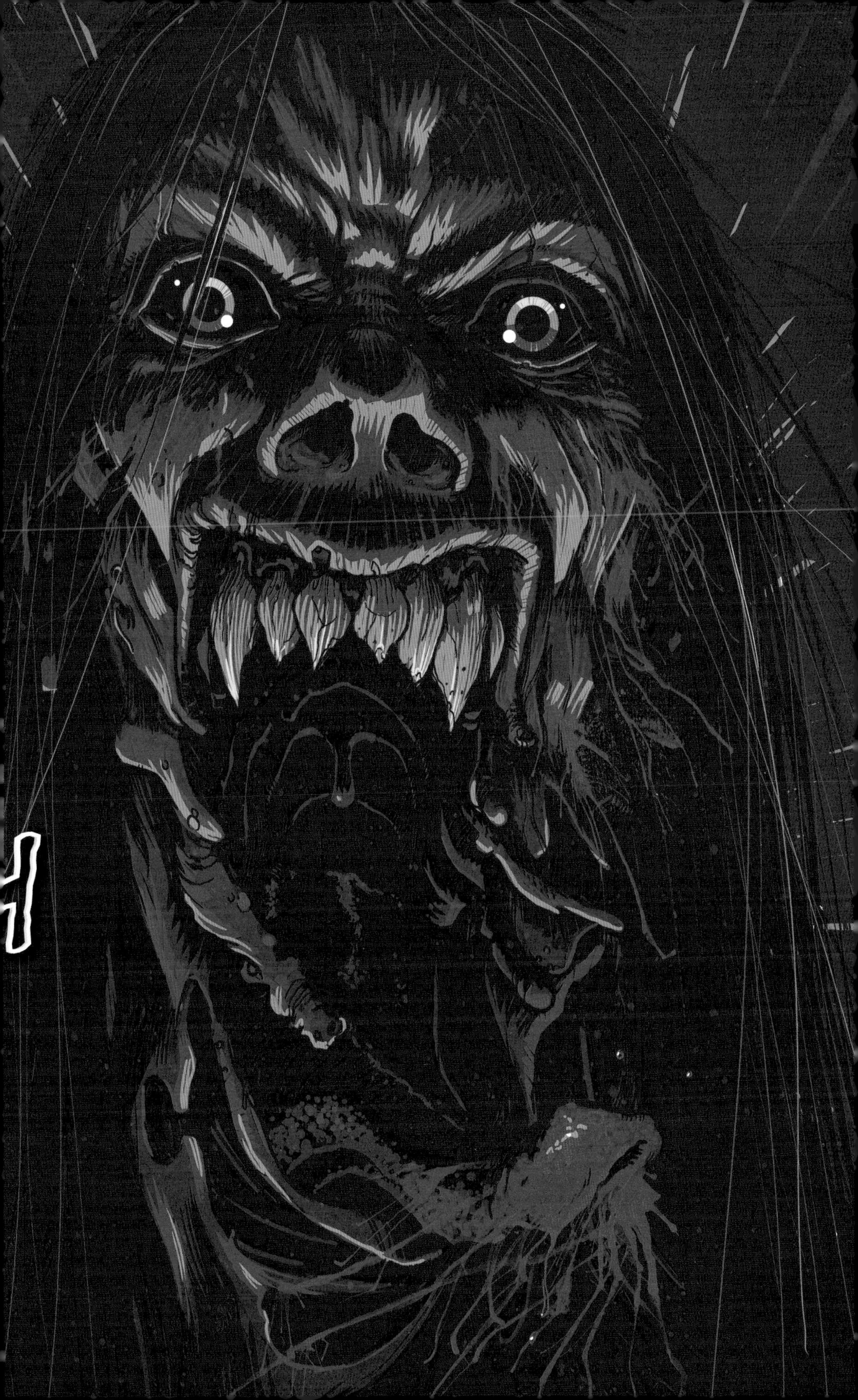

YAEEEEI!

HA HA HA HA HA!

AAAA!

UHN!

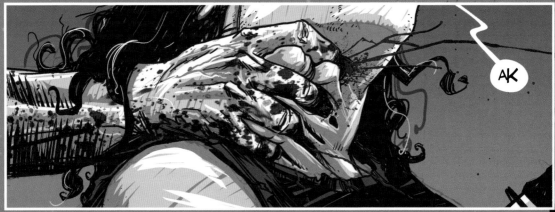

AK

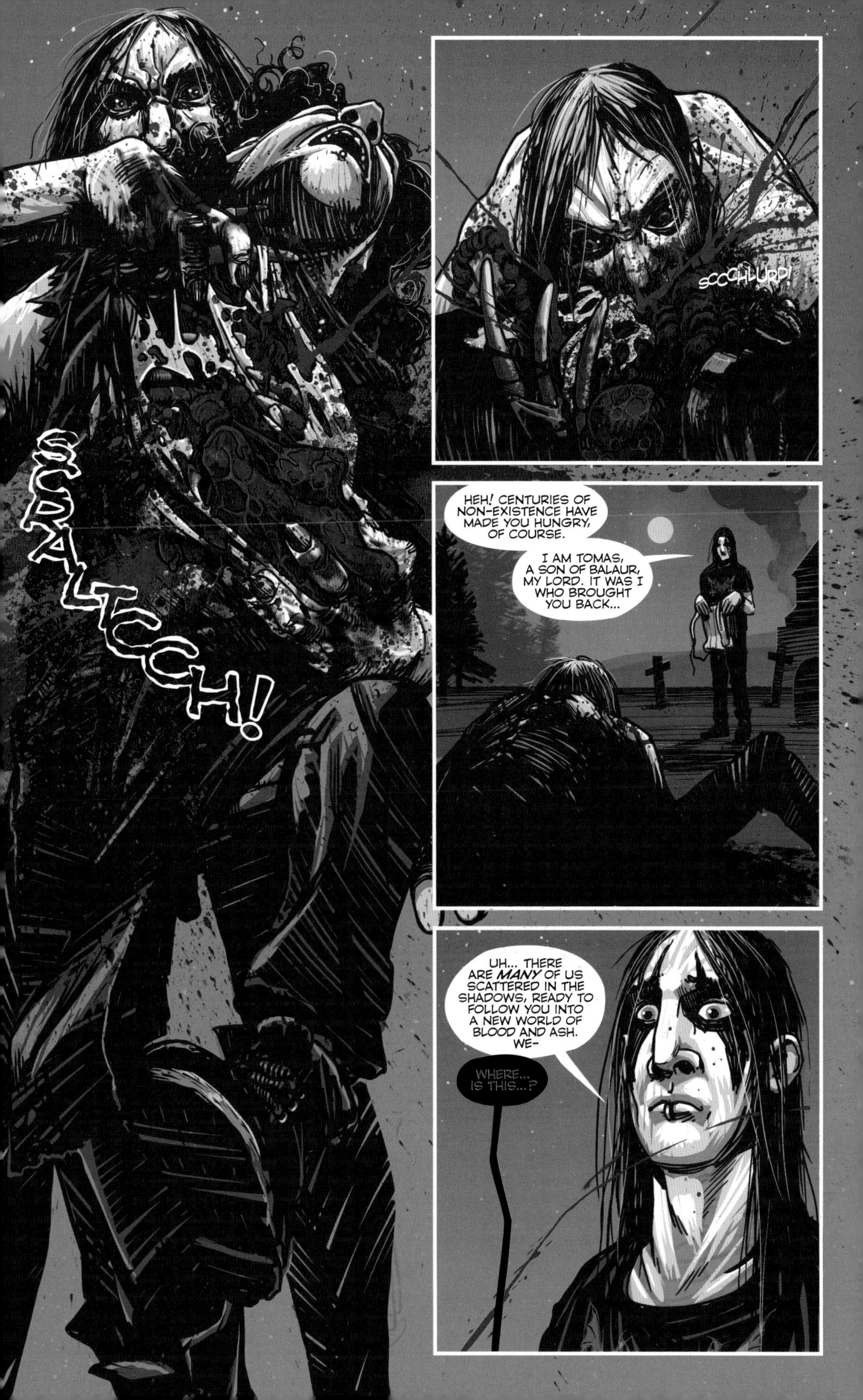
SCRALTCCH!
SCCCHLURP!
HEH! CENTURIES OF NON-EXISTENCE HAVE MADE YOU HUNGRY, OF COURSE.
I AM TOMAS, A SON OF BALAUR, MY LORD. IT WAS I WHO BROUGHT YOU BACK...
UH... THERE ARE MANY OF US SCATTERED IN THE SHADOWS, READY TO FOLLOW YOU INTO A NEW WORLD OF BLOOD AND ASH. WE-
WHERE... IS THIS...?

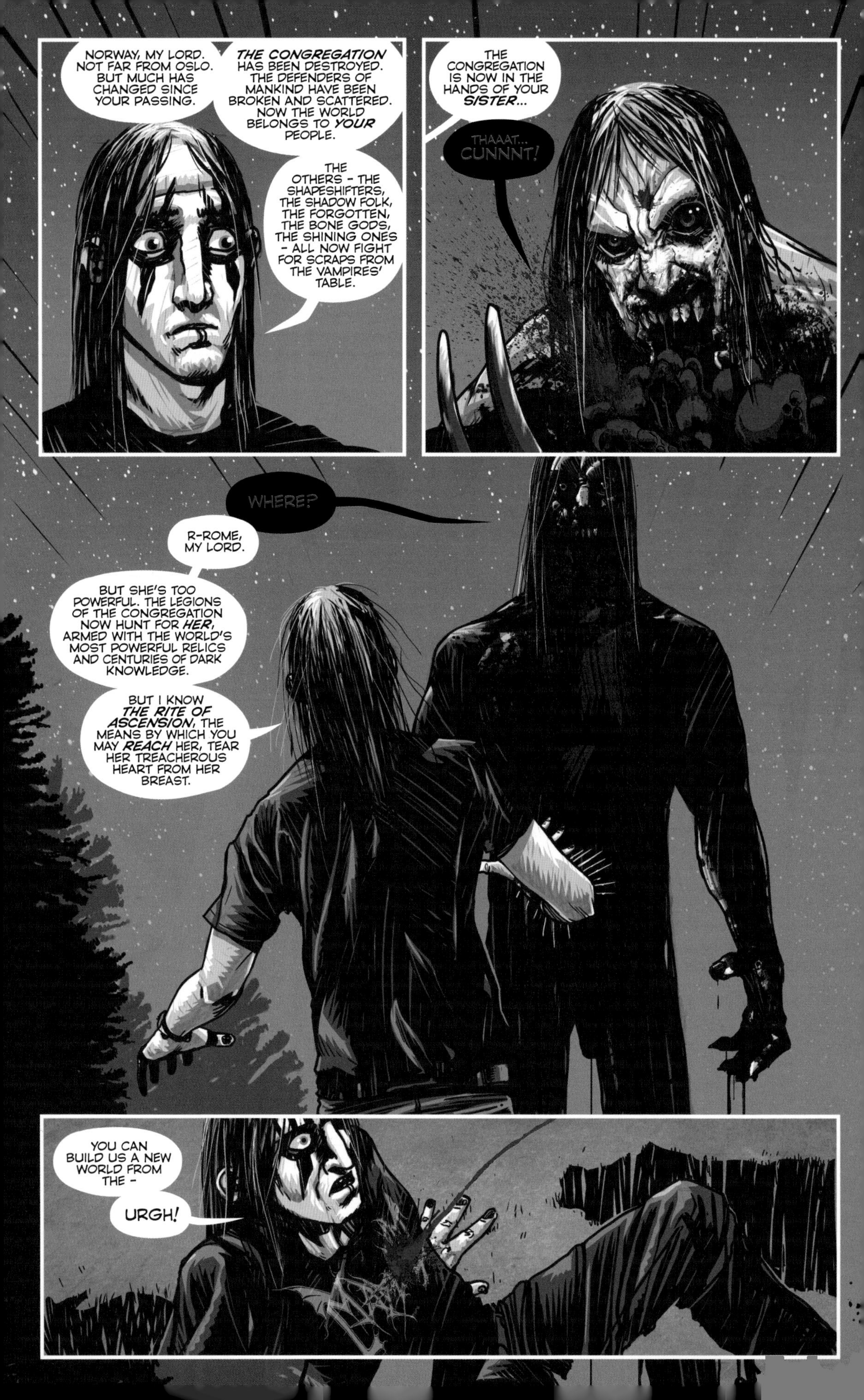
NORWAY, MY LORD. NOT FAR FROM OSLO. BUT MUCH HAS CHANGED SINCE YOUR PASSING.
THE CONGREGATION HAS BEEN DESTROYED. THE DEFENDERS OF MANKIND HAVE BEEN BROKEN AND SCATTERED. NOW THE WORLD BELONGS TO YOUR PEOPLE.
THE OTHERS - THE SHAPESHIFTERS, THE SHADOW FOLK, THE FORGOTTEN, THE BONE GODS, THE SHINING ONES - ALL NOW FIGHT FOR SCRAPS FROM THE VAMPIRES' TABLE.
THE CONGREGATION IS NOW IN THE HANDS OF YOUR SISTER...
THAAAT... CUNNNT!
WHERE?
R-ROME, MY LORD.
BUT SHE'S TOO POWERFUL. THE LEGIONS OF THE CONGREGATION NOW HUNT FOR HER, ARMED WITH THE WORLD'S MOST POWERFUL RELICS AND CENTURIES OF DARK KNOWLEDGE.
BUT I KNOW THE RITE OF ASCENSION, THE MEANS BY WHICH YOU MAY REACH HER, TEAR HER TREACHEROUS HEART FROM HER BREAST.
YOU CAN BUILD US A NEW WORLD FROM THE -
URGH!

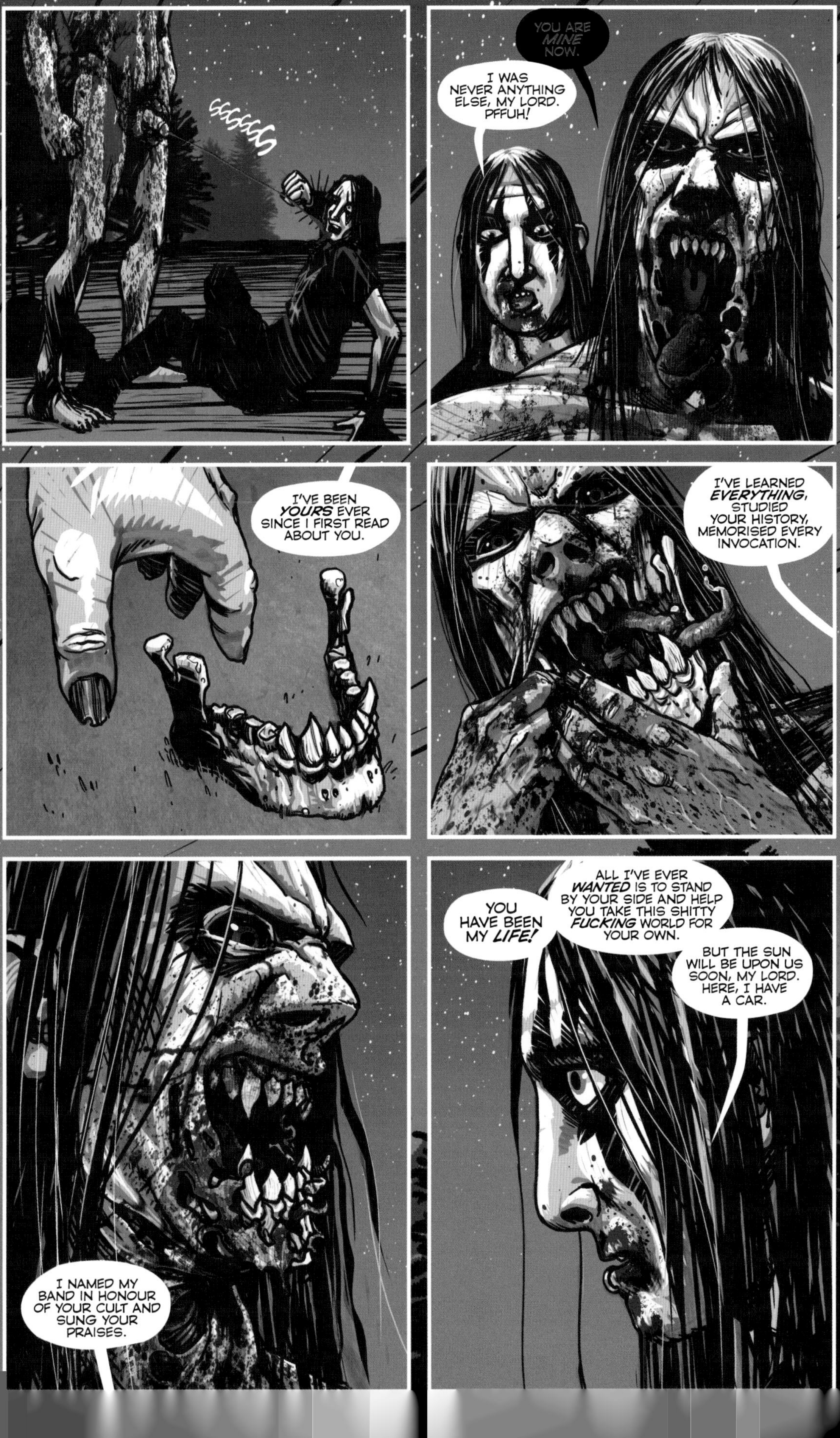
SSSSSSS
YOU ARE MINE NOW.
I WAS NEVER ANYTHING ELSE, MY LORD. PFFUH!
I'VE BEEN YOURS EVER SINCE I FIRST READ ABOUT YOU.
I'VE LEARNED EVERYTHING, STUDIED YOUR HISTORY, MEMORISED EVERY INVOCATION.
I NAMED MY BAND IN HONOUR OF YOUR CULT AND SUNG YOUR PRAISES.
YOU HAVE BEEN MY LIFE!
ALL I'VE EVER WANTED IS TO STAND BY YOUR SIDE AND HELP YOU TAKE THIS SHITTY FUCKING WORLD FOR YOUR OWN.
BUT THE SUN WILL BE UPON US SOON, MY LORD. HERE, I HAVE A CAR.

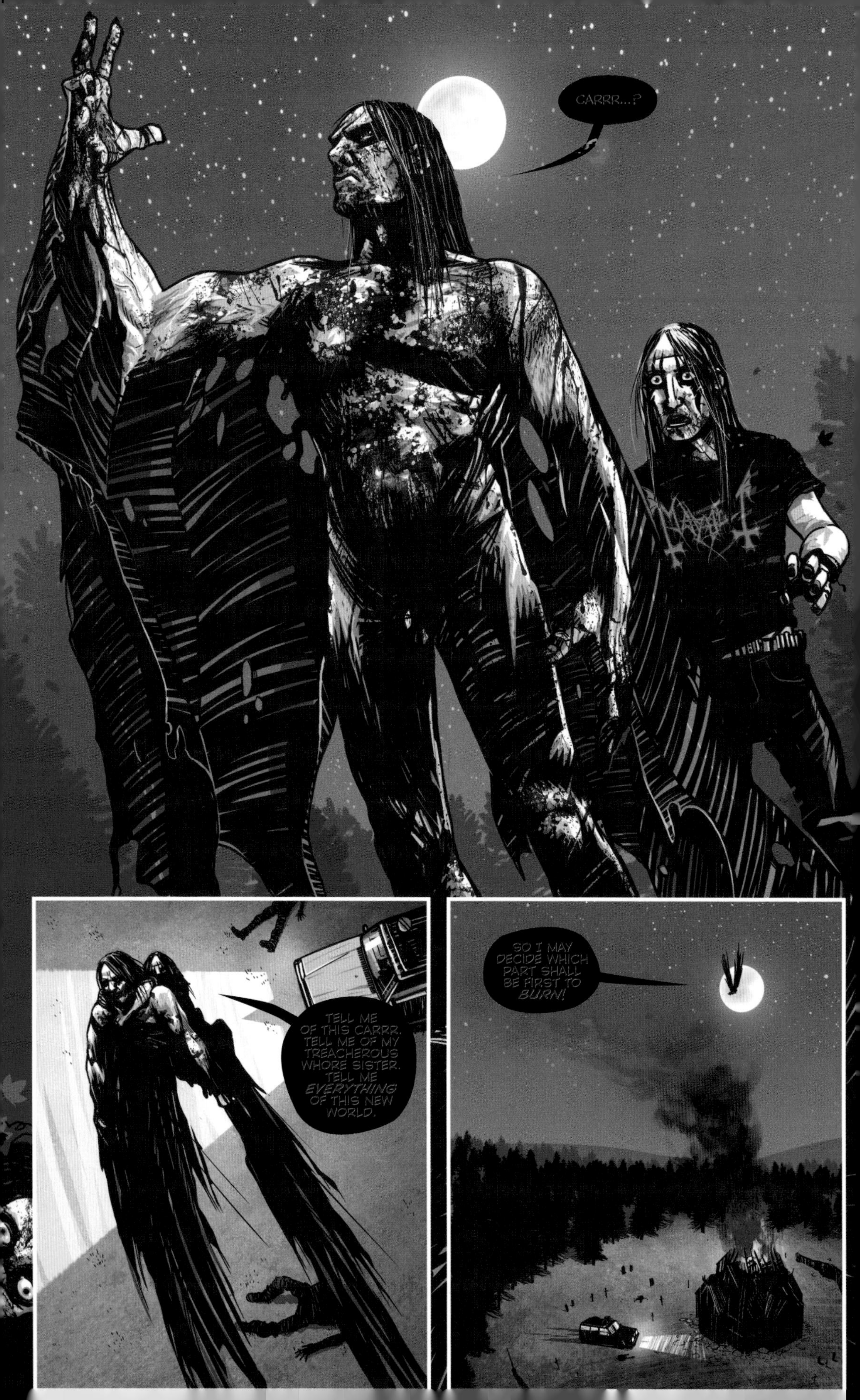
CARRR...?
TELL ME OF THIS CARRR. TELL ME OF MY TREACHEROUS WHORE SISTER. TELL ME *EVERYTHING* OF THIS NEW WORLD.
SO I MAY DECIDE WHICH PART SHALL BE FIRST TO *BURN!*

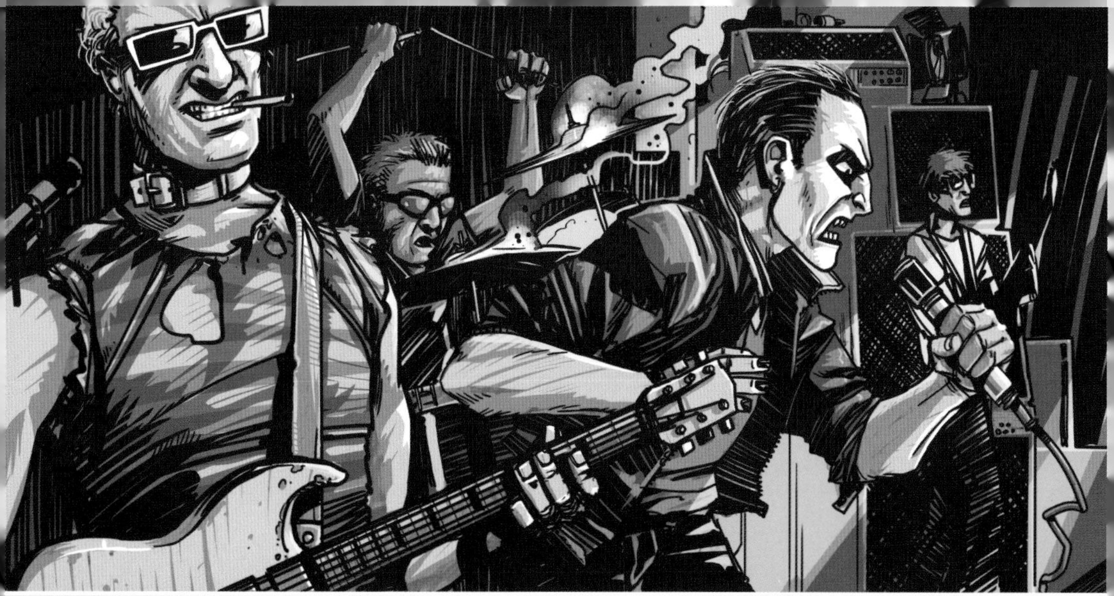

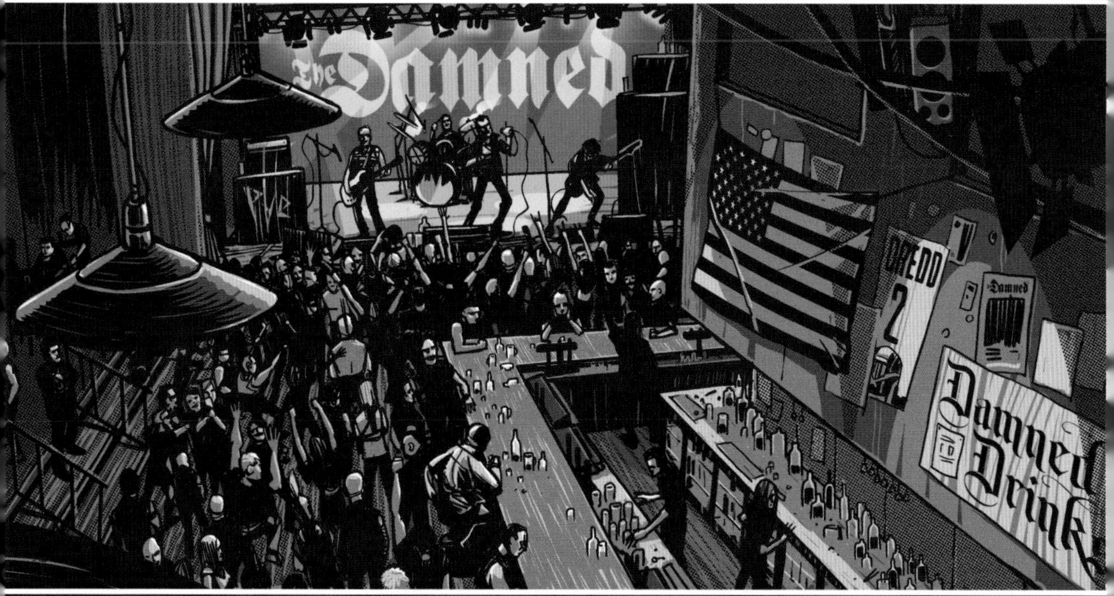
The Damned
DREDD 2
Damned
Damned Drink

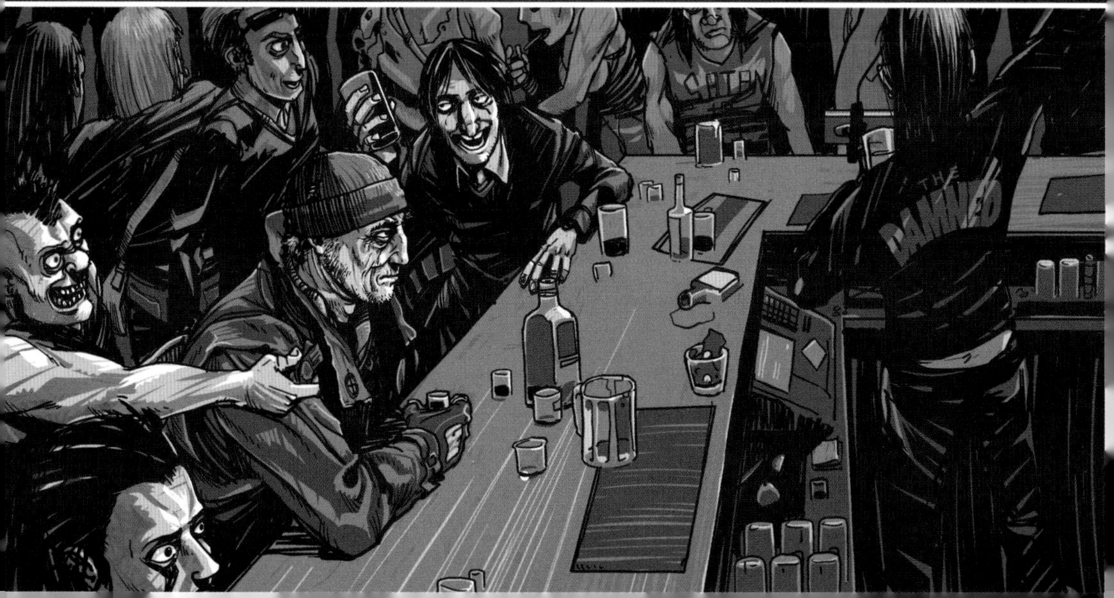
SATAN
THE DAMNED

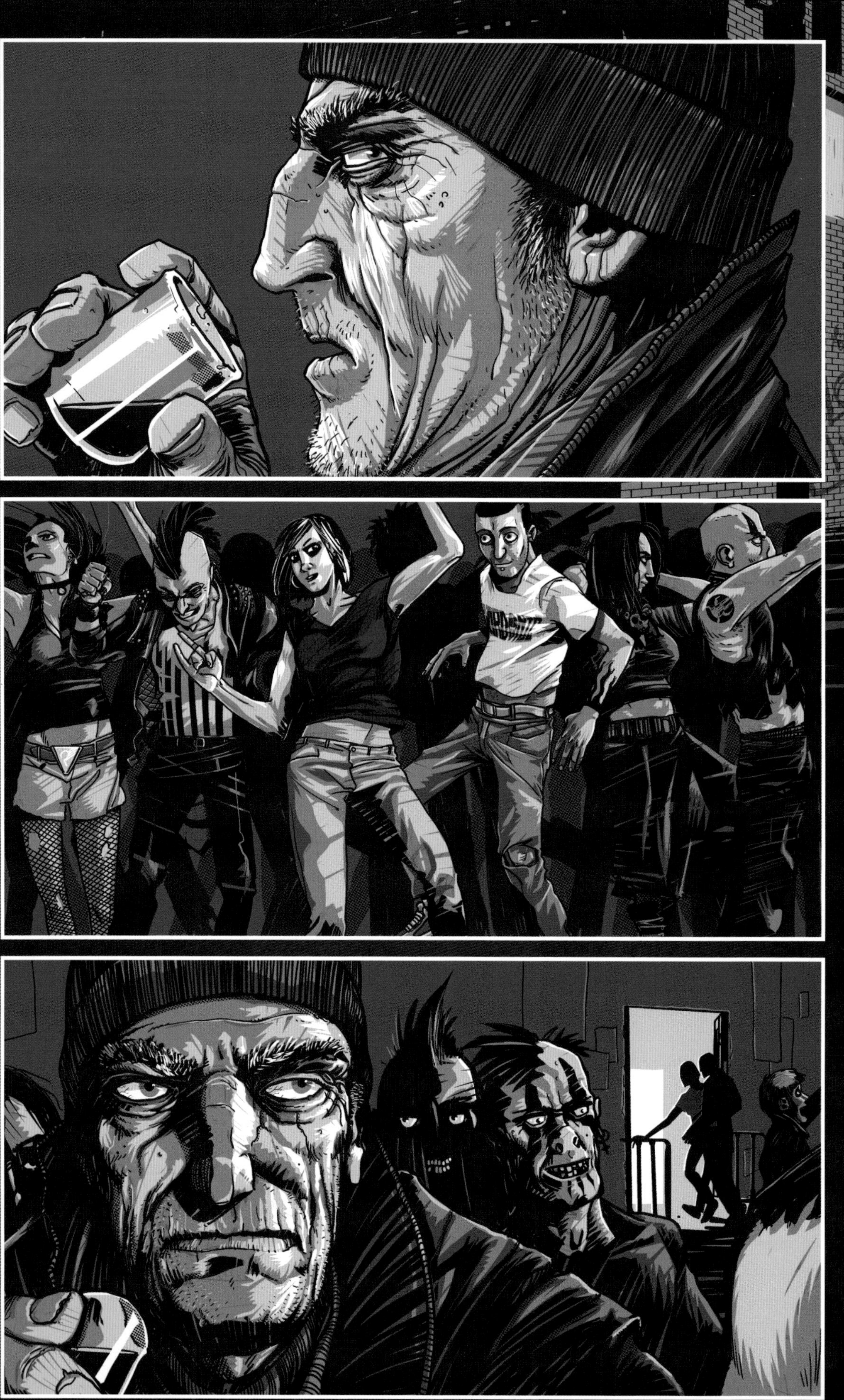

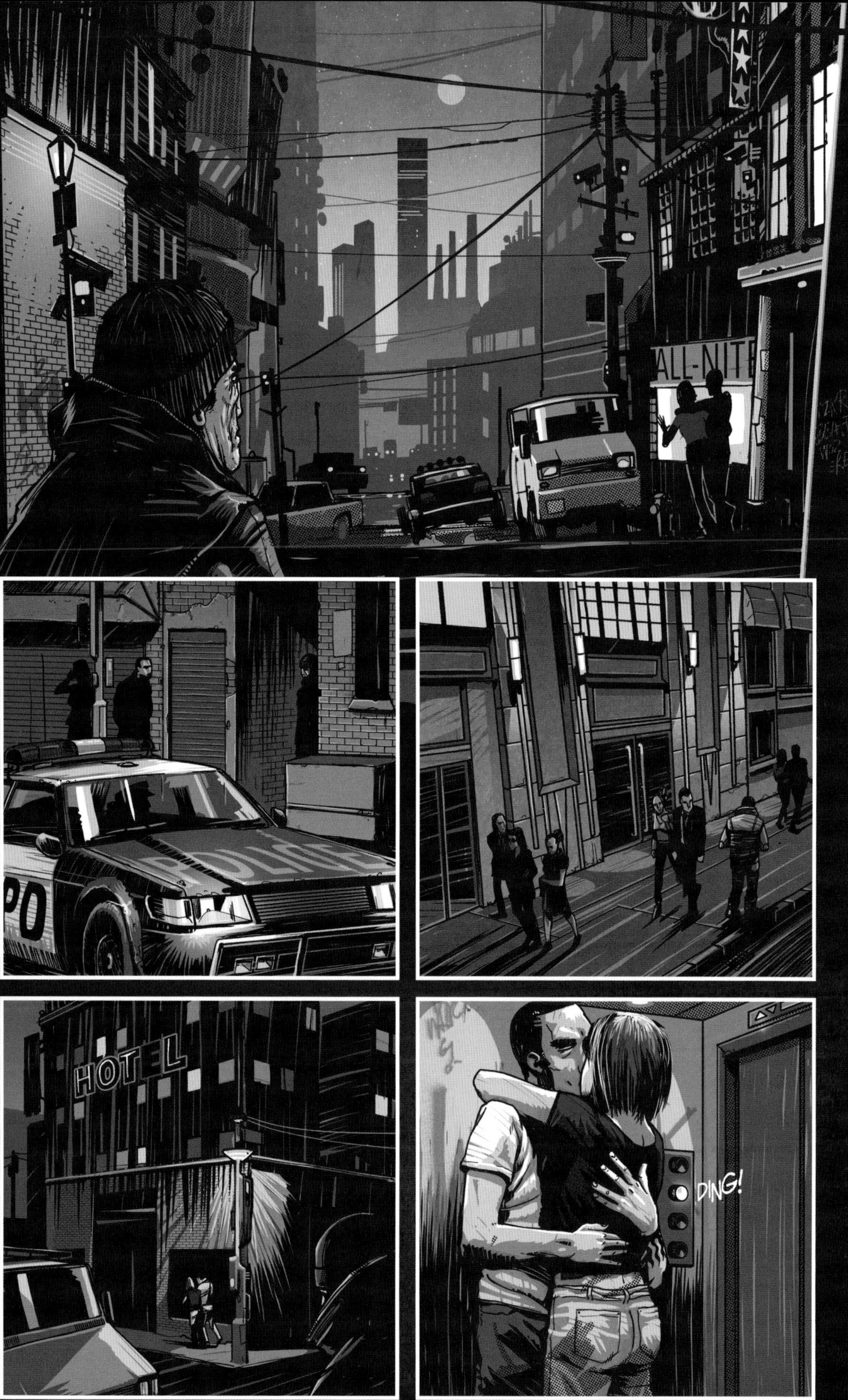
ALL-NITE
POLICE
PD
HOTEL
DING!

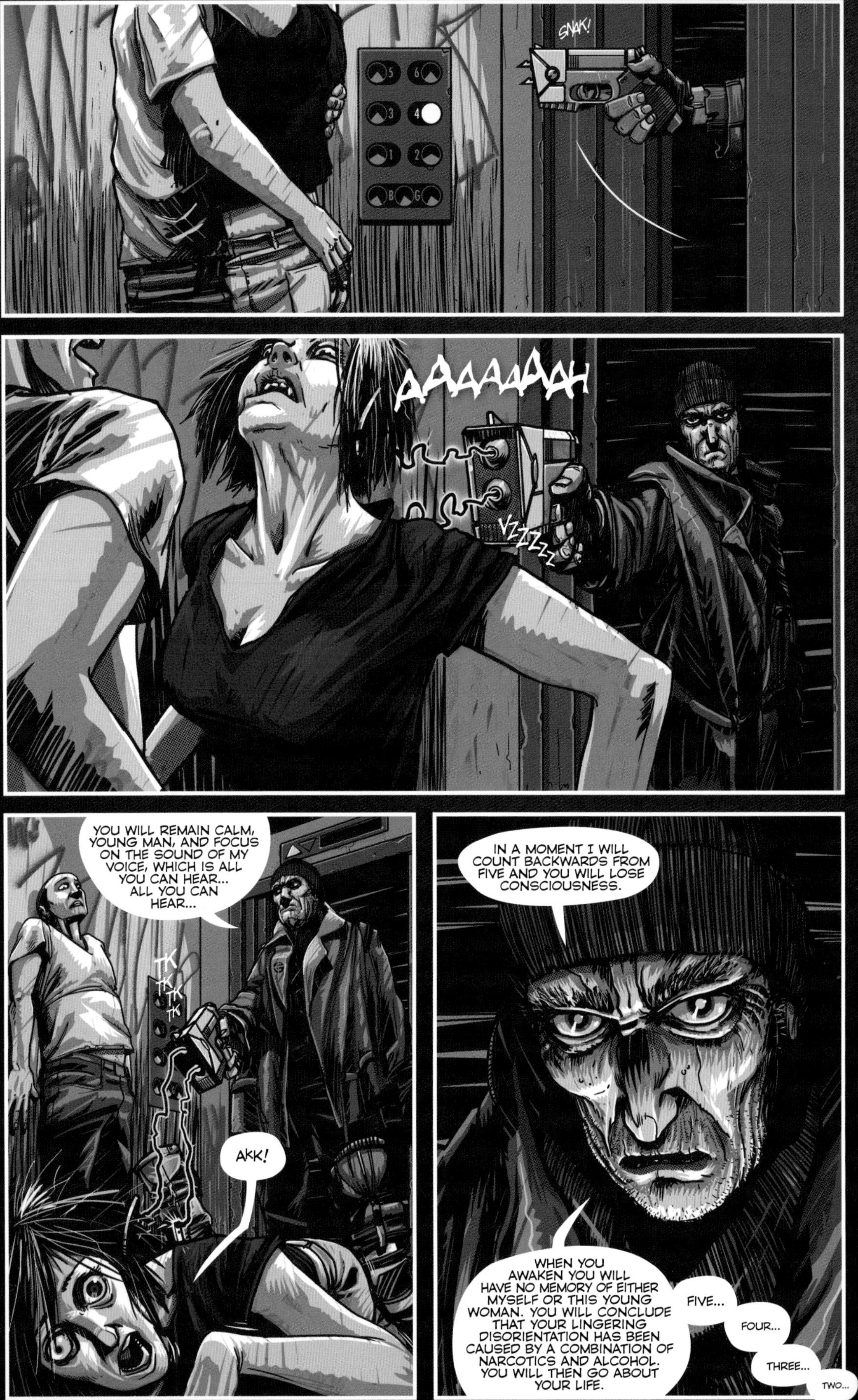
SNAK!
AAAAAAAH
VZZZZZ
YOU WILL REMAIN CALM, YOUNG MAN, AND FOCUS ON THE SOUND OF MY VOICE, WHICH IS ALL YOU CAN HEAR... ALL YOU CAN HEAR...
TK TK TK TK
AKK!
IN A MOMENT I WILL COUNT BACKWARDS FROM FIVE AND YOU WILL LOSE CONSCIOUSNESS.
WHEN YOU AWAKEN YOU WILL HAVE NO MEMORY OF EITHER MYSELF OR THIS YOUNG WOMAN. YOU WILL CONCLUDE THAT YOUR LINGERING DISORIENTATION HAS BEEN CAUSED BY A COMBINATION OF NARCOTICS AND ALCOHOL. YOU WILL THEN GO ABOUT YOUR LIFE.
FIVE...
FOUR...
THREE...
TWO...

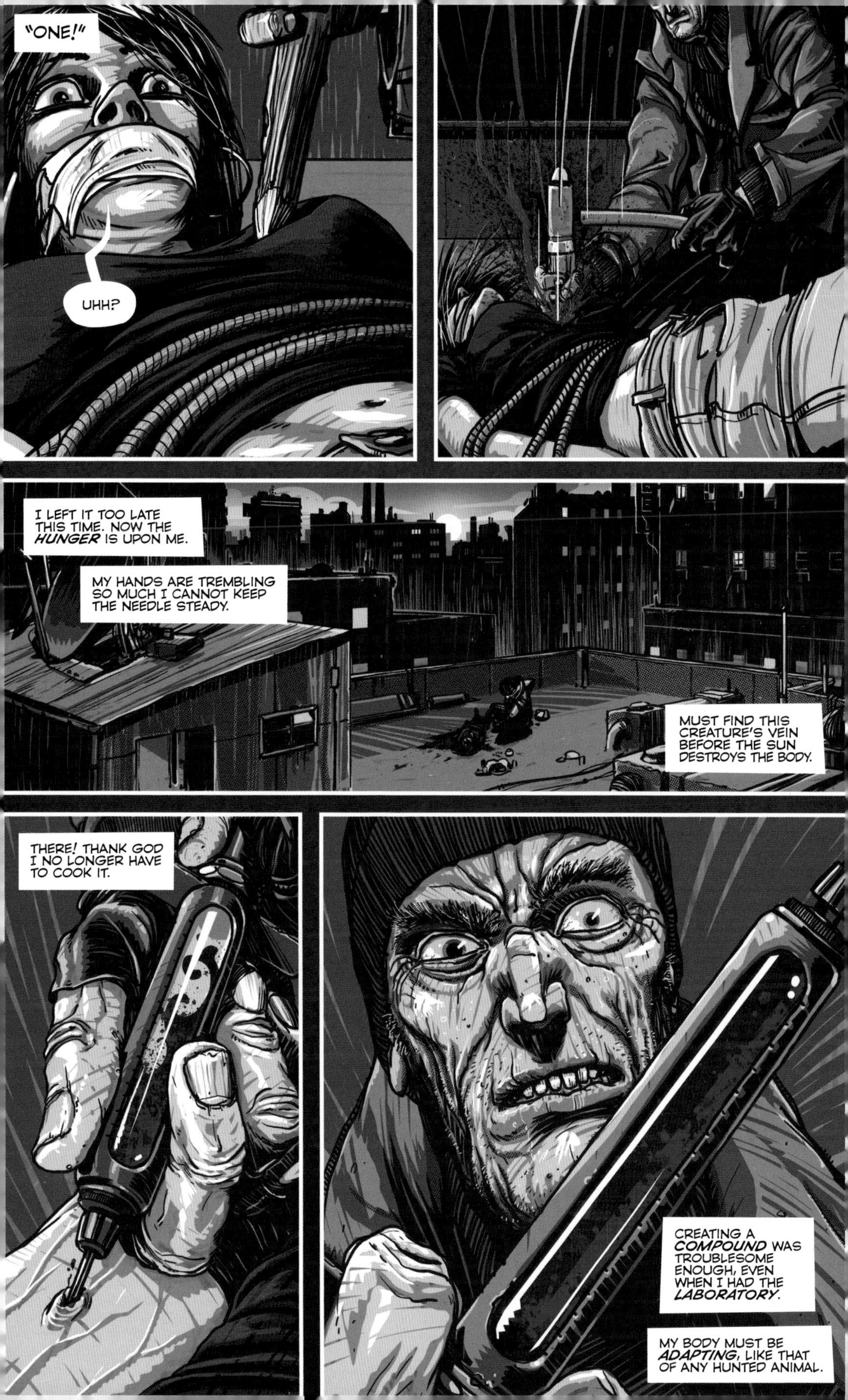
"ONE!"
UHH?
I LEFT IT TOO LATE THIS TIME. NOW THE *HUNGER* IS UPON ME.
MY HANDS ARE TREMBLING SO MUCH I CANNOT KEEP THE NEEDLE STEADY.
MUST FIND THIS CREATURE'S VEIN BEFORE THE SUN DESTROYS THE BODY.
THERE! THANK GOD I NO LONGER HAVE TO COOK IT.
CREATING A *COMPOUND* WAS TROUBLESOME ENOUGH, EVEN WHEN I HAD THE *LABORATORY*.
MY BODY MUST BE *ADAPTING*, LIKE THAT OF ANY HUNTED ANIMAL.

FORGIVE ME, LORD.

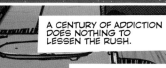

A CENTURY OF ADDICTION DOES NOTHING TO LESSEN THE RUSH.

THE STOLEN BLOOD MELTS INTO ME, SOFTENING THE STIFFNESS IN MY JOINTS, ILLUMINATING THE DARKNESS OF THE WORLD. THEN THE LIVES OF THE CREATURE'S VICTIMS FLASH BEFORE MY EYES...

FASCINATING HOW THE VAMPIRE APPEARS TO ABSORB SOME PORTION OF THE SOUL WHEN IT FEEDS. BUT ITS MIND IS COLD AND PREDATORY, AND SO THE EXPERIENCE WASHES OVER IT LIKE A STREAM OVER STONES.

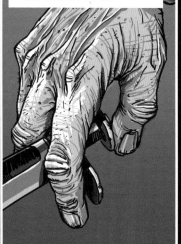

ALAS, I AM BUT MORTAL, AND MY MIND FILLS WITH FOREIGN MEMORIES UNTIL I CAN BARELY DISTINGUISH MY OWN.

AND ANOTHER PART OF ME FALLS AWAY LIKE A HANDFUL OF DEAD LEAVES.

I RECALL BEING SOMETHING OF A PHILOSOPHER IN MY YOUTH.

I WONDER WHAT THAT YOUNG MAN WOULD HAVE MADE OF *THIS* ENQUIRY: WHEN A MAN ABANDONS HIMSELF TO DUTY, WHAT THEN REMAINS OF THE MAN...?

WHAT DOES HE BECOME...?

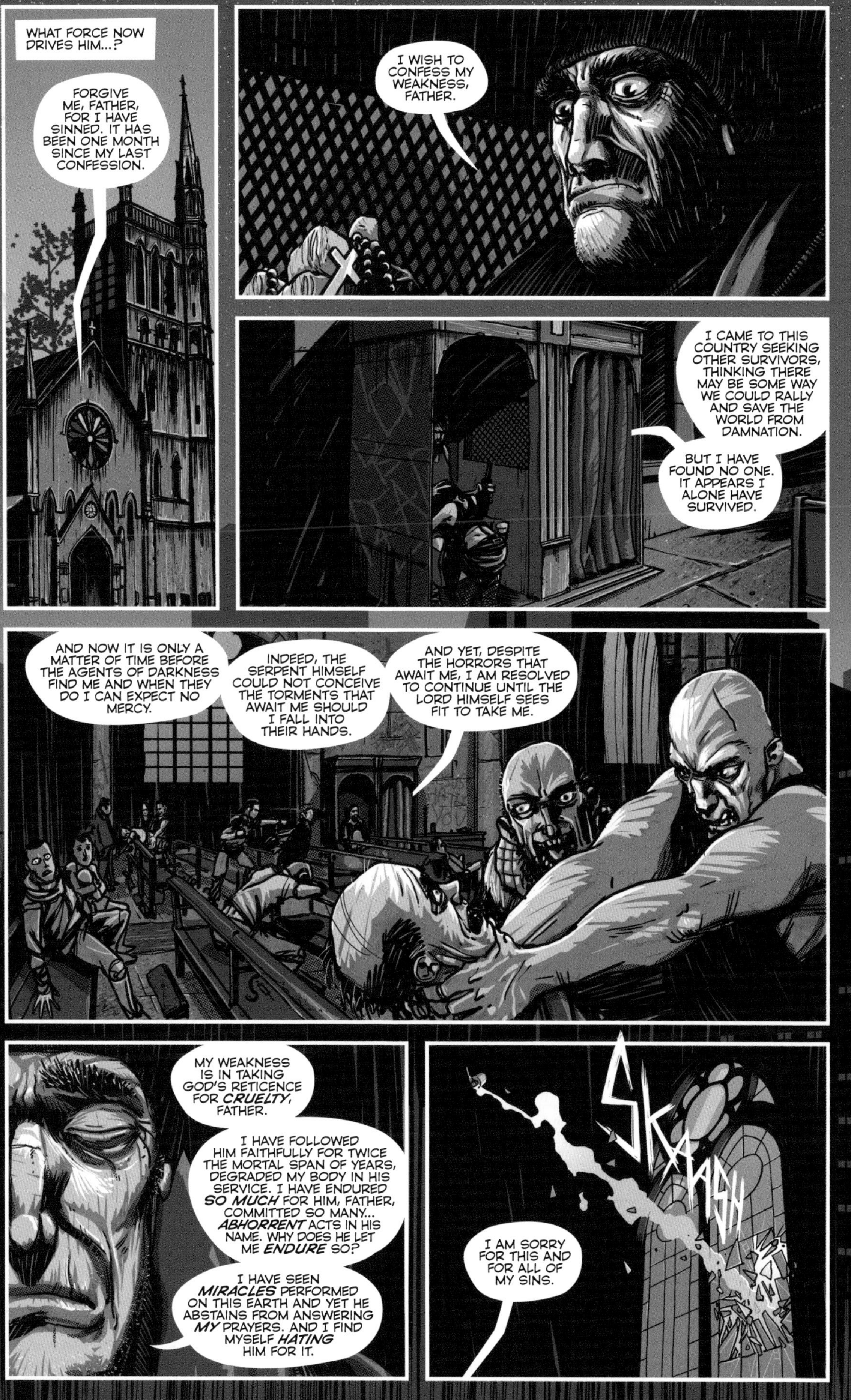
WHAT FORCE NOW DRIVES HIM...?
FORGIVE ME, FATHER, FOR I HAVE SINNED. IT HAS BEEN ONE MONTH SINCE MY LAST CONFESSION.
I WISH TO CONFESS MY WEAKNESS, FATHER.
I CAME TO THIS COUNTRY SEEKING OTHER SURVIVORS, THINKING THERE MAY BE SOME WAY WE COULD RALLY AND SAVE THE WORLD FROM DAMNATION.
BUT I HAVE FOUND NO ONE. IT APPEARS I ALONE HAVE SURVIVED.
AND NOW IT IS ONLY A MATTER OF TIME BEFORE THE AGENTS OF DARKNESS FIND ME AND WHEN THEY DO I CAN EXPECT NO MERCY.
INDEED, THE SERPENT HIMSELF COULD NOT CONCEIVE THE TORMENTS THAT AWAIT ME SHOULD I FALL INTO THEIR HANDS.
AND YET, DESPITE THE HORRORS THAT AWAIT ME, I AM RESOLVED TO CONTINUE UNTIL THE LORD HIMSELF SEES FIT TO TAKE ME.
MY WEAKNESS IS IN TAKING GOD'S RETICENCE FOR *CRUELTY*, FATHER.
I HAVE FOLLOWED HIM FAITHFULLY FOR TWICE THE MORTAL SPAN OF YEARS, DEGRADED MY BODY IN HIS SERVICE. I HAVE ENDURED ***SO MUCH*** FOR HIM, FATHER, COMMITTED SO MANY... ***ABHORRENT*** ACTS IN HIS NAME. WHY DOES HE LET ME ***ENDURE*** SO?
I HAVE SEEN ***MIRACLES*** PERFORMED ON THIS EARTH AND YET HE ABSTAINS FROM ANSWERING ***MY*** PRAYERS. AND I FIND MYSELF ***HATING*** HIM FOR IT.
SKAASH
I AM SORRY FOR THIS AND FOR ALL OF MY SINS.

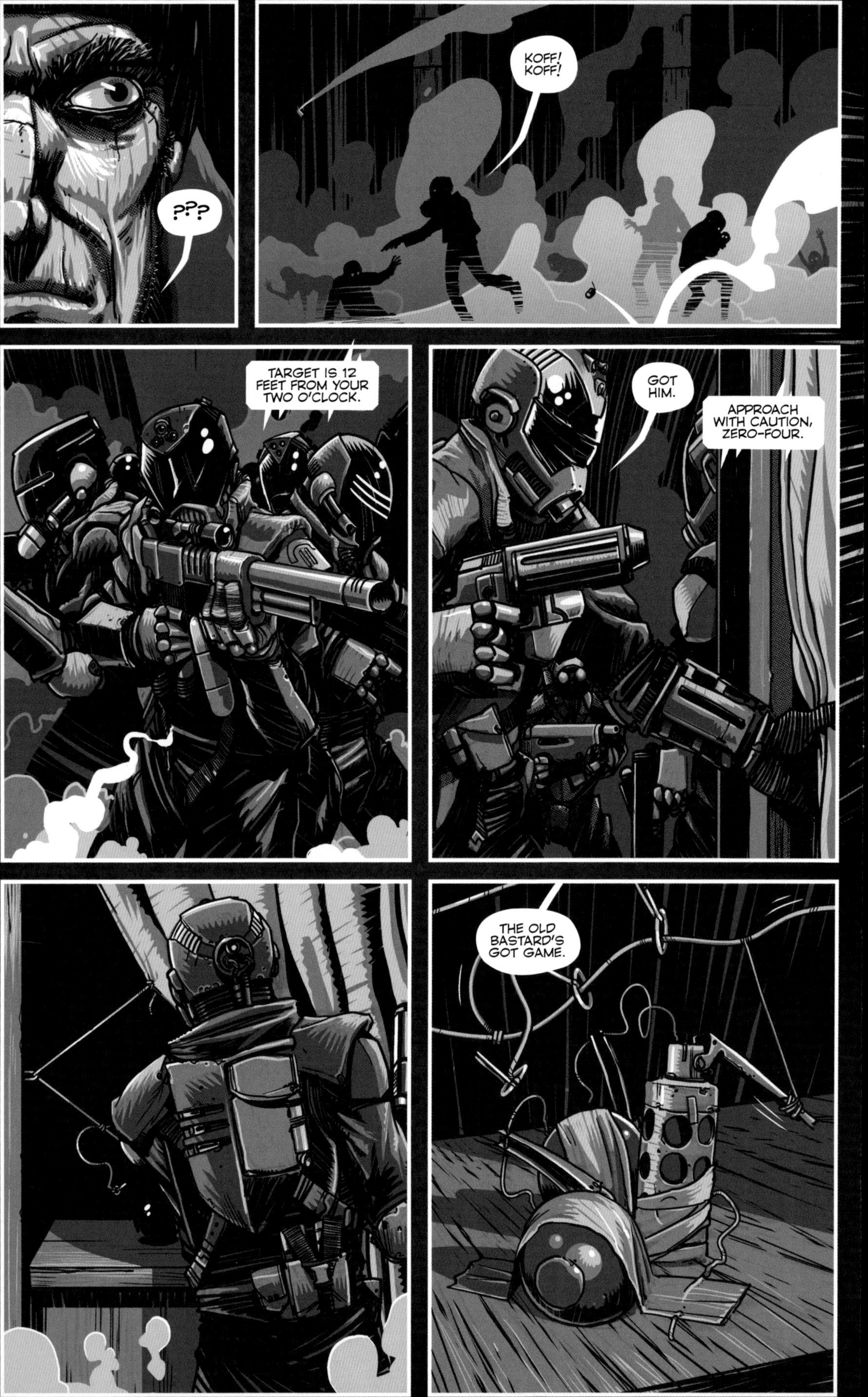
???
KOFF! KOFF!
TARGET IS 12 FEET FROM YOUR TWO O'CLOCK.
GOT HIM.
APPROACH WITH CAUTION, ZERO-FOUR.
THE OLD BASTARD'S GOT GAME.

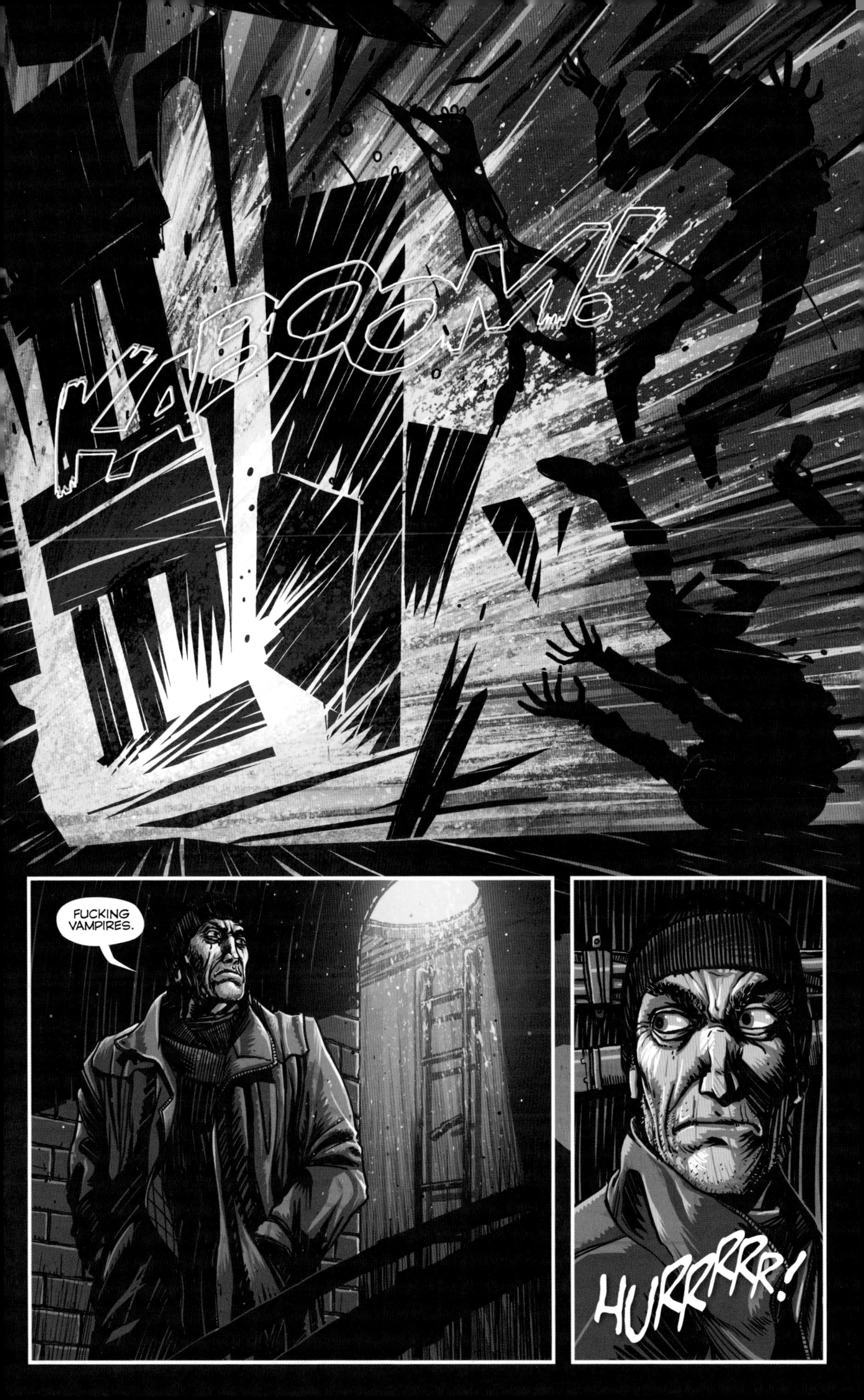
KABOOM!
FUCKING VAMPIRES.
HURRRRR!

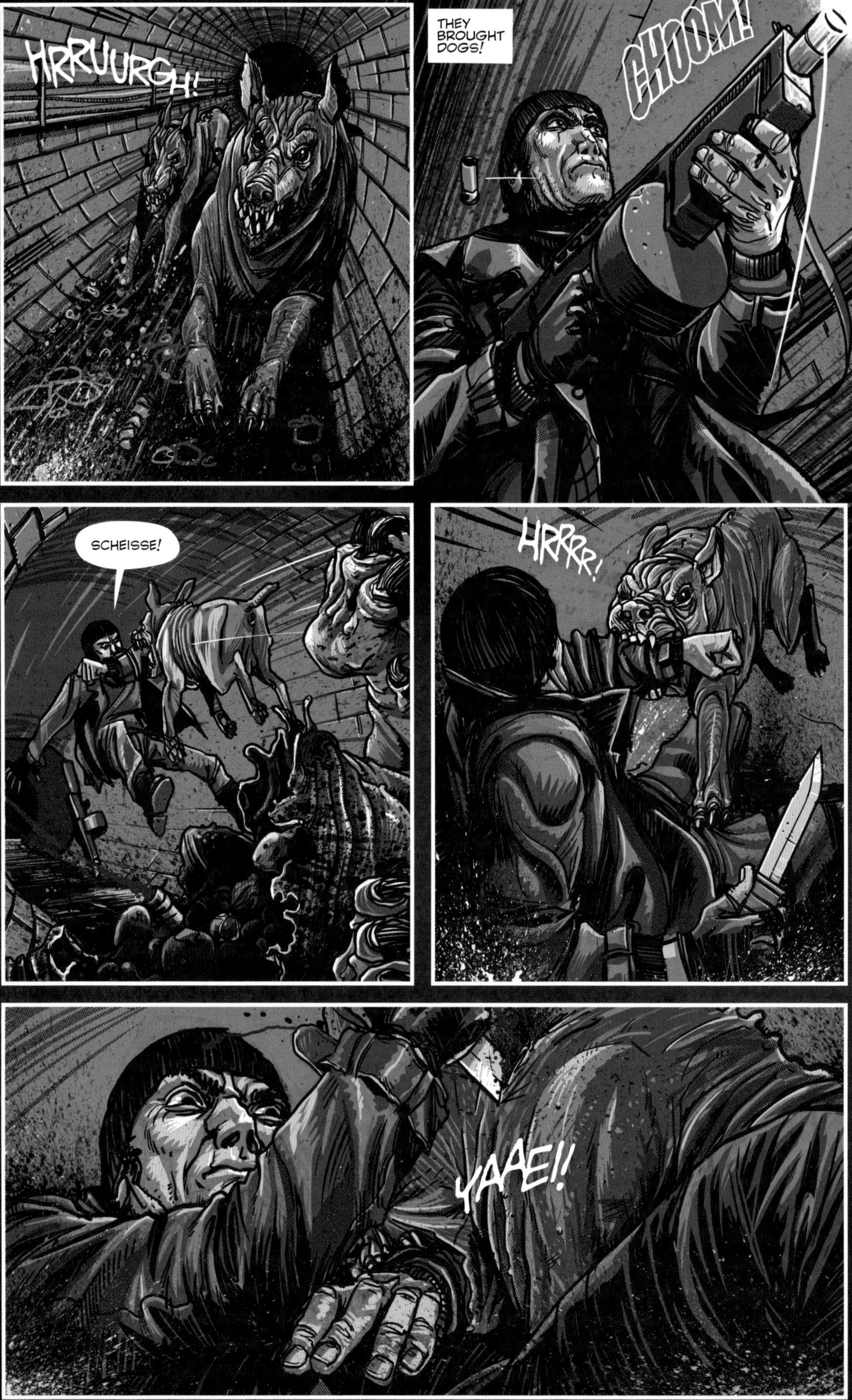
HRRUUURGH!
THEY BROUGHT DOGS!
CHOOM!
SCHEISSE!
HRRRR!
YAAE!!

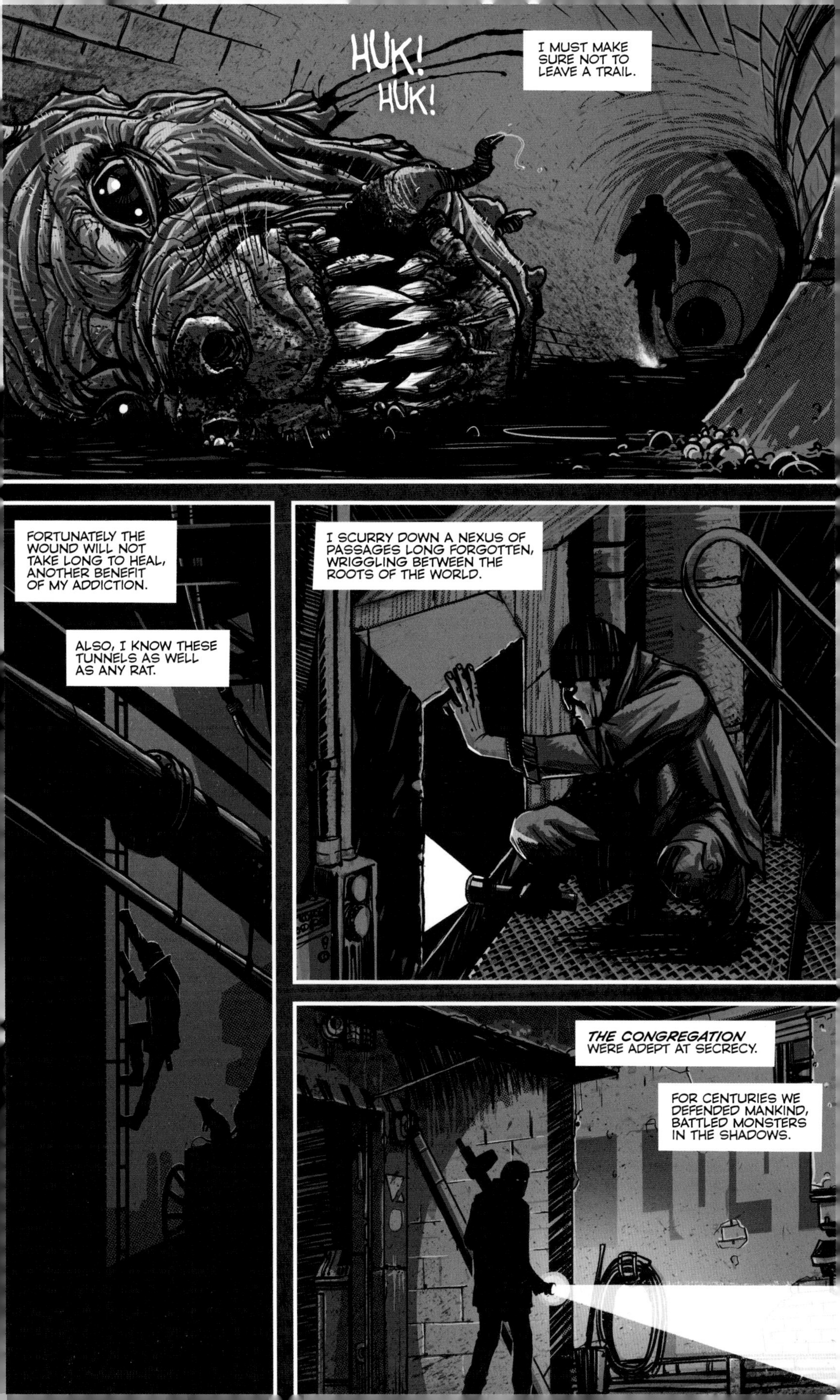
HUK!
HUK!
I MUST MAKE SURE NOT TO LEAVE A TRAIL.
FORTUNATELY THE WOUND WILL NOT TAKE LONG TO HEAL, ANOTHER BENEFIT OF MY ADDICTION.
ALSO, I KNOW THESE TUNNELS AS WELL AS ANY RAT.
I SCURRY DOWN A NEXUS OF PASSAGES LONG FORGOTTEN, WRIGGLING BETWEEN THE ROOTS OF THE WORLD.
THE CONGREGATION WERE ADEPT AT SECRECY.
FOR CENTURIES WE DEFENDED MANKIND, BATTLED MONSTERS IN THE SHADOWS.

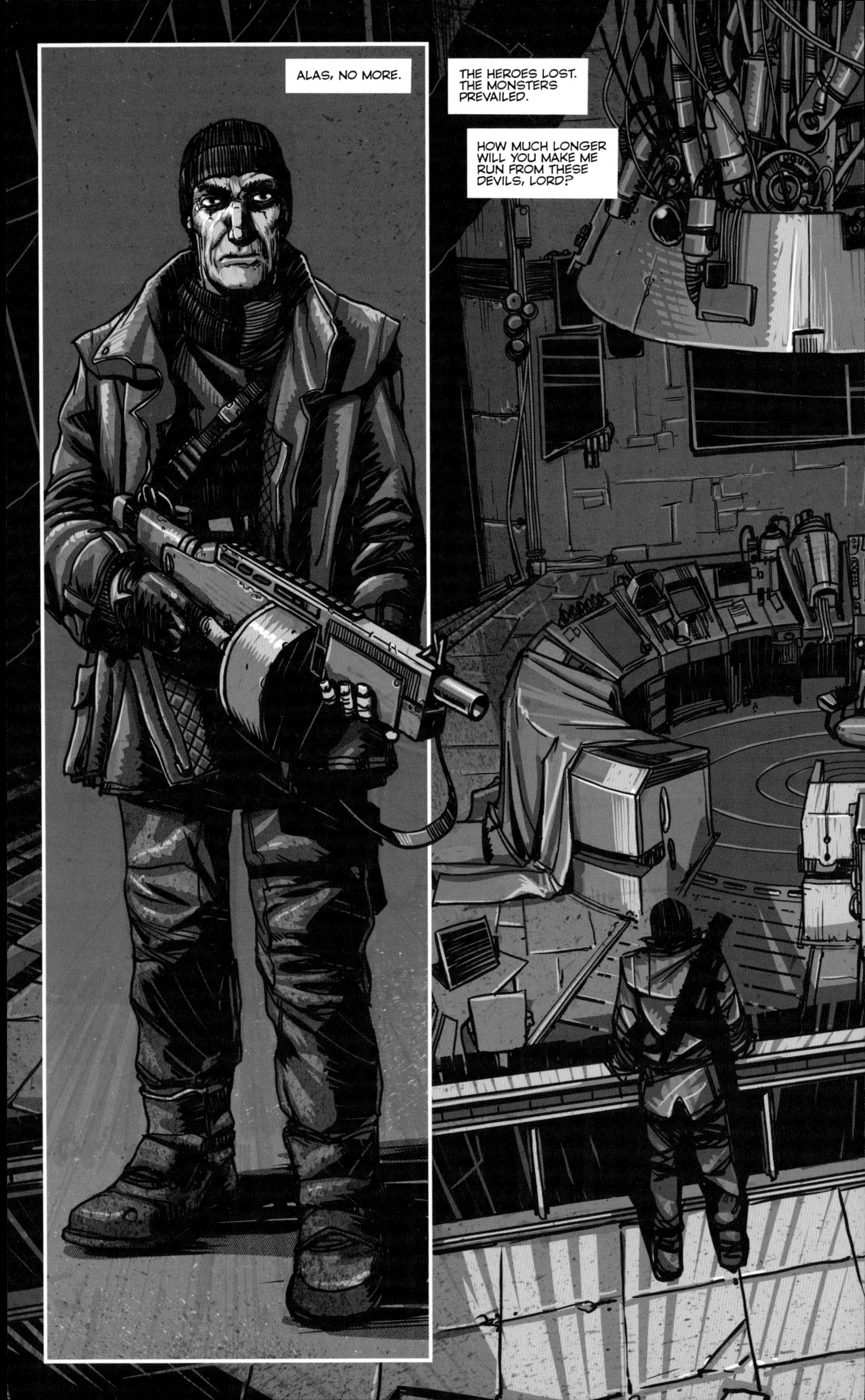
ALAS, NO MORE.
THE HEROES LOST. THE MONSTERS PREVAILED.
HOW MUCH LONGER WILL YOU MAKE ME RUN FROM THESE DEVILS, LORD?

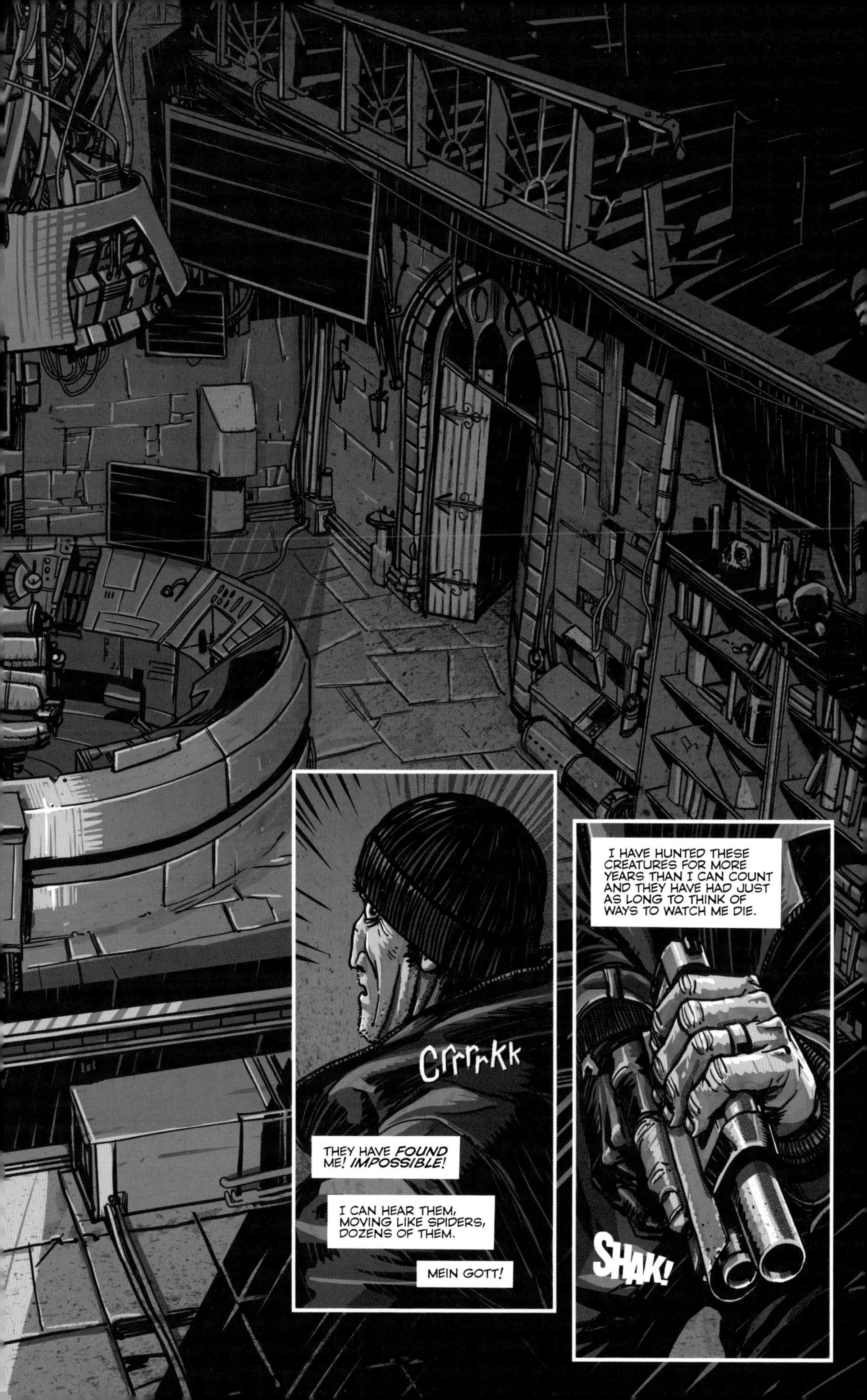
Crrrrkk
THEY HAVE FOUND ME! IMPOSSIBLE!
I CAN HEAR THEM, MOVING LIKE SPIDERS, DOZENS OF THEM.
MEIN GOTT!
I HAVE HUNTED THESE CREATURES FOR MORE YEARS THAN I CAN COUNT AND THEY HAVE HAD JUST AS LONG TO THINK OF WAYS TO WATCH ME DIE.
SHAK!

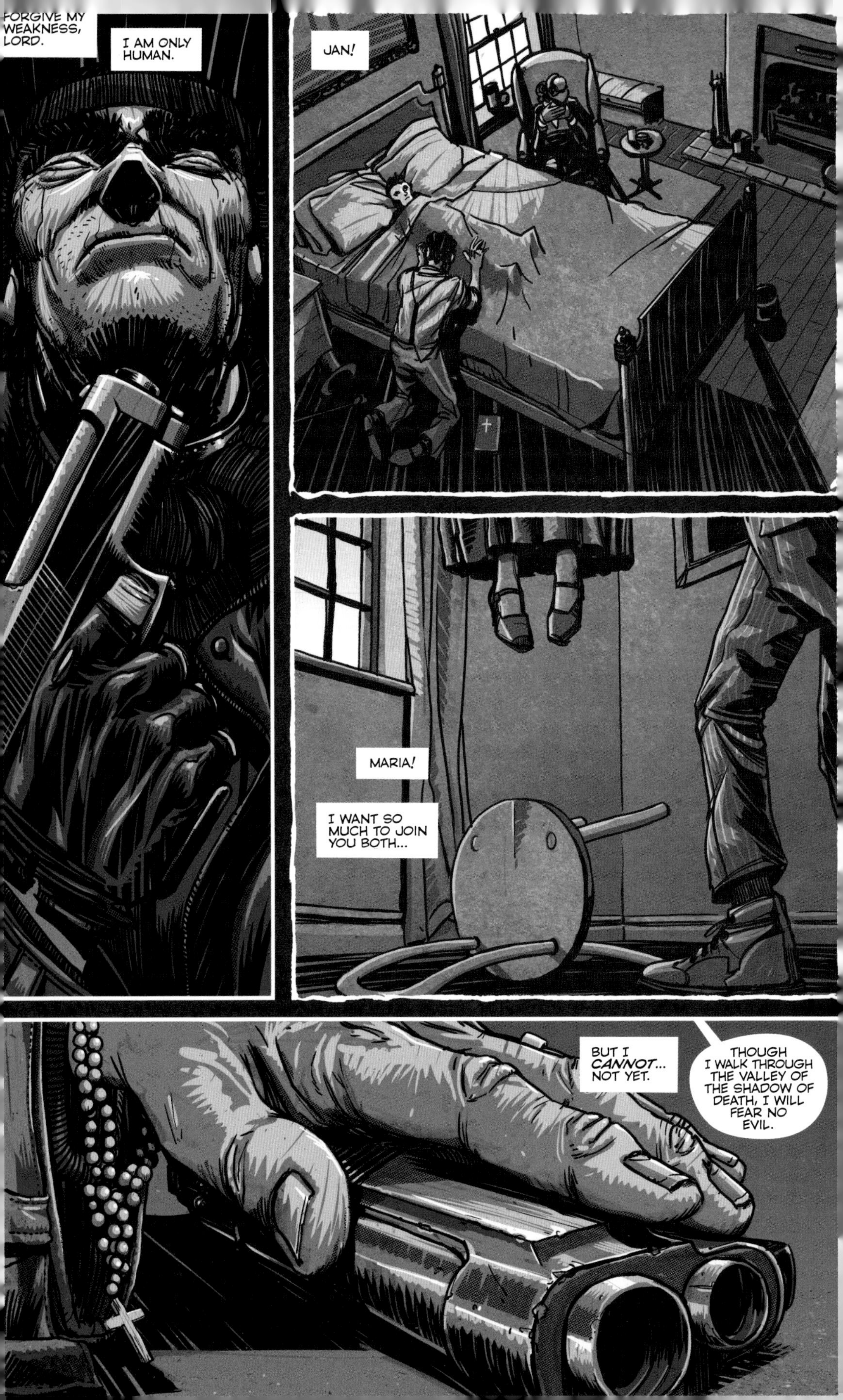
FORGIVE MY WEAKNESS, LORD.
I AM ONLY HUMAN.
JAN!
MARIA!
I WANT SO MUCH TO JOIN YOU BOTH...
BUT I CANNOT... NOT YET.
THOUGH I WALK THROUGH THE VALLEY OF THE SHADOW OF DEATH, I WILL FEAR NO EVIL.

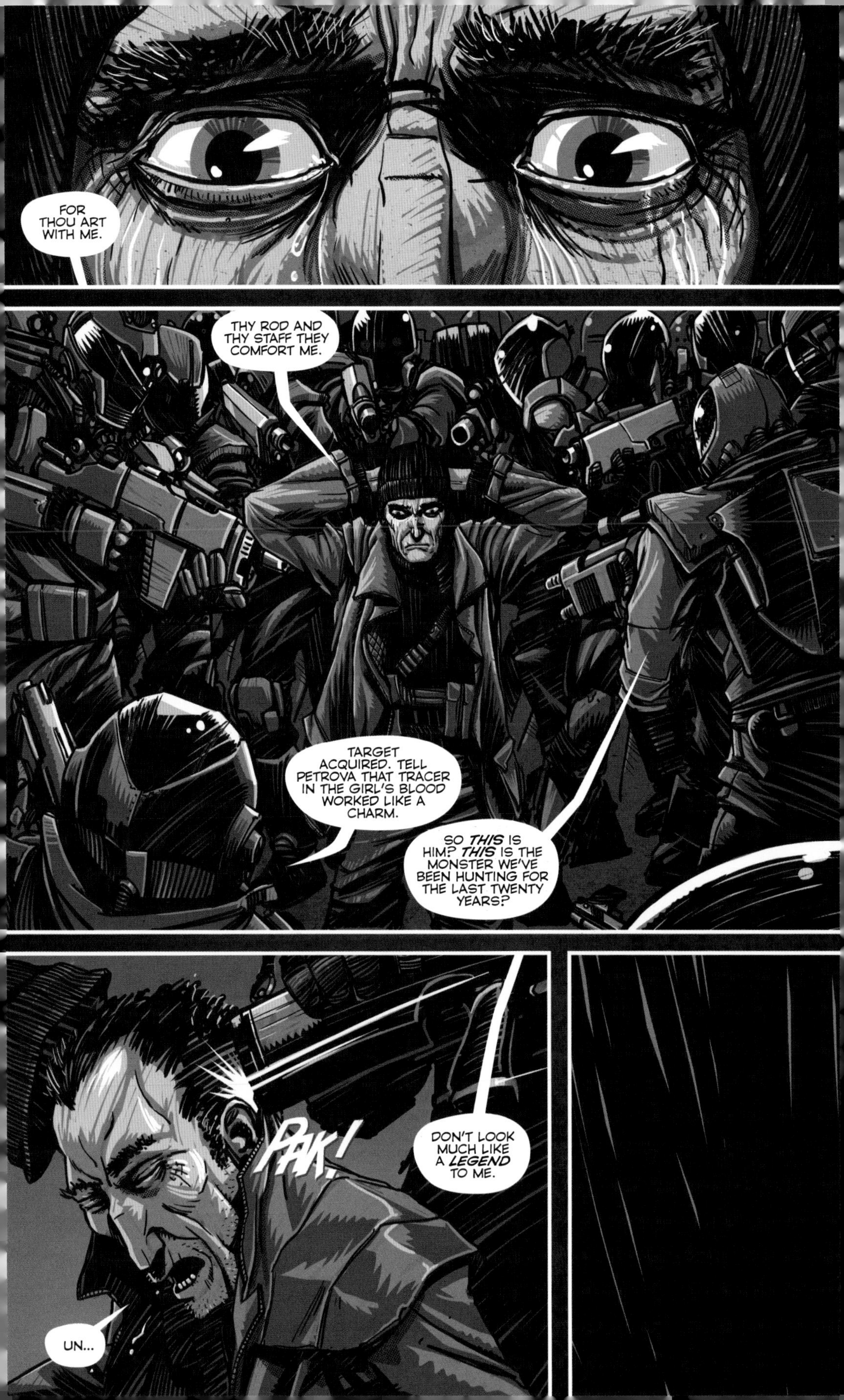
FOR THOU ART WITH ME.
THY ROD AND THY STAFF THEY COMFORT ME.
TARGET ACQUIRED. TELL PETROVA THAT TRACER IN THE GIRL'S BLOOD WORKED LIKE A CHARM.
SO *THIS* IS HIM? *THIS* IS THE MONSTER WE'VE BEEN HUNTING FOR THE LAST TWENTY YEARS?
PAK!
DON'T LOOK MUCH LIKE A *LEGEND* TO ME.
UN...

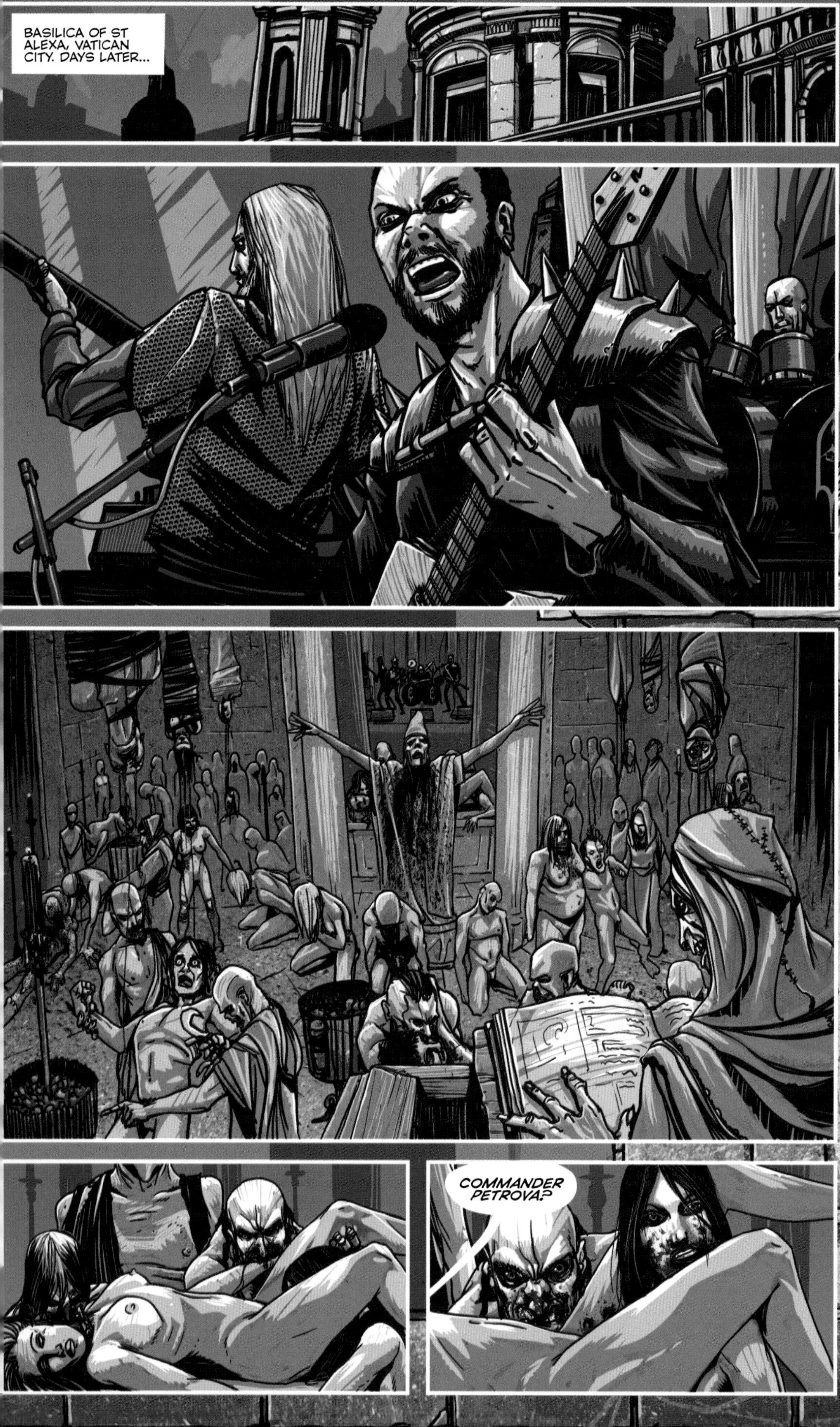
BASILICA OF ST ALEXA, VATICAN CITY. DAYS LATER...
COMMANDER PETROVA?

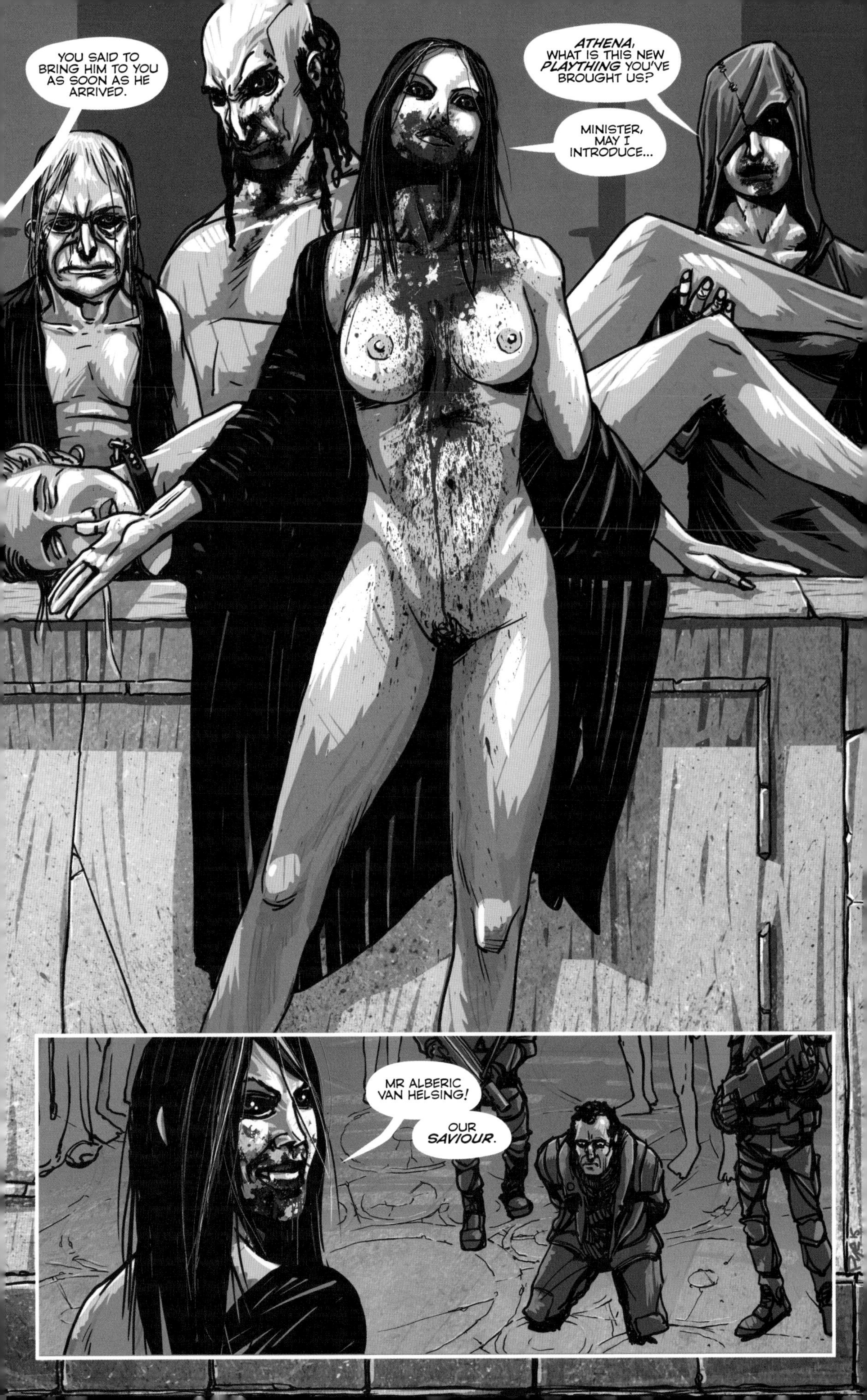
YOU SAID TO BRING HIM TO YOU AS SOON AS HE ARRIVED.
ATHENA, WHAT IS THIS NEW PLAYTHING YOU'VE BROUGHT US?
MINISTER, MAY I INTRODUCE...
MR ALBERIC VAN HELSING!
OUR SAVIOUR.

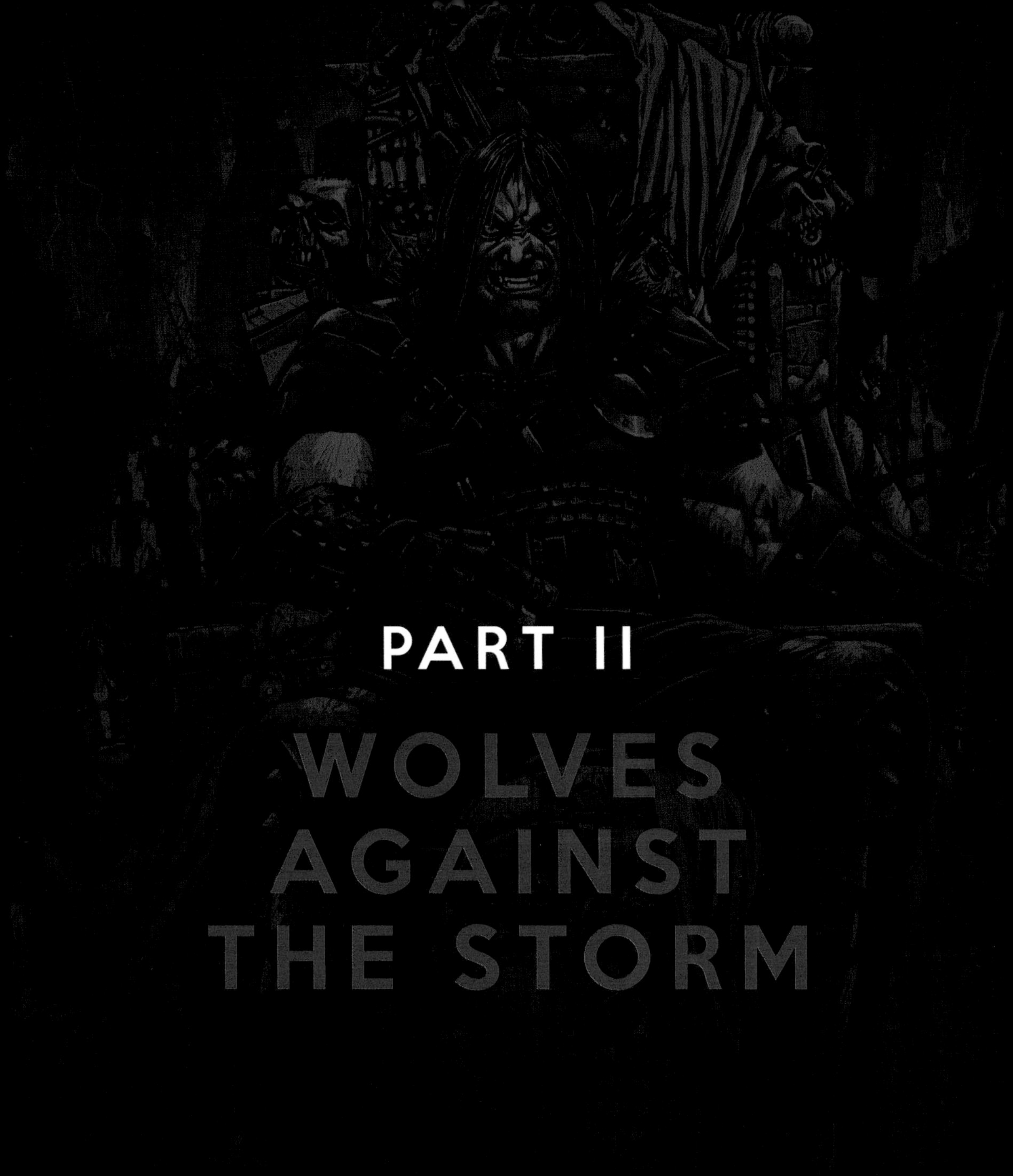

PART II

WOLVES AGAINST THE STORM

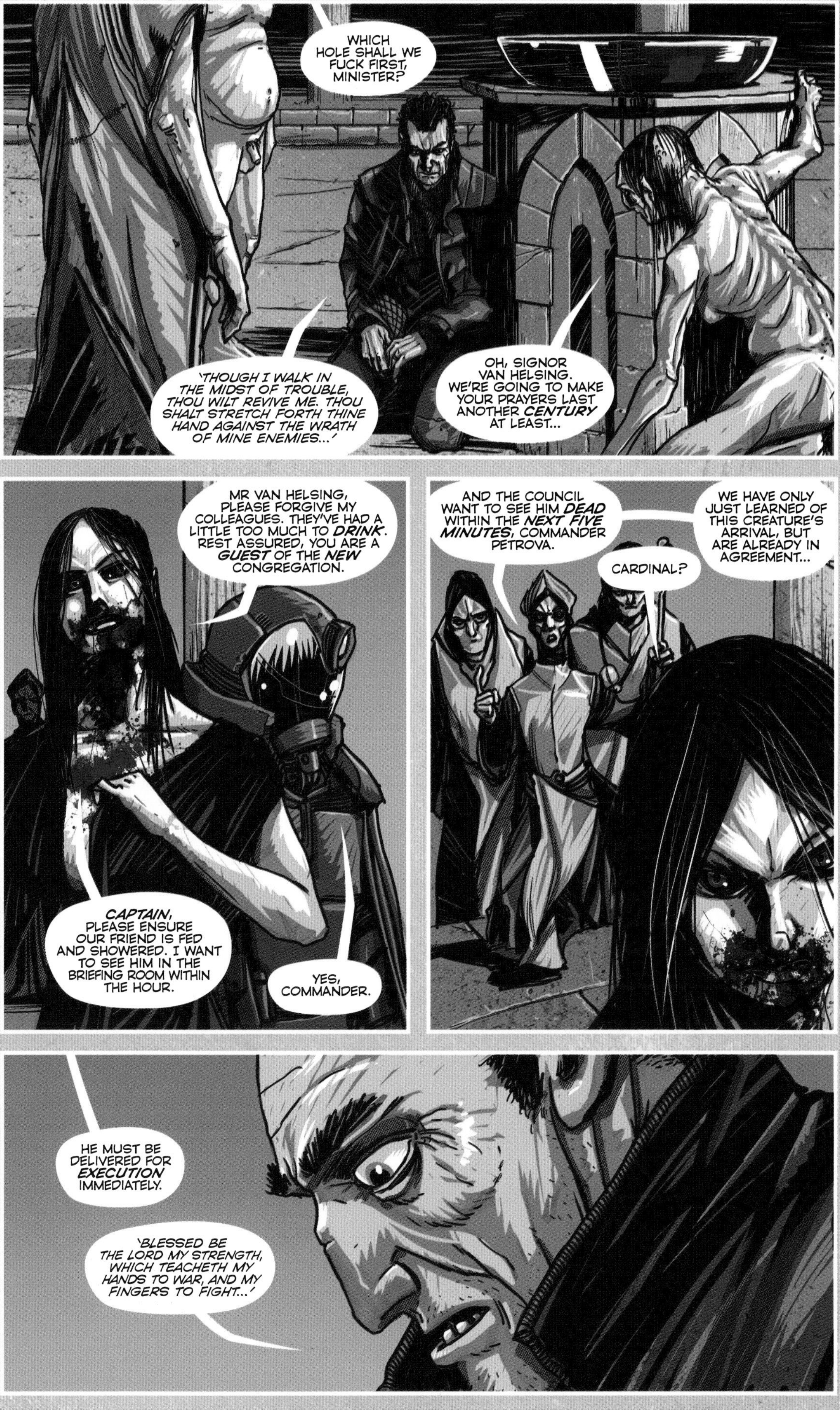
WHICH HOLE SHALL WE FUCK FIRST, MINISTER?
'THOUGH I WALK IN THE MIDST OF TROUBLE, THOU WILT REVIVE ME. THOU SHALT STRETCH FORTH THINE HAND AGAINST THE WRATH OF MINE ENEMIES...'
OH, SIGNOR VAN HELSING. WE'RE GOING TO MAKE YOUR PRAYERS LAST ANOTHER CENTURY AT LEAST...
MR VAN HELSING, PLEASE FORGIVE MY COLLEAGUES. THEY'VE HAD A LITTLE TOO MUCH TO DRINK. REST ASSURED, YOU ARE A GUEST OF THE NEW CONGREGATION.
CAPTAIN, PLEASE ENSURE OUR FRIEND IS FED AND SHOWERED. I WANT TO SEE HIM IN THE BRIEFING ROOM WITHIN THE HOUR.
YES, COMMANDER.
WE HAVE ONLY JUST LEARNED OF THIS CREATURE'S ARRIVAL, BUT ARE ALREADY IN AGREEMENT...
AND THE COUNCIL WANT TO SEE HIM DEAD WITHIN THE NEXT FIVE MINUTES, COMMANDER PETROVA.
CARDINAL?
HE MUST BE DELIVERED FOR EXECUTION IMMEDIATELY.
'BLESSED BE THE LORD MY STRENGTH, WHICH TEACHETH MY HANDS TO WAR, AND MY FINGERS TO FIGHT...'

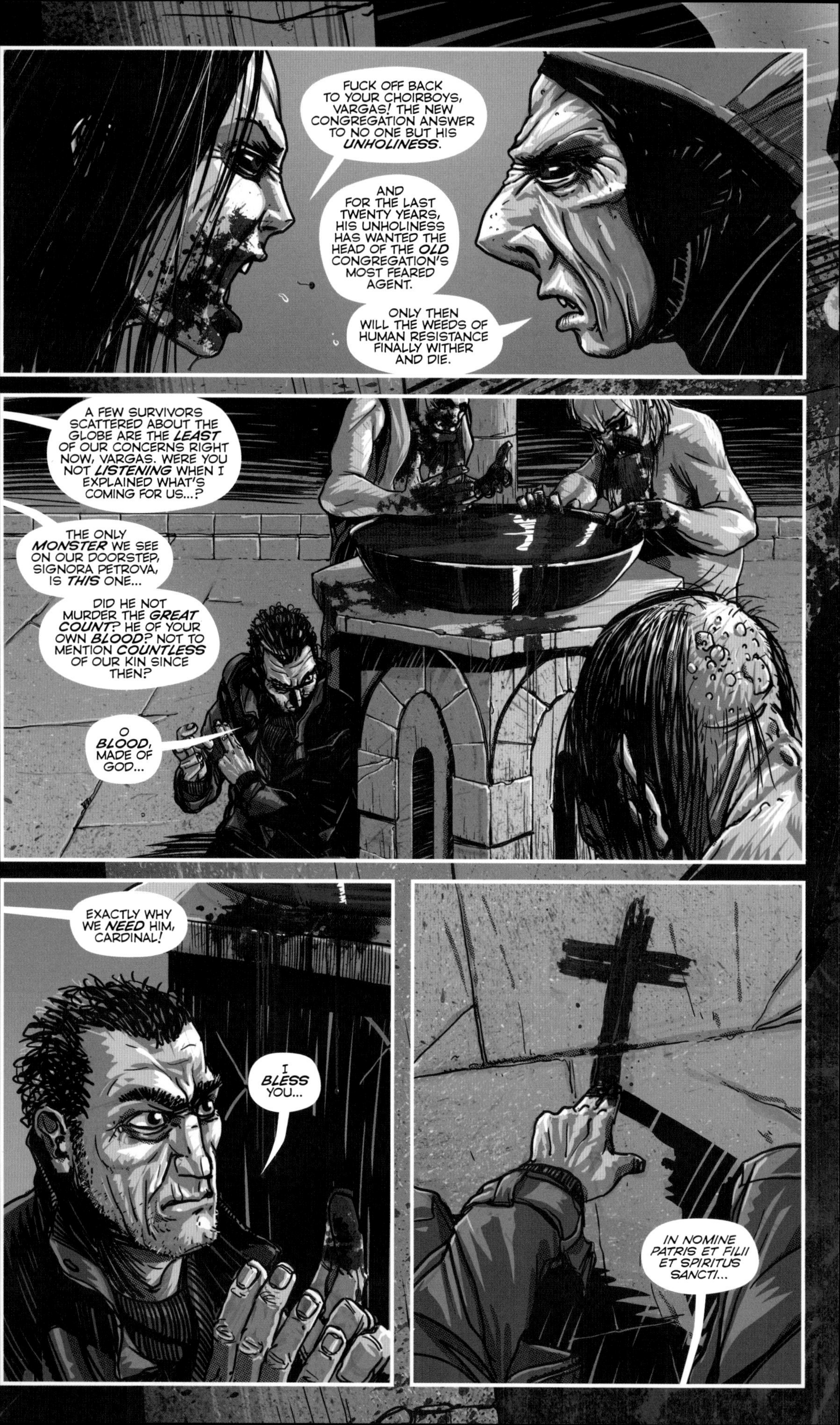
FUCK OFF BACK TO YOUR CHOIRBOYS, VARGAS! THE NEW CONGREGATION ANSWER TO NO ONE BUT HIS UNHOLINESS.
AND FOR THE LAST TWENTY YEARS, HIS UNHOLINESS HAS WANTED THE HEAD OF THE OLD CONGREGATION'S MOST FEARED AGENT.
ONLY THEN WILL THE WEEDS OF HUMAN RESISTANCE FINALLY WITHER AND DIE.
A FEW SURVIVORS SCATTERED ABOUT THE GLOBE ARE THE LEAST OF OUR CONCERNS RIGHT NOW, VARGAS. WERE YOU NOT LISTENING WHEN I EXPLAINED WHAT'S COMING FOR US...?
THE ONLY MONSTER WE SEE ON OUR DOORSTEP, SIGNORA PETROVA, IS THIS ONE...
DID HE NOT MURDER THE GREAT COUNT? HE OF YOUR OWN BLOOD? NOT TO MENTION COUNTLESS OF OUR KIN SINCE THEN?
O BLOOD, MADE OF GOD...
EXACTLY WHY WE NEED HIM, CARDINAL!
I BLESS YOU...
IN NOMINE PATRIS ET FILII ET SPIRITUS SANCTI...

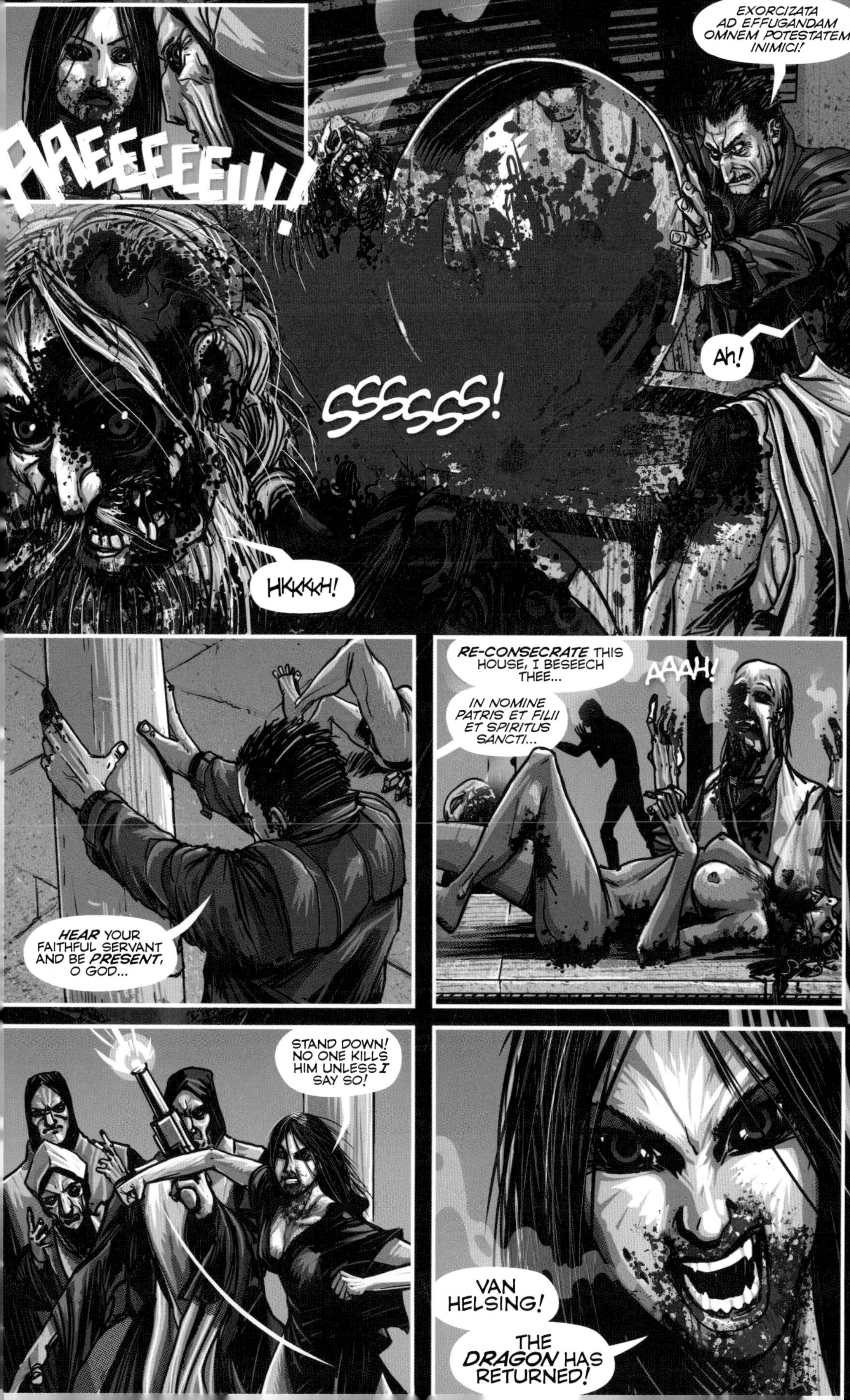
EXORCIZATA AD EFFUGANDAM OMNEM POTESTATEM INIMICI!
Ah!
SSSSSS!
HKKKKH!
HEAR YOUR FAITHFUL SERVANT AND BE PRESENT, O GOD...
RE-CONSECRATE THIS HOUSE, I BESEECH THEE...
IN NOMINE PATRIS ET FILII ET SPIRITUS SANCTI...
AAAH!
STAND DOWN! NO ONE KILLS HIM UNLESS I SAY SO!
VAN HELSING!
THE DRAGON HAS RETURNED!

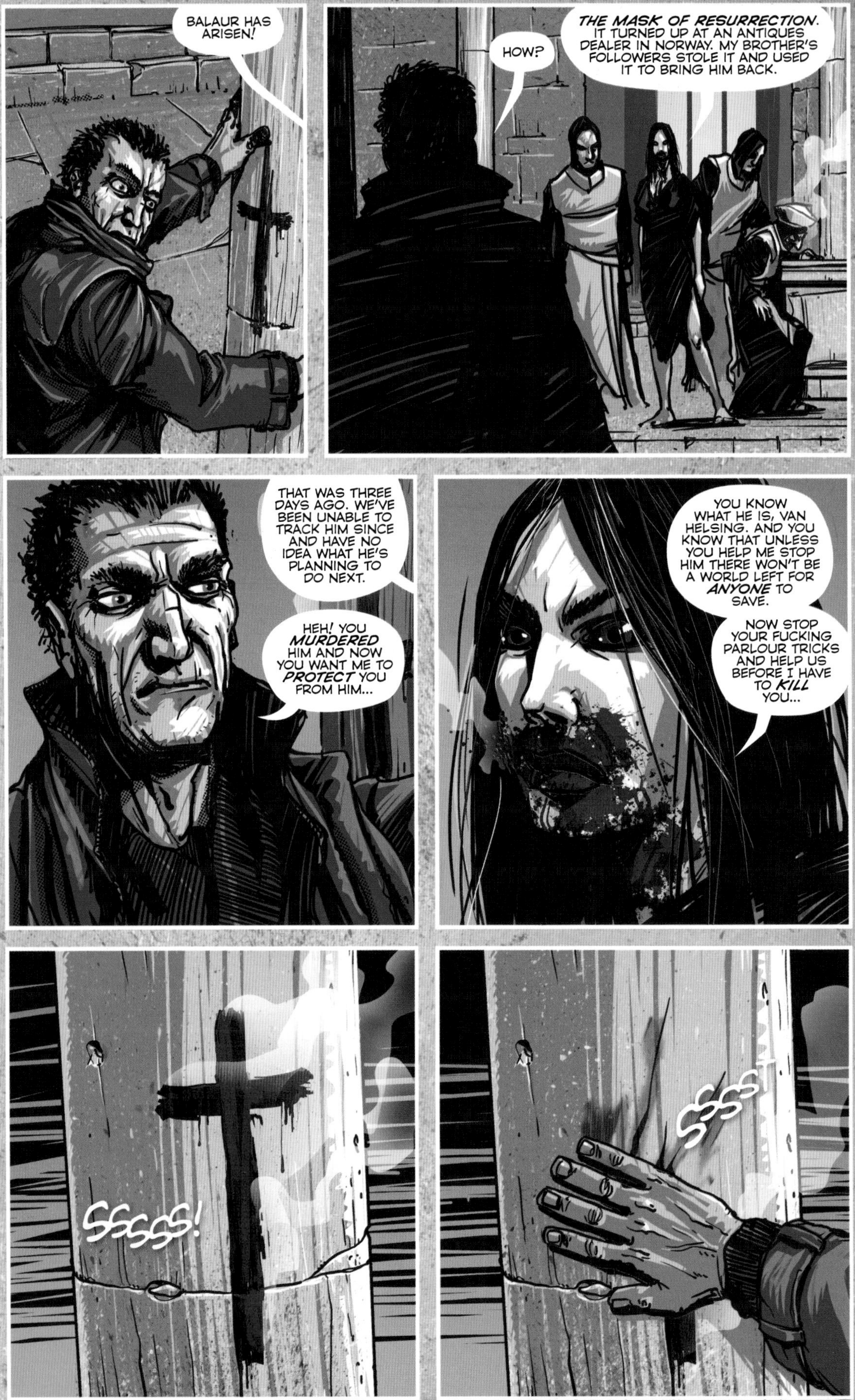
BALAUR HAS ARISEN!
HOW?
THE MASK OF RESURRECTION. IT TURNED UP AT AN ANTIQUES DEALER IN NORWAY. MY BROTHER'S FOLLOWERS STOLE IT AND USED IT TO BRING HIM BACK.
THAT WAS THREE DAYS AGO. WE'VE BEEN UNABLE TO TRACK HIM SINCE AND HAVE NO IDEA WHAT HE'S PLANNING TO DO NEXT.
HEH! YOU MURDERED HIM AND NOW YOU WANT ME TO PROTECT YOU FROM HIM...
YOU KNOW WHAT HE IS, VAN HELSING. AND YOU KNOW THAT UNLESS YOU HELP ME STOP HIM THERE WON'T BE A WORLD LEFT FOR ANYONE TO SAVE.
NOW STOP YOUR FUCKING PARLOUR TRICKS AND HELP US BEFORE I HAVE TO KILL YOU...
SSSSS!
SSSST

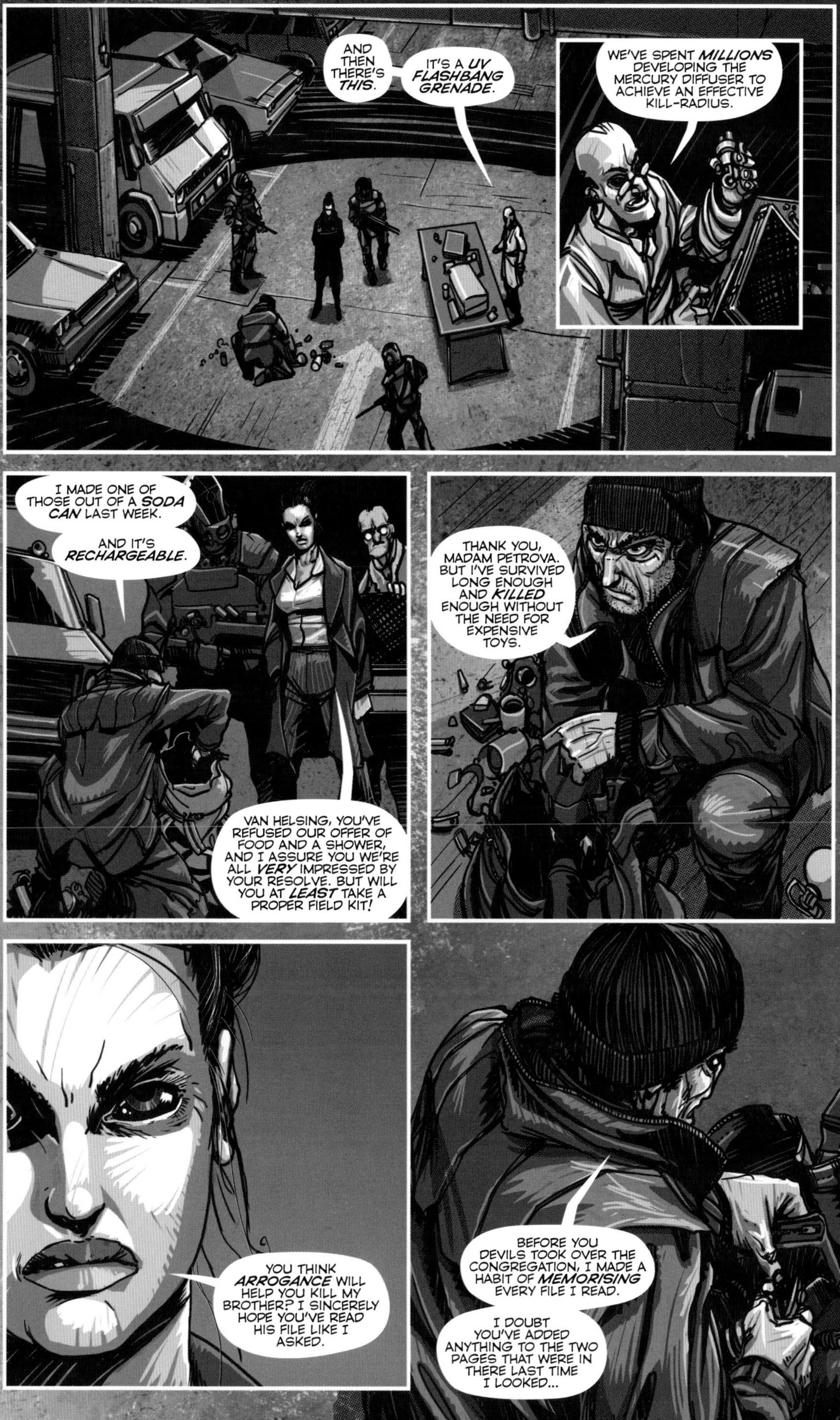
AND THEN THERE'S THIS.
IT'S A UV FLASHBANG GRENADE.
WE'VE SPENT MILLIONS DEVELOPING THE MERCURY DIFFUSER TO ACHIEVE AN EFFECTIVE KILL-RADIUS.
I MADE ONE OF THOSE OUT OF A SODA CAN LAST WEEK.
AND IT'S RECHARGEABLE.
VAN HELSING, YOU'VE REFUSED OUR OFFER OF FOOD AND A SHOWER, AND I ASSURE YOU WE'RE ALL VERY IMPRESSED BY YOUR RESOLVE. BUT WILL YOU AT LEAST TAKE A PROPER FIELD KIT!
THANK YOU, MADAM PETROVA. BUT I'VE SURVIVED LONG ENOUGH AND KILLED ENOUGH WITHOUT THE NEED FOR EXPENSIVE TOYS.
YOU THINK ARROGANCE WILL HELP YOU KILL MY BROTHER? I SINCERELY HOPE YOU'VE READ HIS FILE LIKE I ASKED.
BEFORE YOU DEVILS TOOK OVER THE CONGREGATION, I MADE A HABIT OF MEMORISING EVERY FILE I READ.
I DOUBT YOU'VE ADDED ANYTHING TO THE TWO PAGES THAT WERE IN THERE LAST TIME I LOOKED...

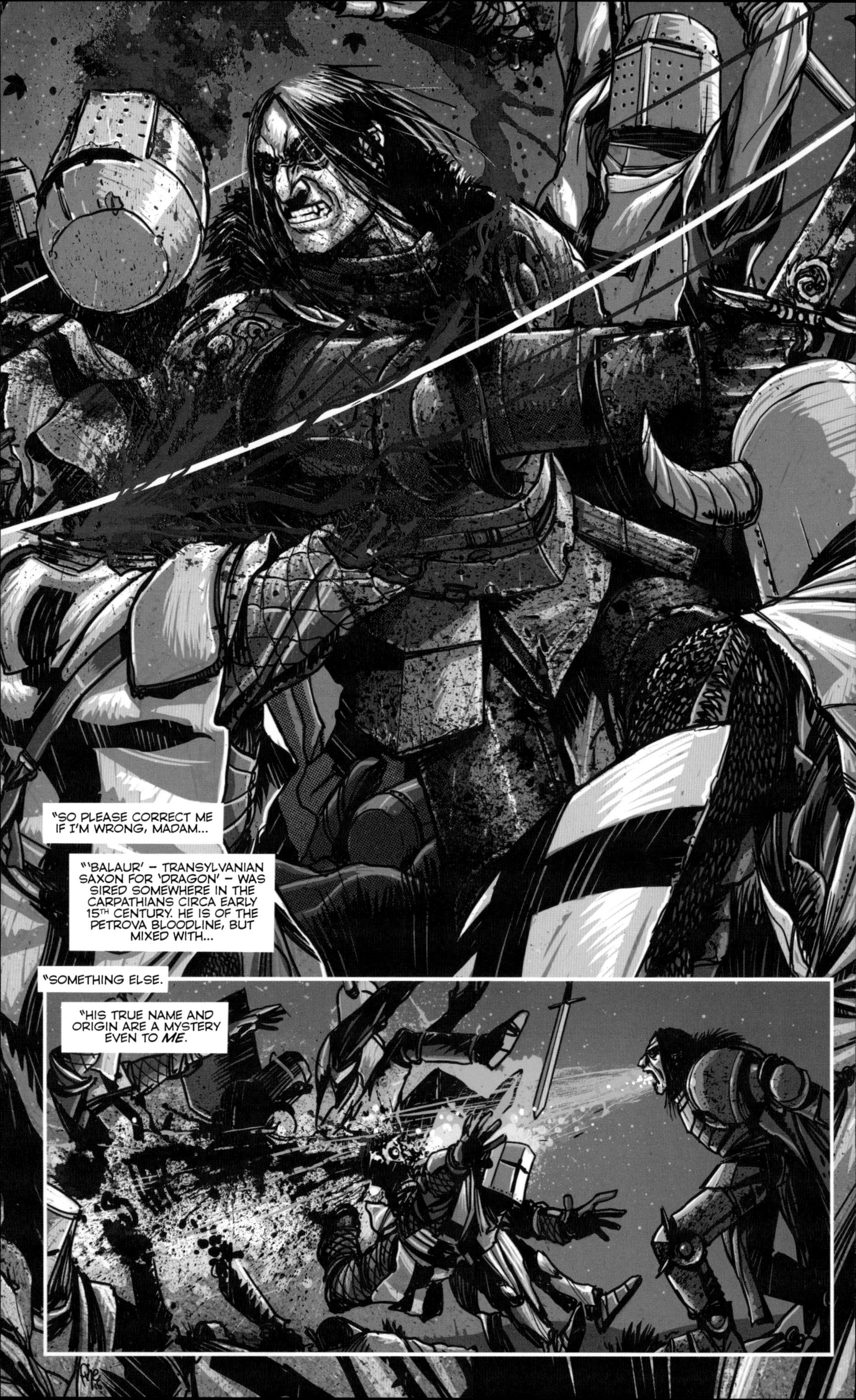

"SO PLEASE CORRECT ME IF I'M WRONG, MADAM...
"'BALAUR' – TRANSYLVANIAN SAXON FOR 'DRAGON' – WAS SIRED SOMEWHERE IN THE CARPATHIANS CIRCA EARLY 15TH CENTURY. HE IS OF THE PETROVA BLOODLINE, BUT MIXED WITH...
"SOMETHING ELSE.
"HIS TRUE NAME AND ORIGIN ARE A MYSTERY EVEN TO *ME*.

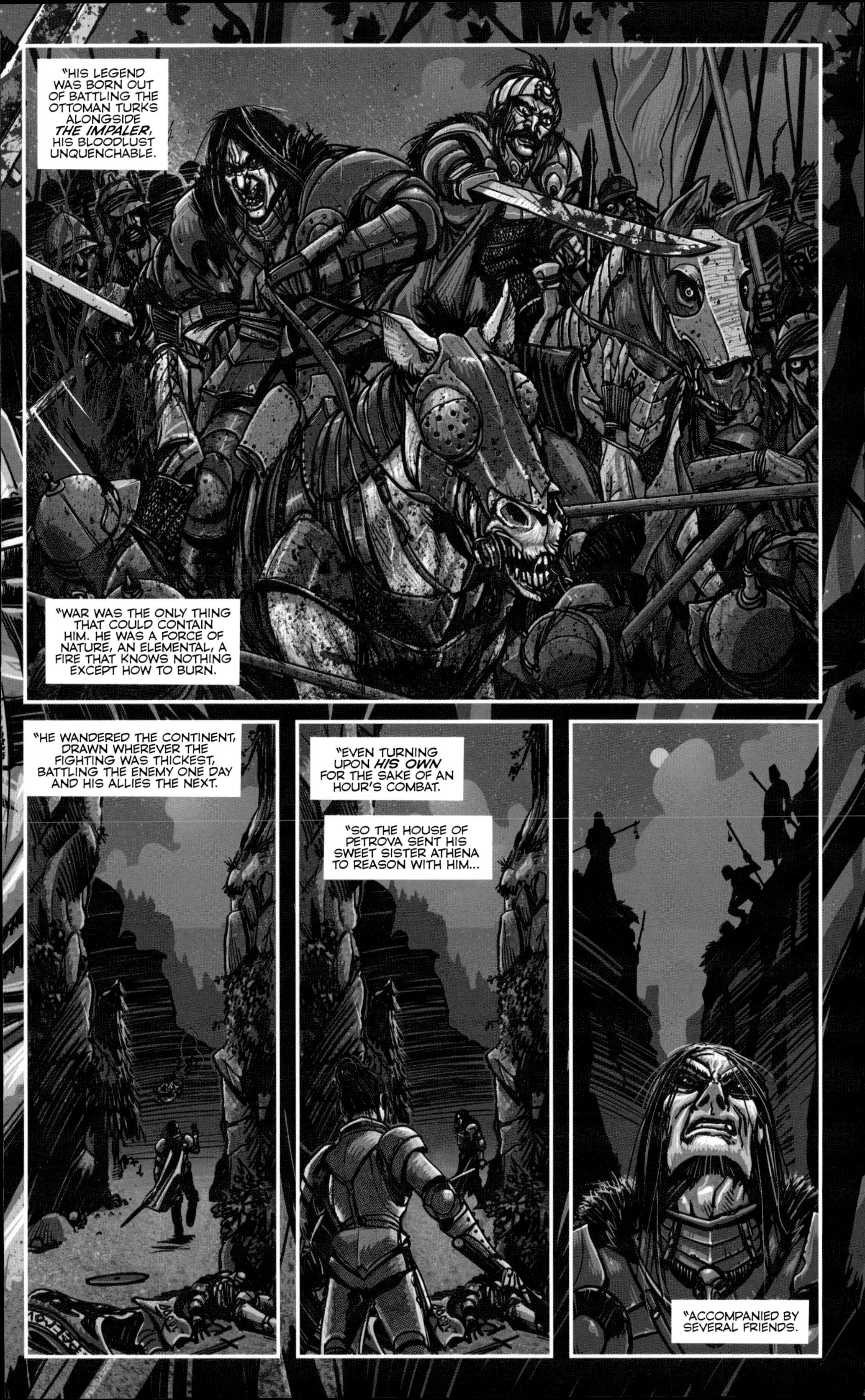
"HIS LEGEND WAS BORN OUT OF BATTLING THE OTTOMAN TURKS ALONGSIDE ***THE IMPALER***, HIS BLOODLUST UNQUENCHABLE.
"WAR WAS THE ONLY THING THAT COULD CONTAIN HIM. HE WAS A FORCE OF NATURE, AN ELEMENTAL, A FIRE THAT KNOWS NOTHING EXCEPT HOW TO BURN.
"HE WANDERED THE CONTINENT, DRAWN WHEREVER THE FIGHTING WAS THICKEST, BATTLING THE ENEMY ONE DAY AND HIS ALLIES THE NEXT.
"EVEN TURNING UPON ***HIS OWN*** FOR THE SAKE OF AN HOUR'S COMBAT.
"SO THE HOUSE OF PETROVA SENT HIS SWEET SISTER ATHENA TO REASON WITH HIM...
"ACCOMPANIED BY SEVERAL FRIENDS.

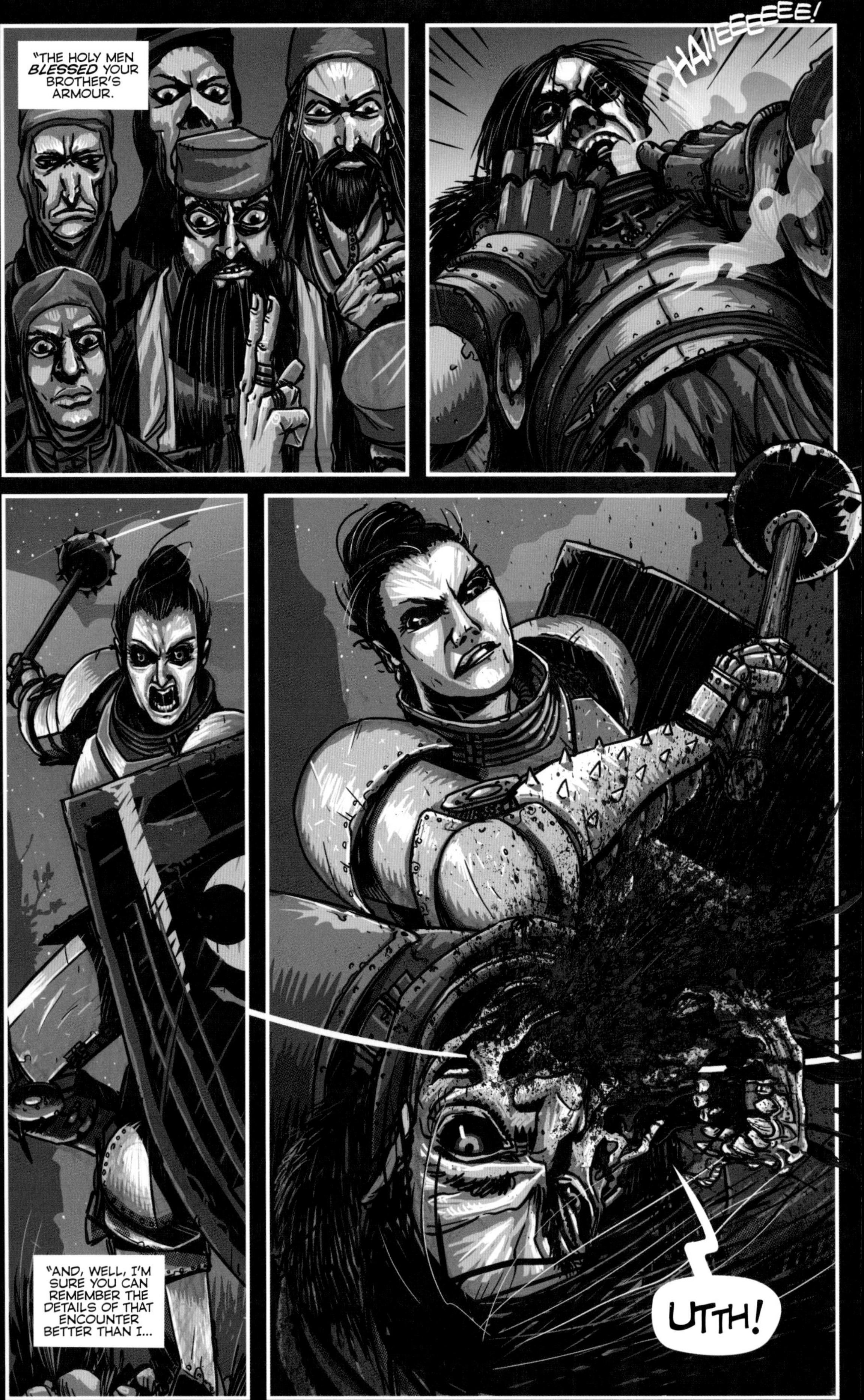
"THE HOLY MEN BLESSED YOUR BROTHER'S ARMOUR.
HAIIEEEEEEE!
"AND, WELL, I'M SURE YOU CAN REMEMBER THE DETAILS OF THAT ENCOUNTER BETTER THAN I...
UTTH!

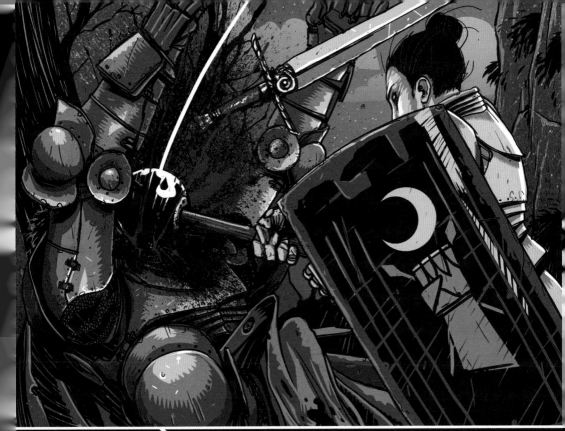

"THE LEGENDS SAID THAT BALAUR'S JAWBONE WAS THE ONLY PART OF HIS UNHOLY FORM NOT BURNED TO ASH BY THE SUN.

"AND THAT A CULT OF FOLLOWERS WHO CALLED THEMSELVES 'THE SONS OF BALAUR' FOUND IT SEVERAL DAYS LATER.

"THEY PRESERVED THIS RELIC INSIDE A MASK ENGRAVED WITH GLYPHS OF RESURRECTION... EARLY NEMORTIAN, IF I RECALL CORRECTLY.

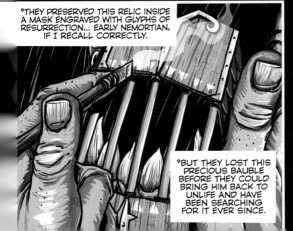

"BUT THEY LOST THIS PRECIOUS BAUBLE BEFORE THEY COULD BRING HIM BACK TO UNLIFE AND HAVE BEEN SEARCHING FOR IT EVER SINCE.

MASK OF BALAUR

"NOW IT SEEMS THEIR PERSISTENCE HAS FINALLY BEEN REWARDED."

I DON'T RECALL ANYTHING IN THAT FILE ABOUT *THE RITE OF ASCENSION*.

THE SONS OF BALAUR ARE SAID TO HAVE SPENT CENTURIES SEARCHING FOR A WAY TO GRANT THEIR MASTER SOME KIND OF *KINGLY POWER* UPON HIS RETURN.

I HOPE THE PROSPECT OF AN ALL-POWERFUL VAMPIRE MADMAN WAS ONE TAKEN *SERIOUSLY* SINCE YOU TOOK OVER THE CONGREGATION...

WE'VE HAD BETTER THINGS TO DO THAN OBSESS OVER FOLK TALES, VAN HELSING. BALAUR'S RETURN IS SOMETHING NONE OF US COULD HAVE PREDICTED.

'BETTER THINGS'?

LIKE *SLAUGHTERING* MY PEOPLE AND ENSURING THE *EXTINCTION* AND *ENSLAVEMENT* OF HUMANITY? YOU SHOULD BEWARE, MADAM...

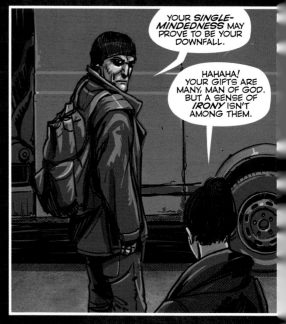

YOUR *SINGLE-MINDEDNESS* MAY PROVE TO BE YOUR DOWNFALL.

HAHAHA! YOUR GIFTS ARE MANY, MAN OF GOD. BUT A SENSE OF *IRONY* ISN'T AMONG THEM.

NOW THAT YOU'VE FINISHED CHECKING YOUR EQUIPMENT FOR TRACKING DEVICES, HAVE YOU WONDERED AT ALL WHY WE'RE LETTING YOU BACK INTO THE FIELD *ALONE*?

BECAUSE YOU KNOW I'LL *KILL* ANYONE YOU SEND WITH ME THE FIRST CHANCE I GET.

WELL, THAT TOO. BUT REMEMBER THAT *TRACER* IN YOUR BLOOD? I'M GUESSING YOU WERE THINKING OF FLUSHING IT OUT WITH SOME KIND OF *TRANSFUSION*, YES?

THE TRUTH IS IT'S NOW *BONDED* WITH YOUR DNA. *PERMANENTLY*. WE CAN FIND YOU NOW *WHEREVER* YOU ARE IN THE WORLD.

OR YOU COULD BE *LYING*.

RUN AND YOU'LL FIND OUT.

BUT DO YOU *REALLY* WANT TO SPEND THE REST OF YOUR DAYS BEING *HUNTED*? SOILING YOUR VEINS WITH STOLEN BLOOD 'TIL GOD ALMIGHTY *FINALLY* DECIDES TO END YOUR MISERY?

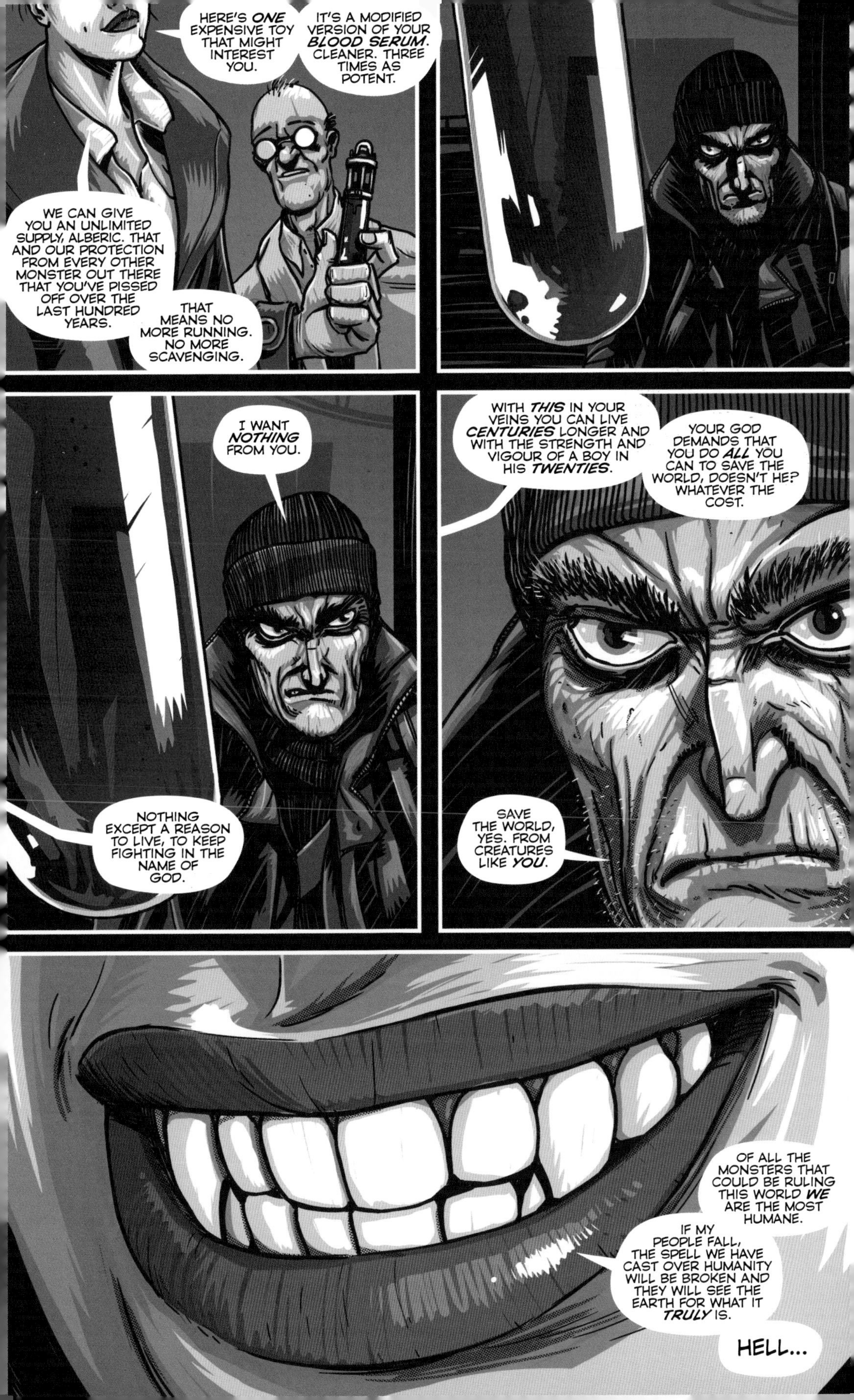
HERE'S ONE EXPENSIVE TOY THAT MIGHT INTEREST YOU.
IT'S A MODIFIED VERSION OF YOUR BLOOD SERUM. CLEANER. THREE TIMES AS POTENT.
WE CAN GIVE YOU AN UNLIMITED SUPPLY, ALBERIC. THAT AND OUR PROTECTION FROM EVERY OTHER MONSTER OUT THERE THAT YOU'VE PISSED OFF OVER THE LAST HUNDRED YEARS.
THAT MEANS NO MORE RUNNING. NO MORE SCAVENGING.
I WANT NOTHING FROM YOU.
NOTHING EXCEPT A REASON TO LIVE, TO KEEP FIGHTING IN THE NAME OF GOD.
WITH THIS IN YOUR VEINS YOU CAN LIVE CENTURIES LONGER AND WITH THE STRENGTH AND VIGOUR OF A BOY IN HIS TWENTIES.
YOUR GOD DEMANDS THAT YOU DO ALL YOU CAN TO SAVE THE WORLD, DOESN'T HE? WHATEVER THE COST.
SAVE THE WORLD, YES. FROM CREATURES LIKE YOU.
OF ALL THE MONSTERS THAT COULD BE RULING THIS WORLD WE ARE THE MOST HUMANE.
IF MY PEOPLE FALL, THE SPELL WE HAVE CAST OVER HUMANITY WILL BE BROKEN AND THEY WILL SEE THE EARTH FOR WHAT IT TRULY IS.
HELL...

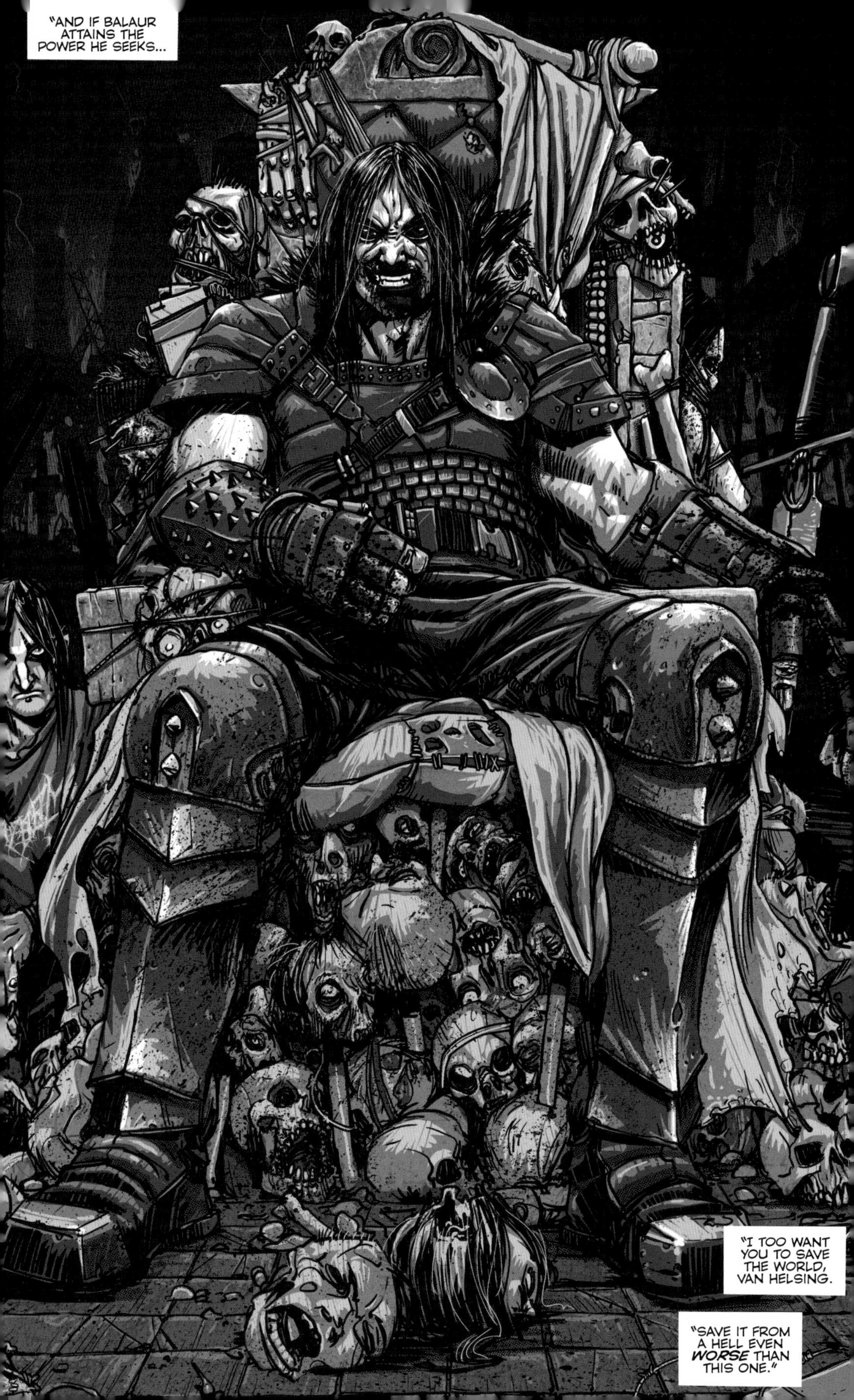
"AND IF BALAUR ATTAINS THE POWER HE SEEKS...
"I TOO WANT YOU TO SAVE THE WORLD, VAN HELSING.
"SAVE IT FROM A HELL EVEN WORSE THAN THIS ONE."

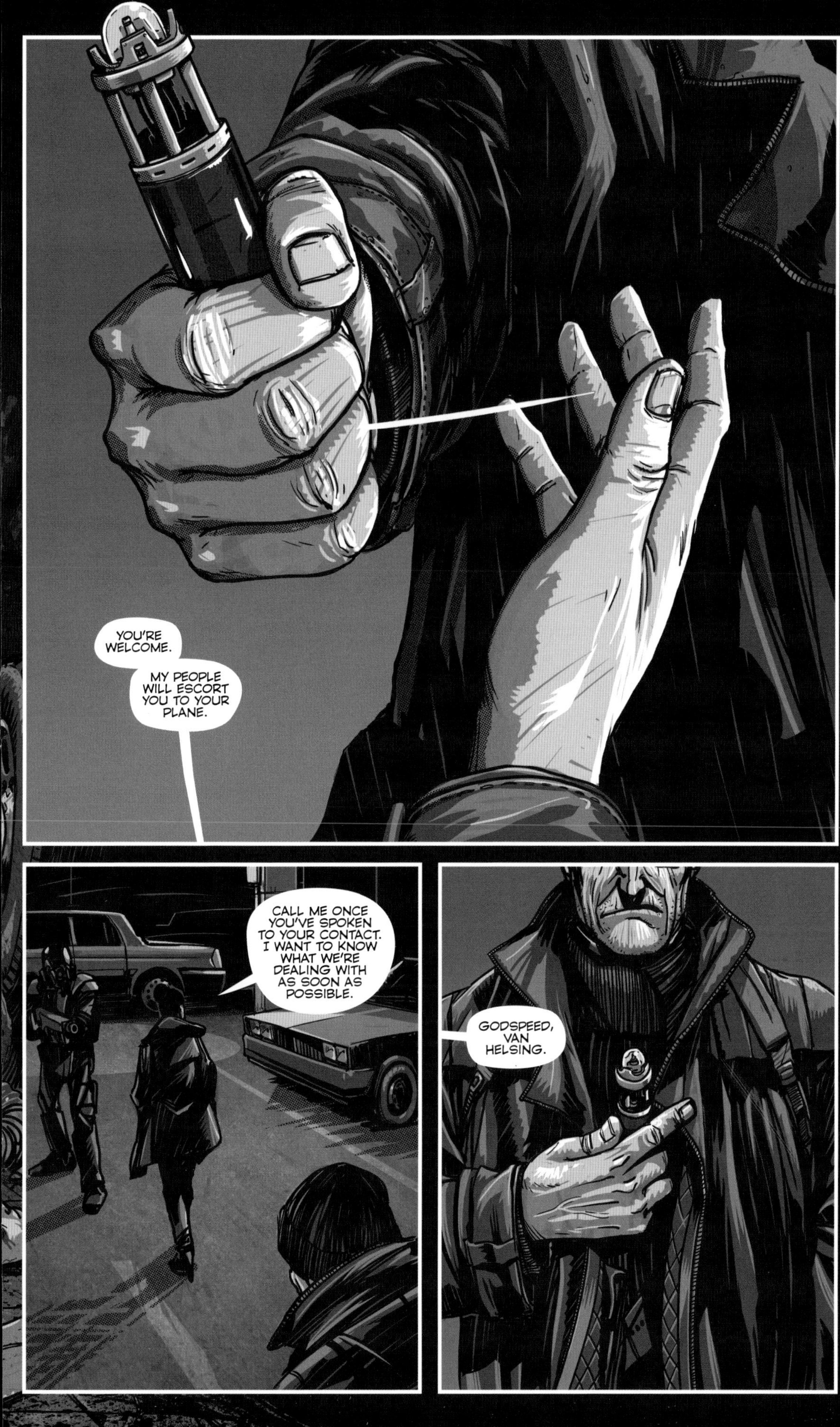

YOU'RE WELCOME.
MY PEOPLE WILL ESCORT YOU TO YOUR PLANE.
CALL ME ONCE YOU'VE SPOKEN TO YOUR CONTACT. I WANT TO KNOW WHAT WE'RE DEALING WITH AS SOON AS POSSIBLE.
GODSPEED, VAN HELSING.

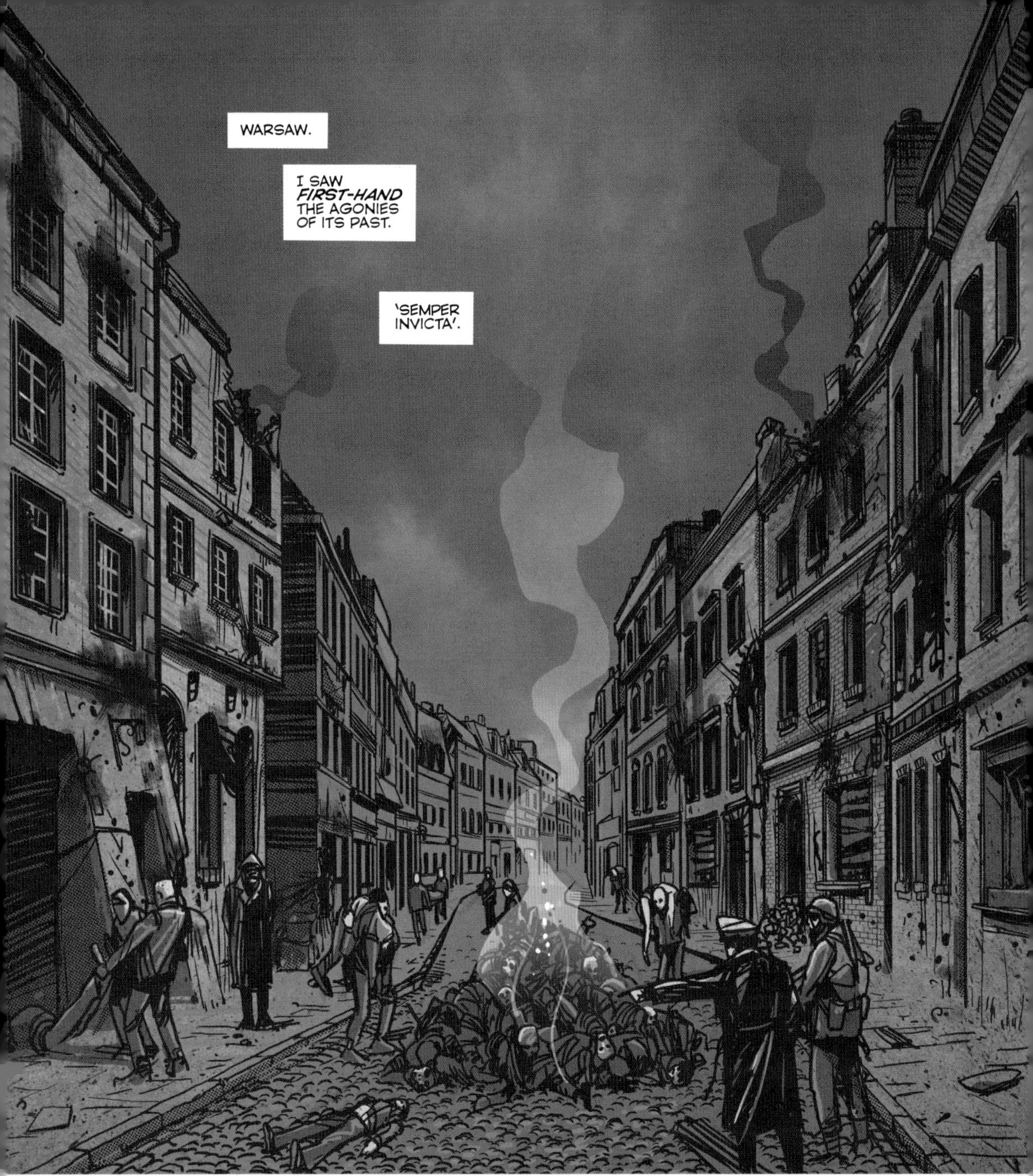
WARSAW.
I SAW *FIRST-HAND* THE AGONIES OF ITS PAST.
'SEMPER INVICTA'.

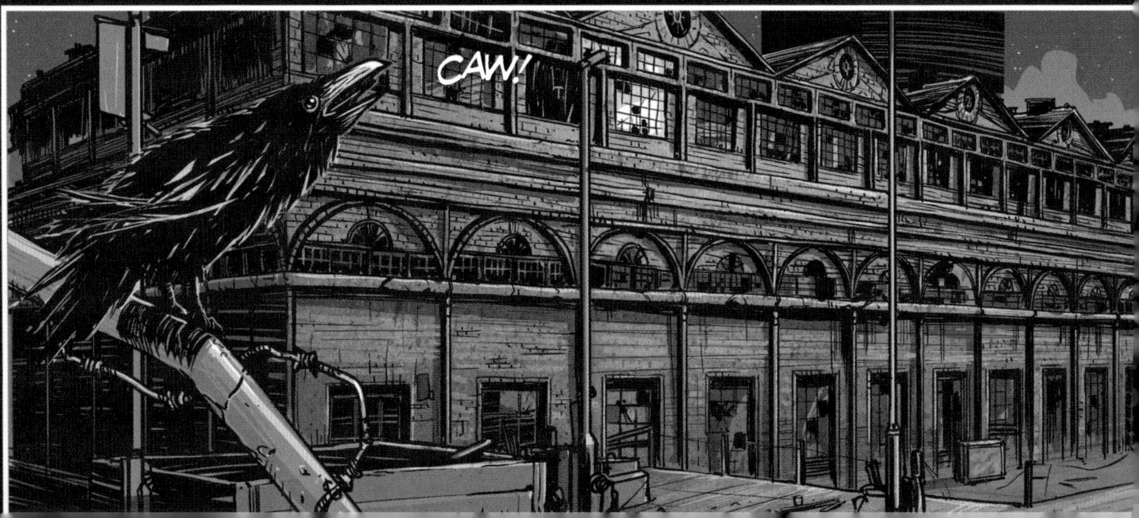
CAW!

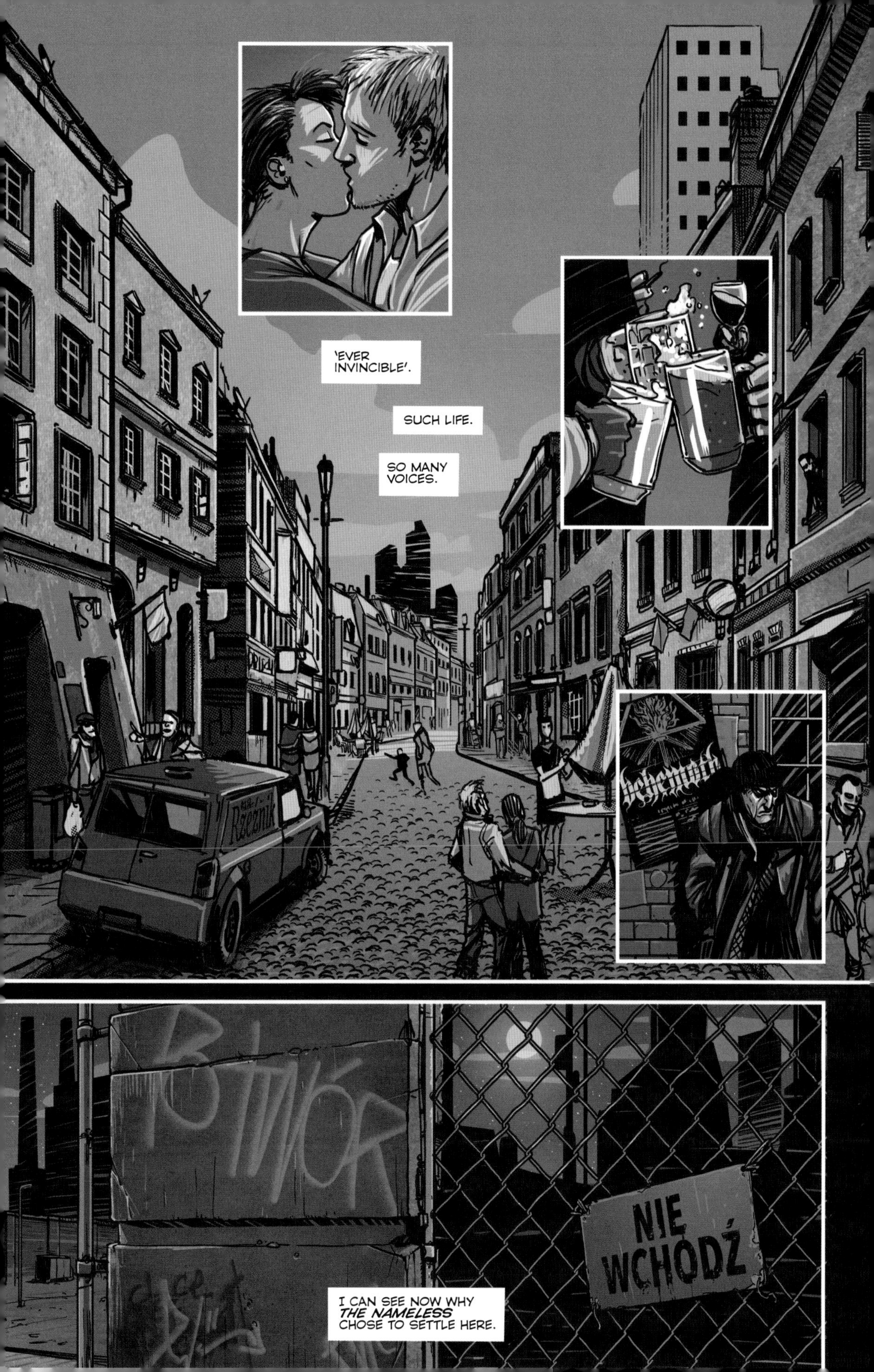

'EVER INVINCIBLE'.
SUCH LIFE.
SO MANY VOICES.
Rzeźnik
NIE WCHODŹ
I CAN SEE NOW WHY *THE NAMELESS* CHOSE TO SETTLE HERE.

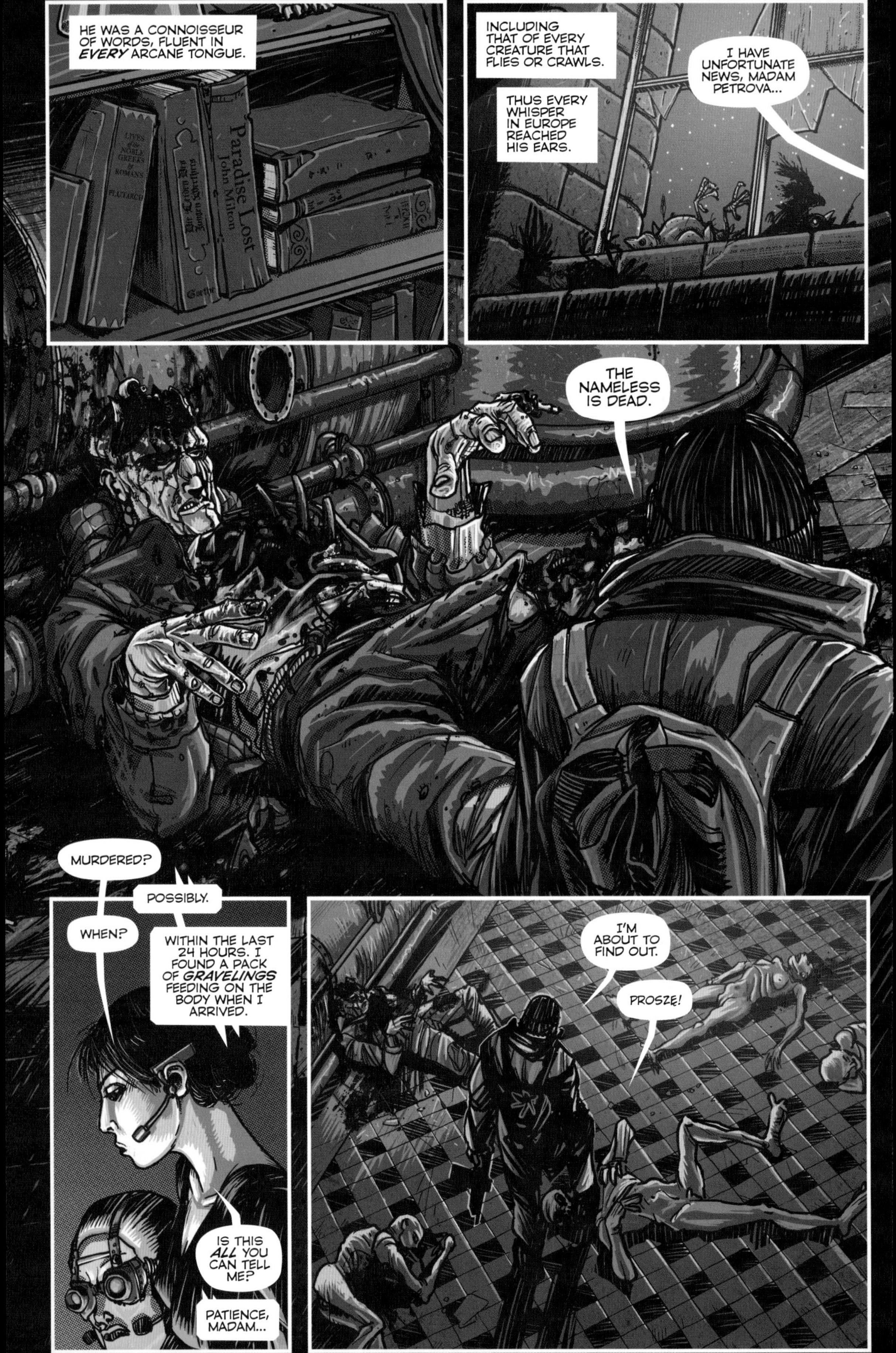
HE WAS A CONNOISSEUR OF WORDS, FLUENT IN *EVERY* ARCANE TONGUE.
LIVES of the NOBLE GREEKS & ROMANS PLUTARCH
Paradise Lost John Milton
INCLUDING THAT OF EVERY CREATURE THAT FLIES OR CRAWLS.
THUS EVERY WHISPER IN EUROPE REACHED HIS EARS.
I HAVE UNFORTUNATE NEWS, MADAM PETROVA...
THE NAMELESS IS DEAD.
MURDERED?
POSSIBLY.
WHEN?
WITHIN THE LAST 24 HOURS. I FOUND A PACK OF *GRAVELINGS* FEEDING ON THE BODY WHEN I ARRIVED.
IS THIS *ALL* YOU CAN TELL ME?
PATIENCE, MADAM...
I'M ABOUT TO FIND OUT.
PROSZĘ!

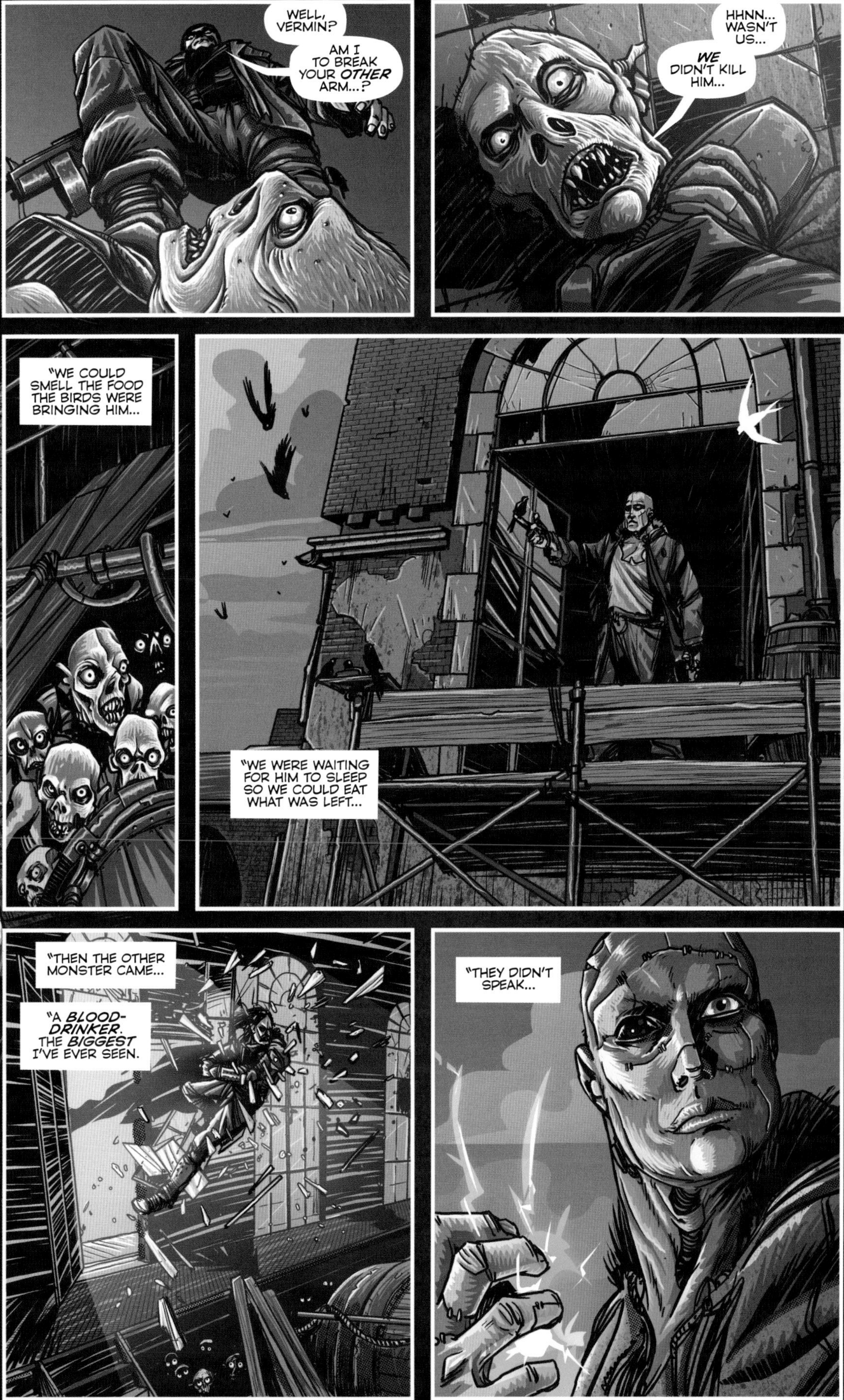
WELL, VERMIN?
AM I TO BREAK YOUR OTHER ARM...?
HHNN... WASN'T US...
WE DIDN'T KILL HIM...
"WE COULD SMELL THE FOOD THE BIRDS WERE BRINGING HIM...
"WE WERE WAITING FOR HIM TO SLEEP SO WE COULD EAT WHAT WAS LEFT...
"THEN THE OTHER MONSTER CAME...
"A BLOOD-DRINKER. THE BIGGEST I'VE EVER SEEN.
"THEY DIDN'T SPEAK...

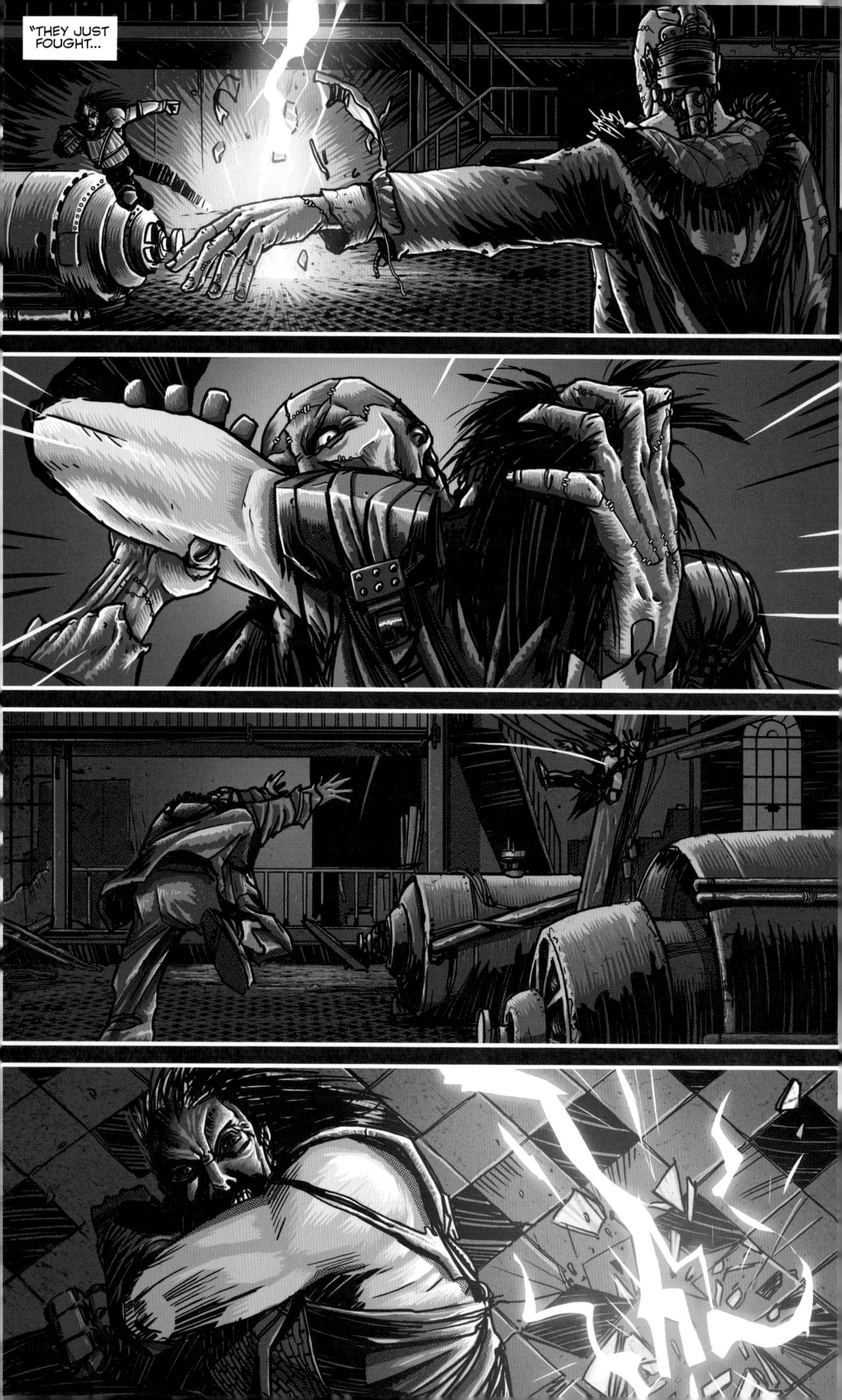
"THEY JUST FOUGHT...

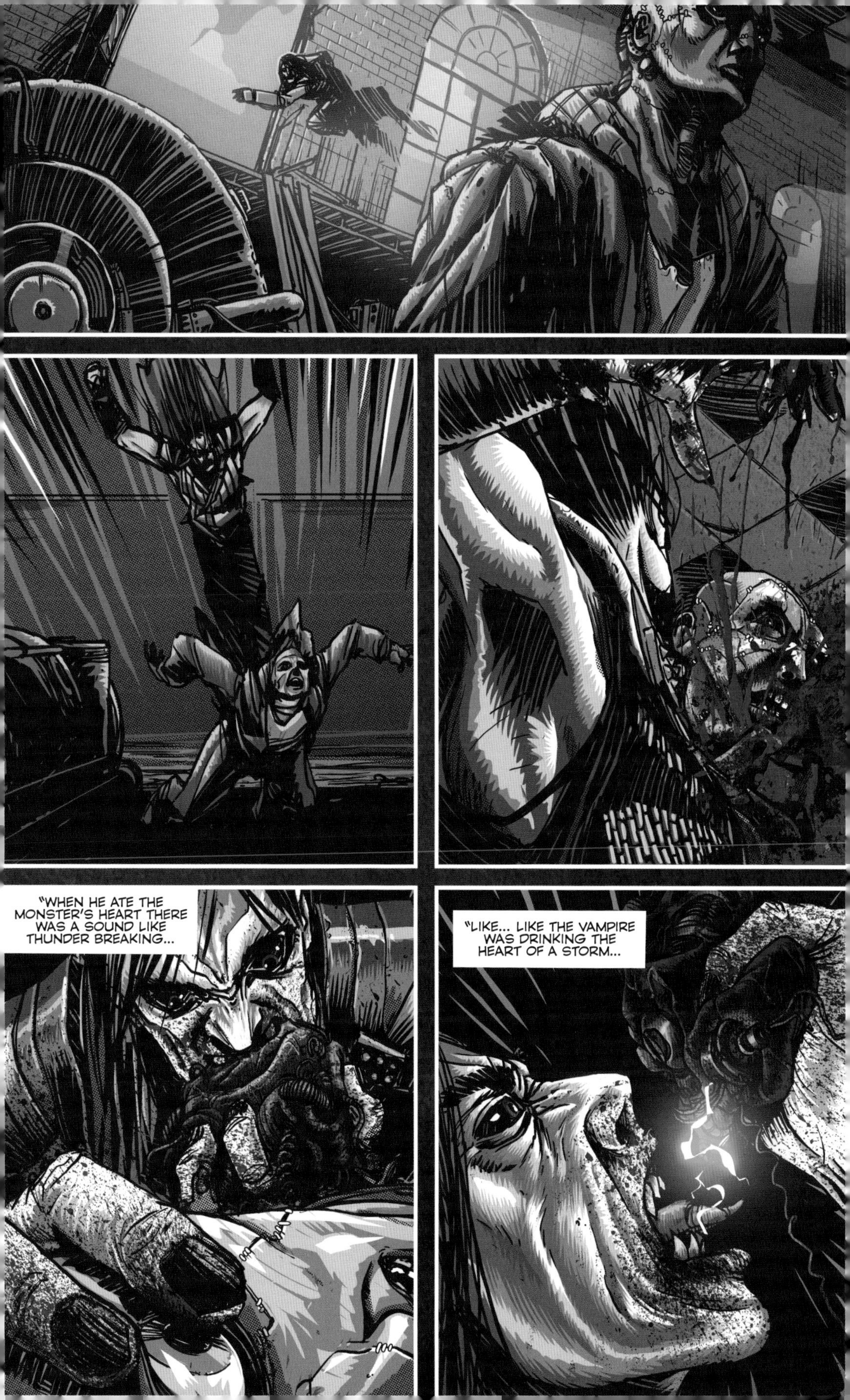
"WHEN HE ATE THE MONSTER'S HEART THERE WAS A SOUND LIKE THUNDER BREAKING...
"LIKE... LIKE THE VAMPIRE WAS DRINKING THE HEART OF A STORM...

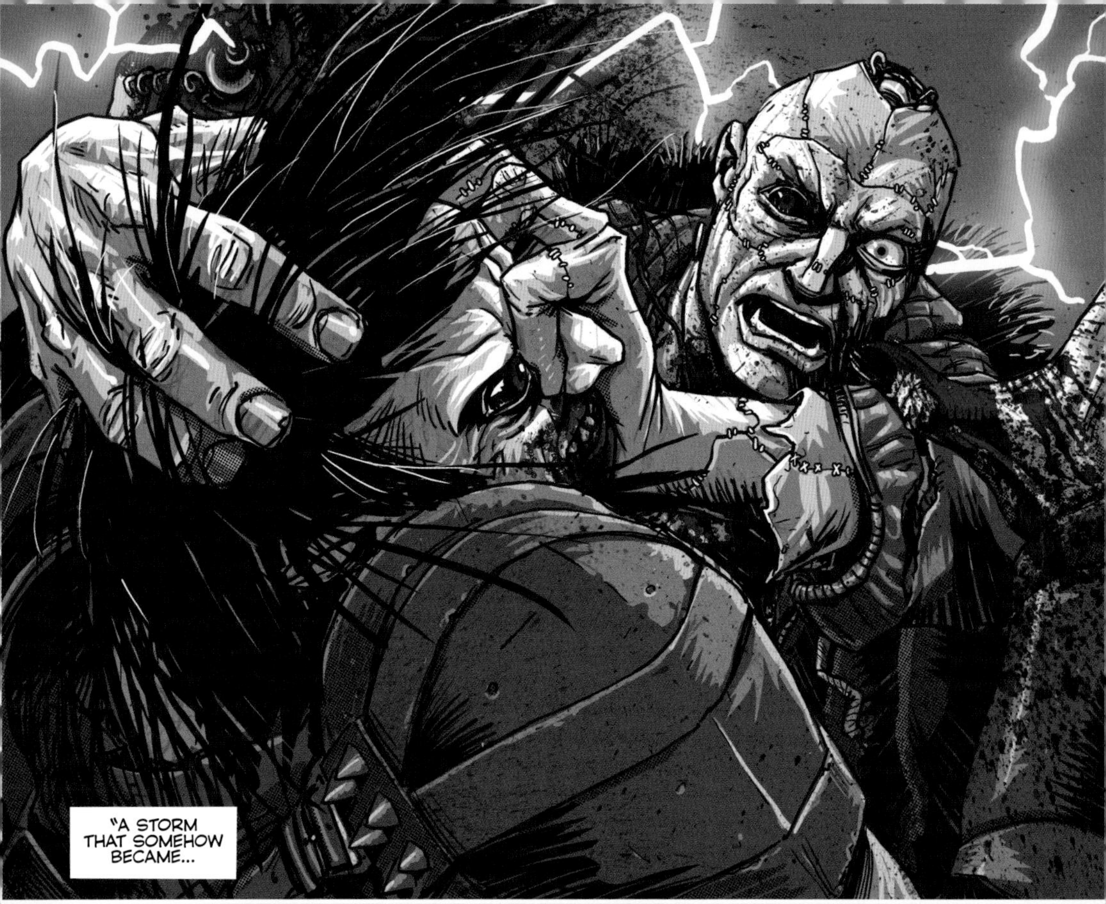
"A STORM THAT SOMEHOW BECAME...

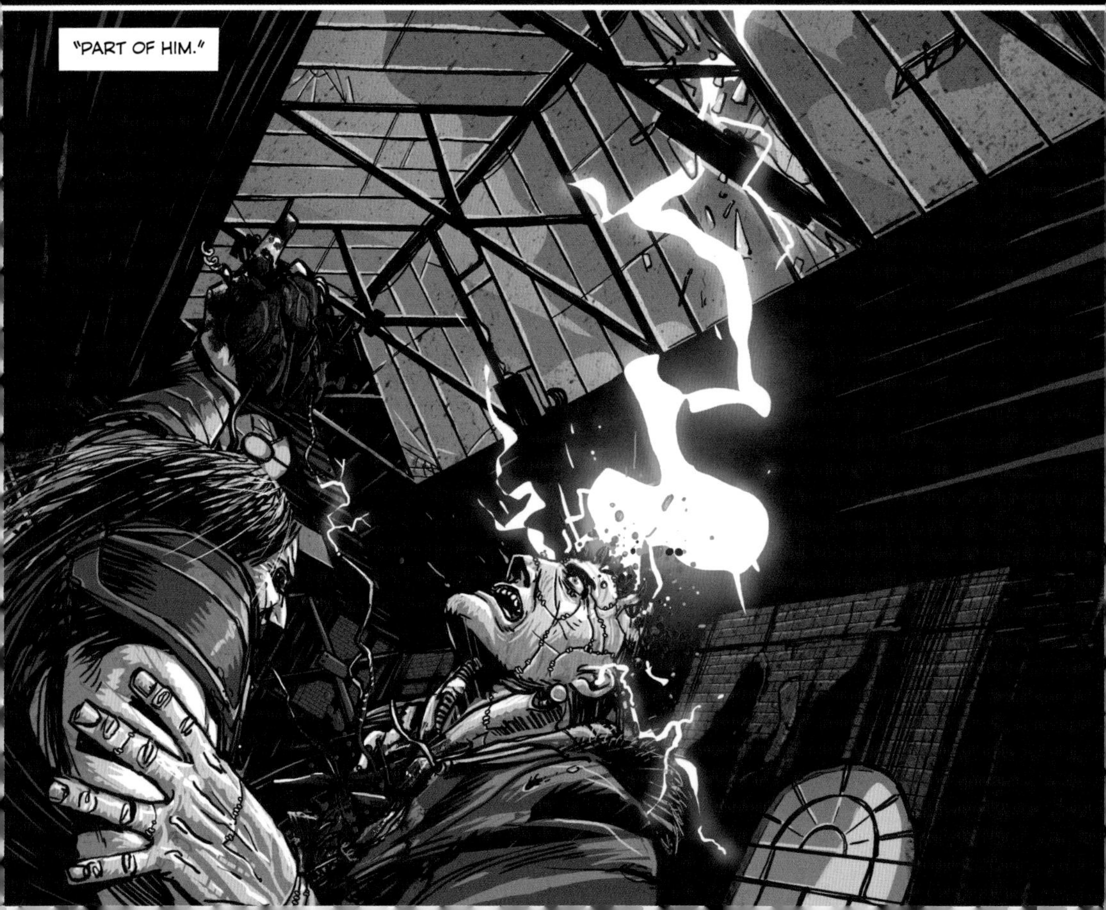
"PART OF HIM."

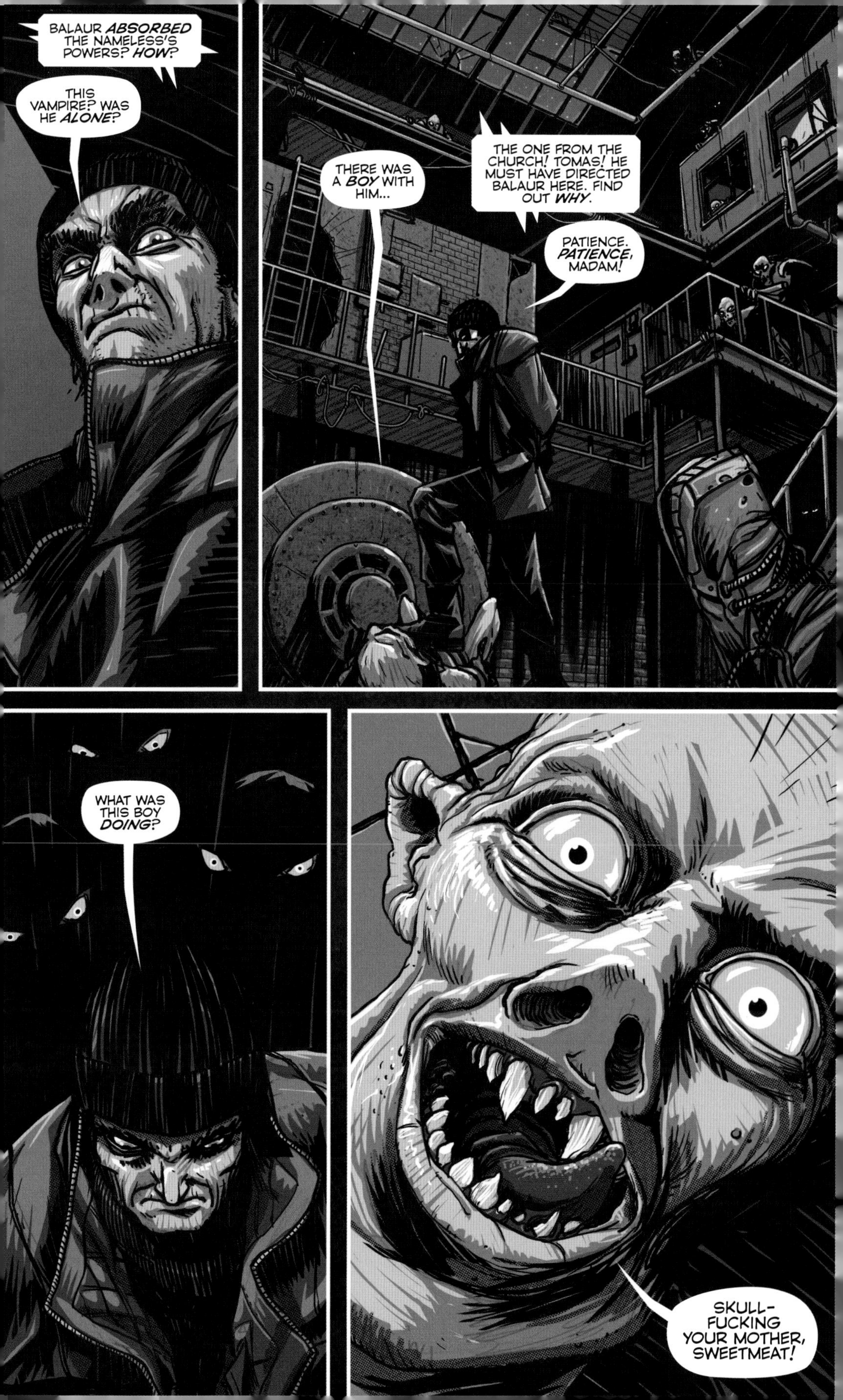
BALAUR ABSORBED THE NAMELESS'S POWERS? HOW?
THIS VAMPIRE? WAS HE ALONE?
THERE WAS A BOY WITH HIM...
THE ONE FROM THE CHURCH! TOMAS! HE MUST HAVE DIRECTED BALAUR HERE. FIND OUT WHY.
PATIENCE. PATIENCE, MADAM!
WHAT WAS THIS BOY DOING?
SKULL-FUCKING YOUR MOTHER, SWEETMEAT!

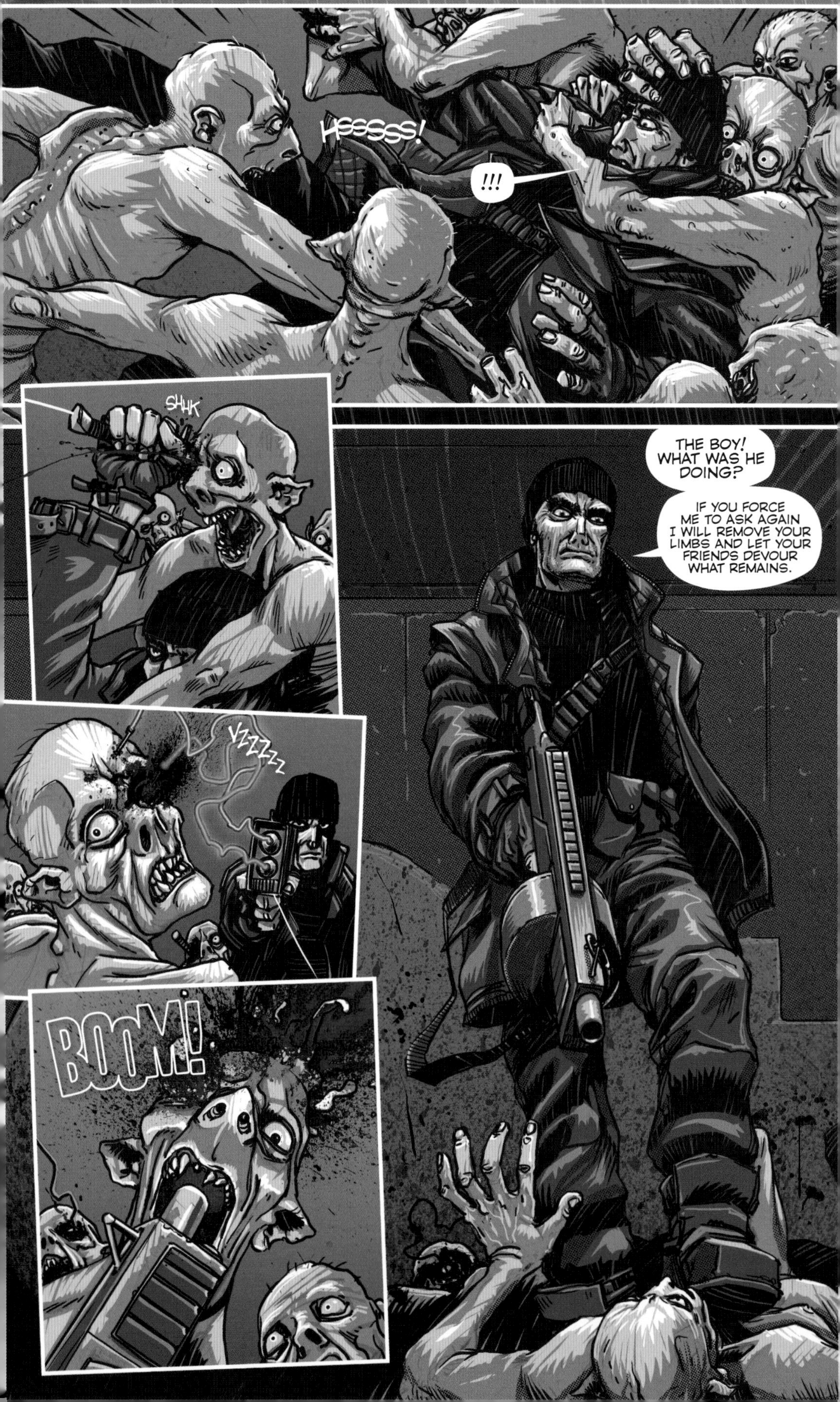
HSSSSS!
!!!
SHHK
THE BOY! WHAT WAS HE DOING?
IF YOU FORCE ME TO ASK AGAIN I WILL REMOVE YOUR LIMBS AND LET YOUR FRIENDS DEVOUR WHAT REMAINS.
VZZZZZ
BOOM!

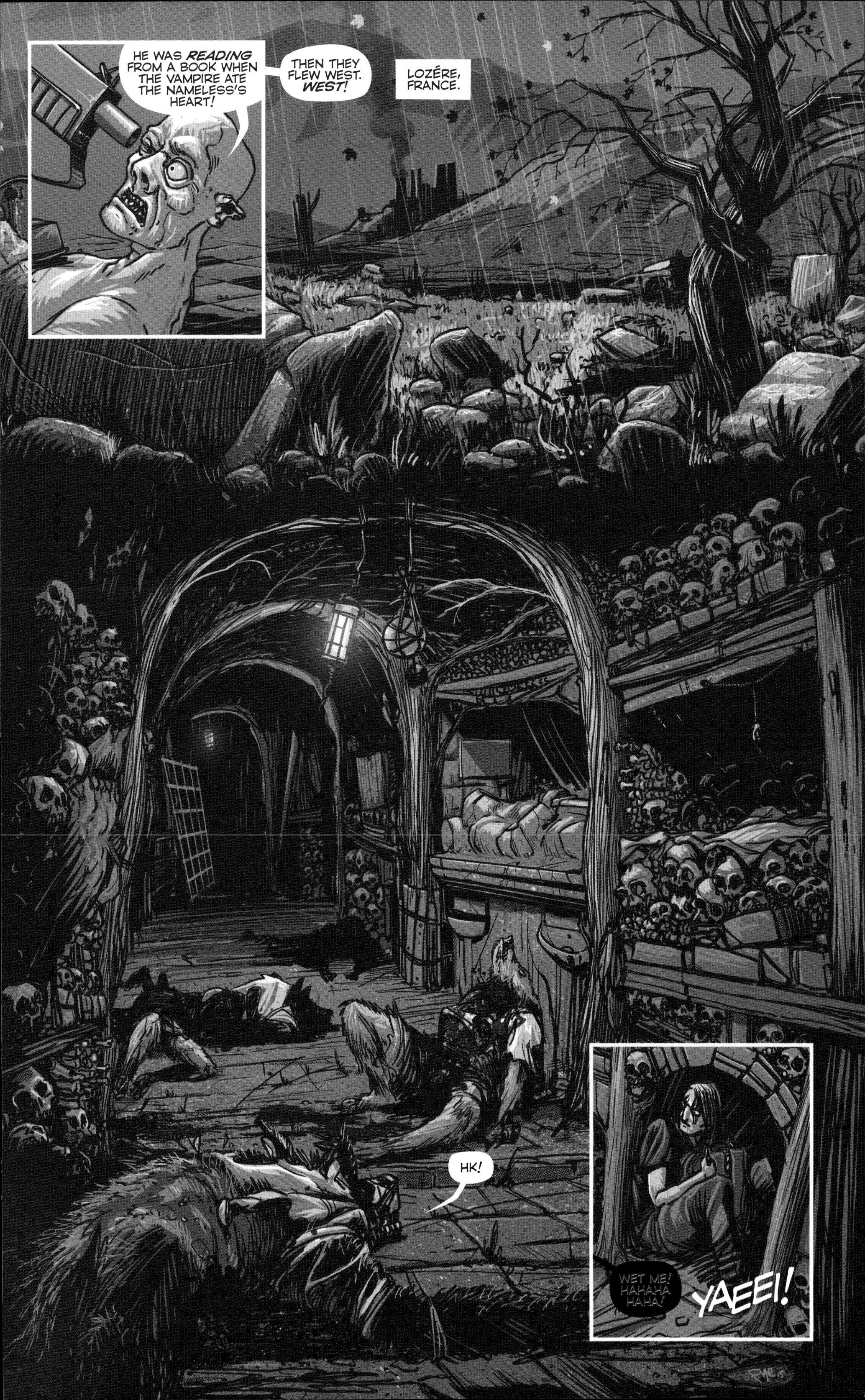
HE WAS READING FROM A BOOK WHEN THE VAMPIRE ATE THE NAMELESS'S HEART!
THEN THEY FLEW WEST. WEST!
LOZÉRE, FRANCE.
HK!
WET ME! HAHAHA HAHA!
YAEEI!

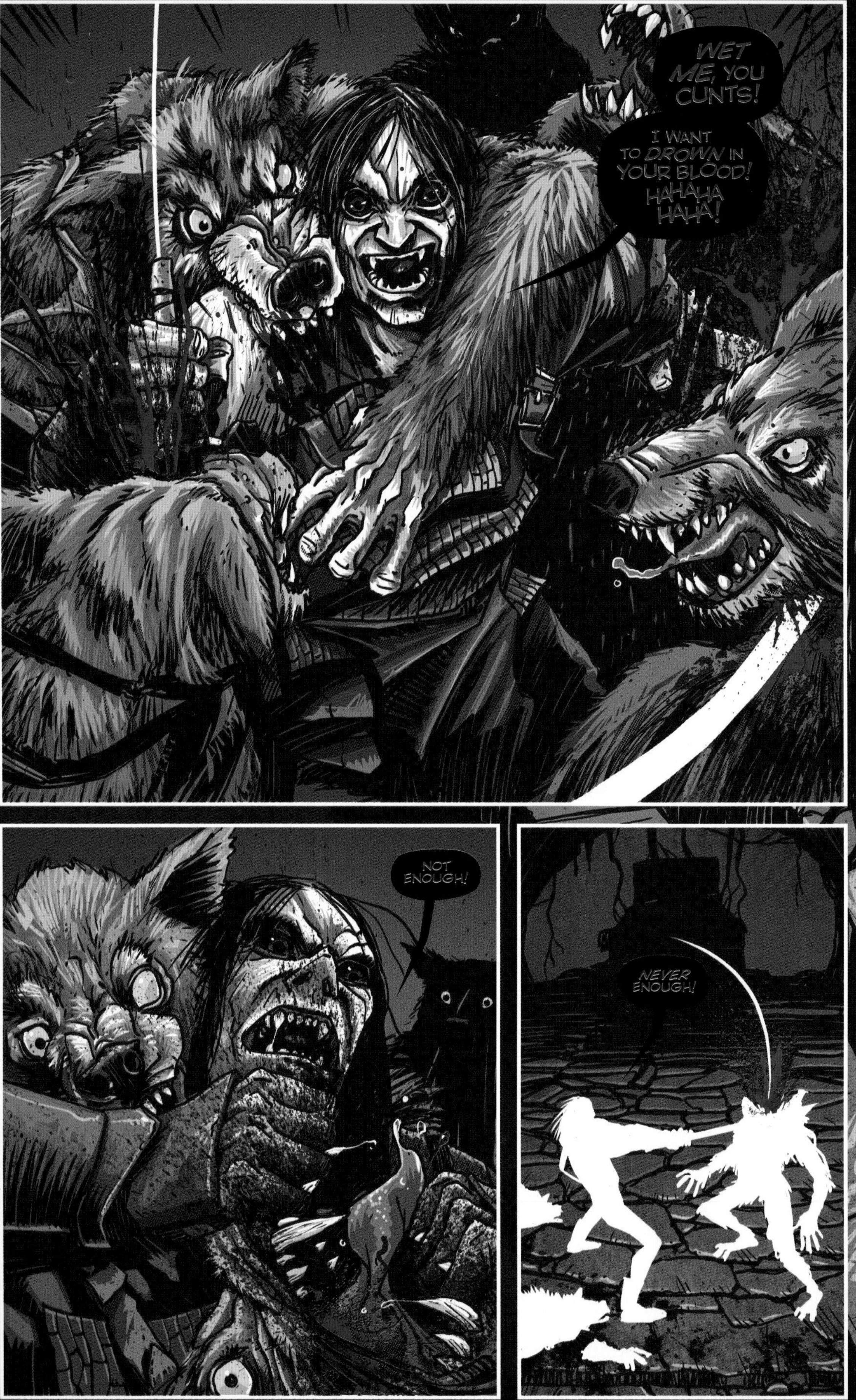
WET ME, YOU CUNTS!
I WANT TO DROWN IN YOUR BLOOD! HAHAHA HAHA!
NOT ENOUGH!
NEVER ENOUGH!

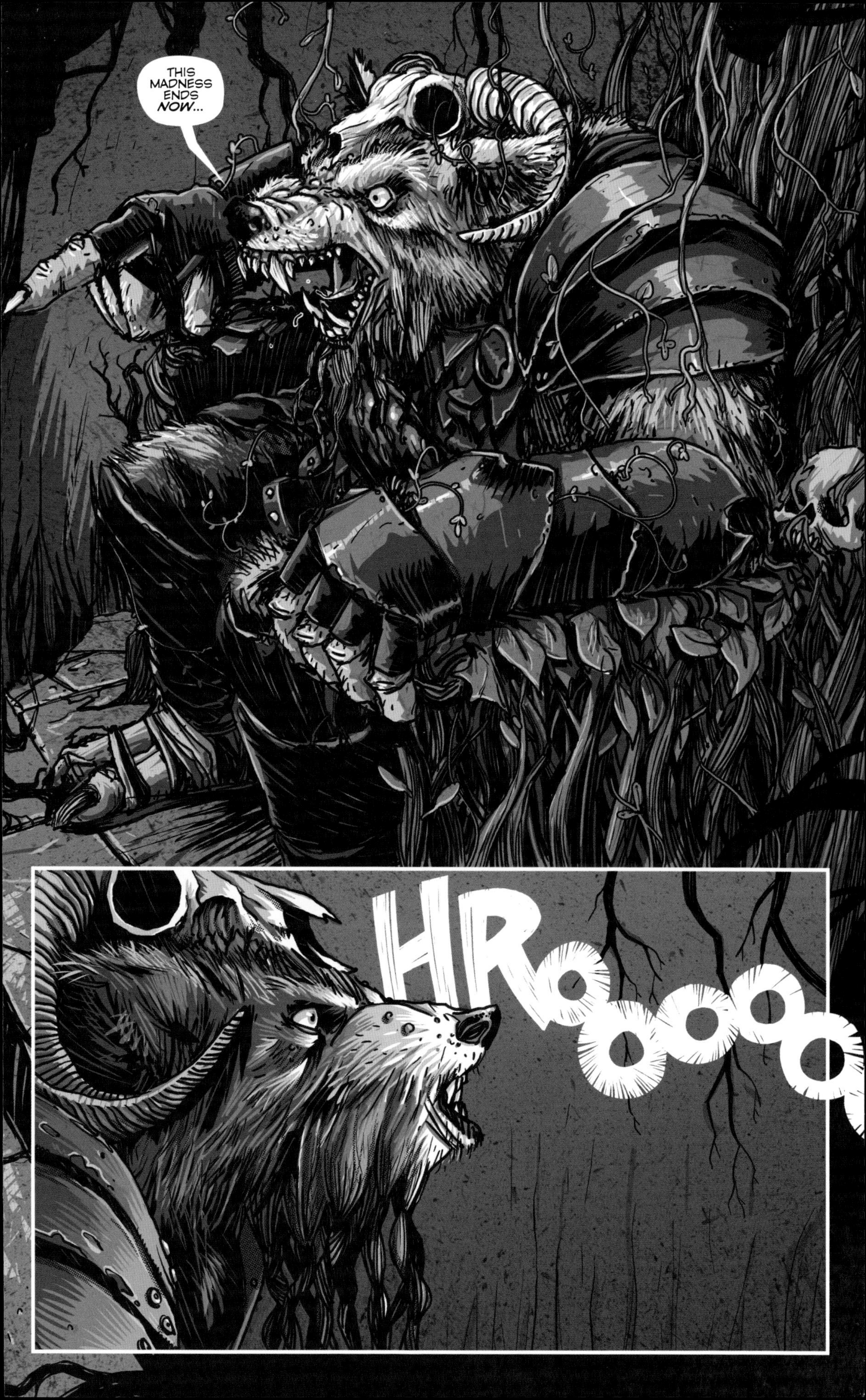
THIS MADNESS ENDS NOW...
HROOOOO

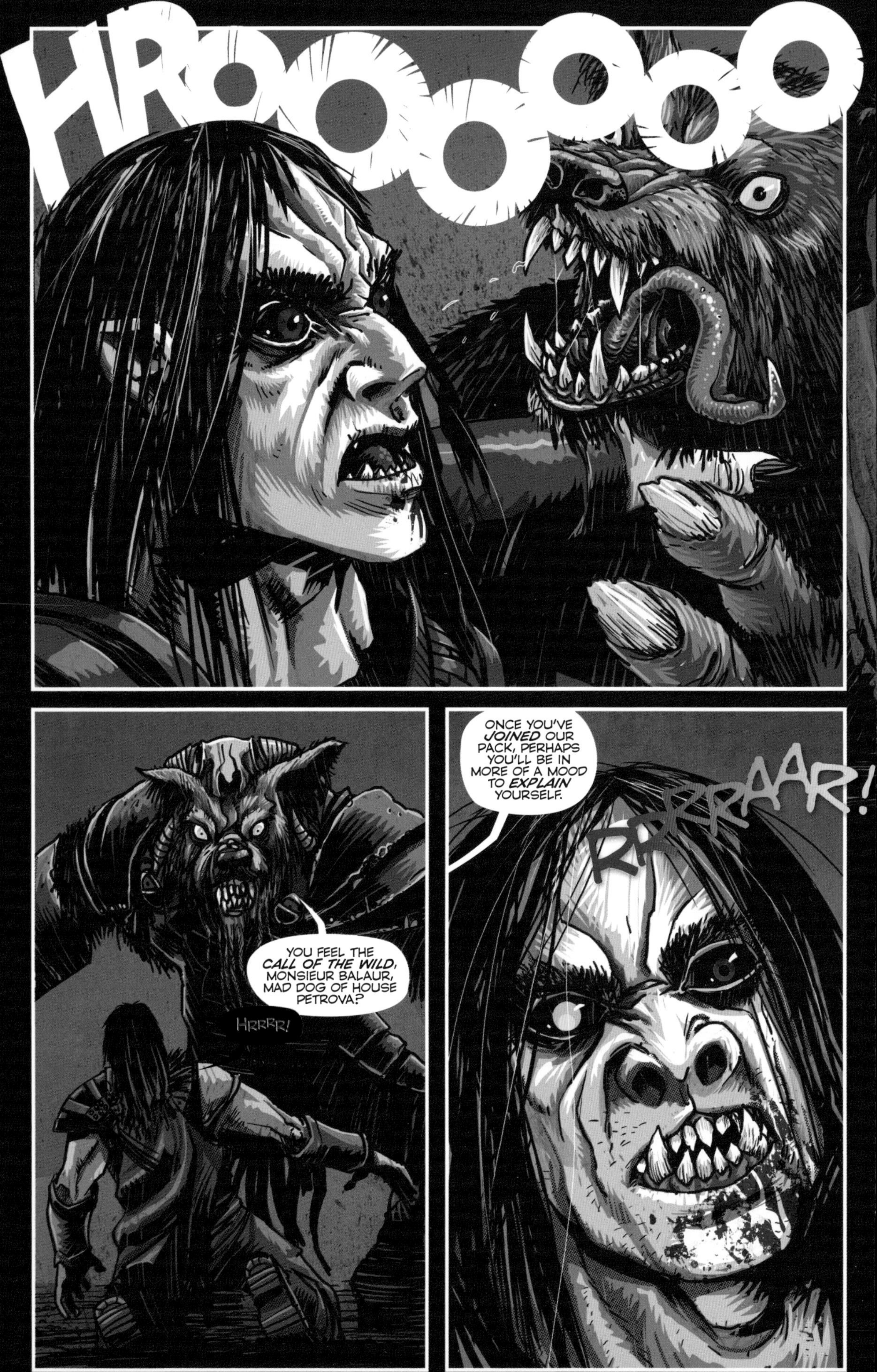
HROOOOOOOO
YOU FEEL THE *CALL OF THE WILD*, MONSIEUR BALAUR, MAD DOG OF HOUSE PETROVA?
HRRRR!
ONCE YOU'VE *JOINED* OUR PACK, PERHAPS YOU'LL BE IN MORE OF A MOOD TO *EXPLAIN* YOURSELF.
RRRRAAR!

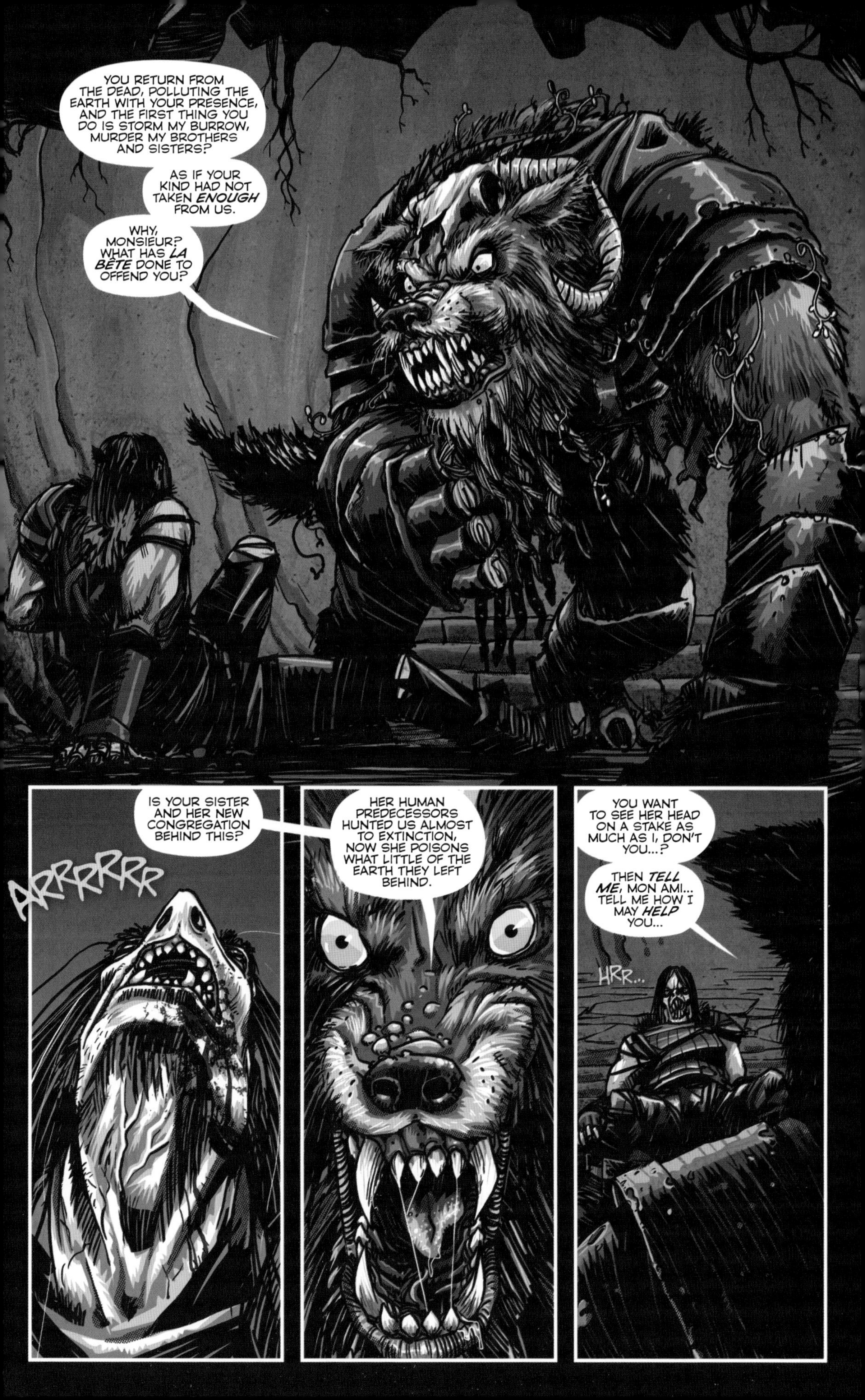

YOU RETURN FROM THE DEAD, POLLUTING THE EARTH WITH YOUR PRESENCE, AND THE FIRST THING YOU DO IS STORM MY BURROW, MURDER MY BROTHERS AND SISTERS?
AS IF YOUR KIND HAD NOT TAKEN *ENOUGH* FROM US.
WHY, MONSIEUR? WHAT HAS *LA BÊTE* DONE TO OFFEND YOU?
IS YOUR SISTER AND HER NEW CONGREGATION BEHIND THIS?
ARRRRRR
HER HUMAN PREDECESSORS HUNTED US ALMOST TO EXTINCTION, NOW SHE POISONS WHAT LITTLE OF THE EARTH THEY LEFT BEHIND.
YOU WANT TO SEE HER HEAD ON A STAKE AS MUCH AS I, DON'T YOU...?
THEN *TELL ME*, MON AMI... TELL ME HOW I MAY *HELP* YOU...
HRR...

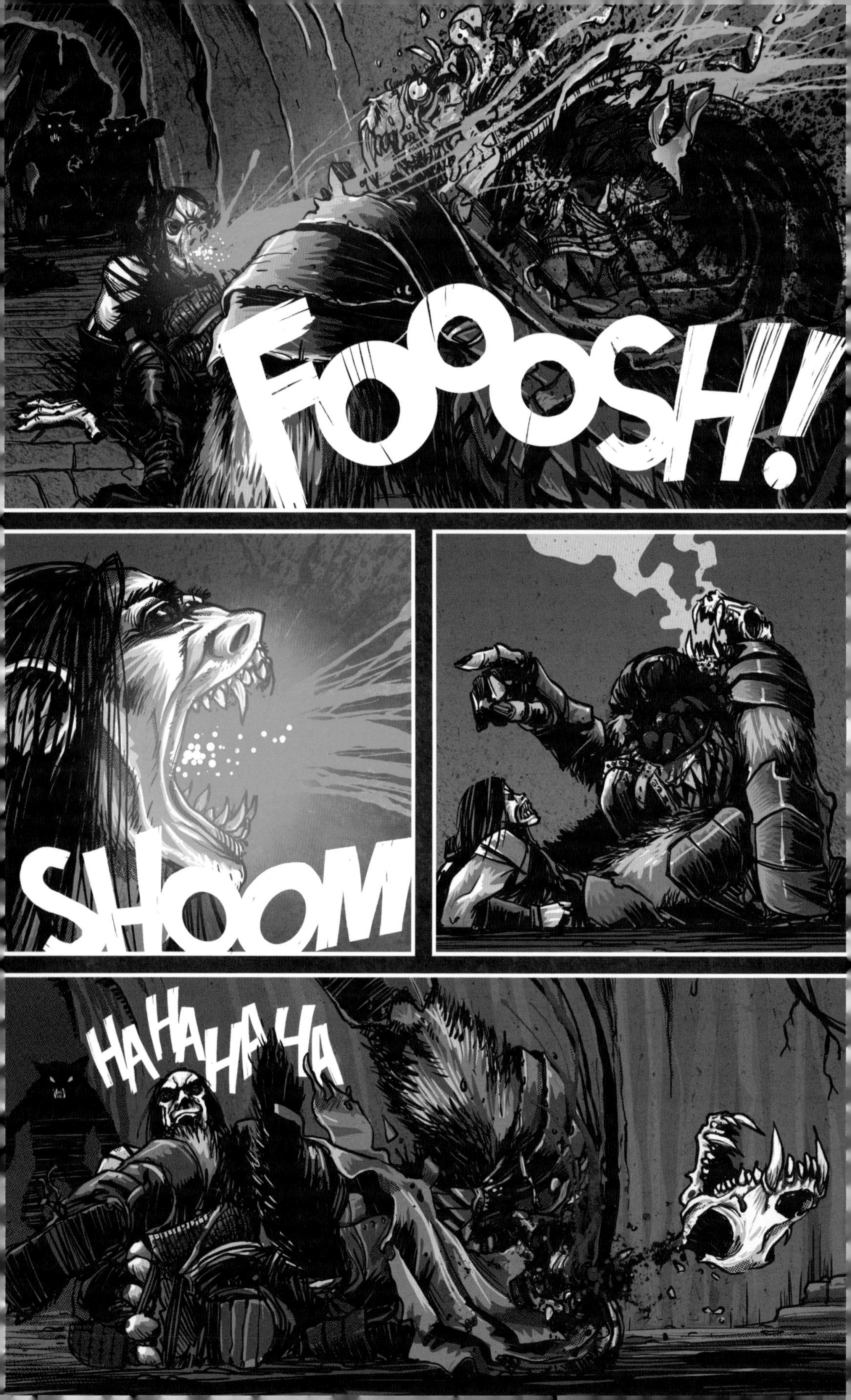
FOOOOSH!!
SHOOM
HAHAHAHA

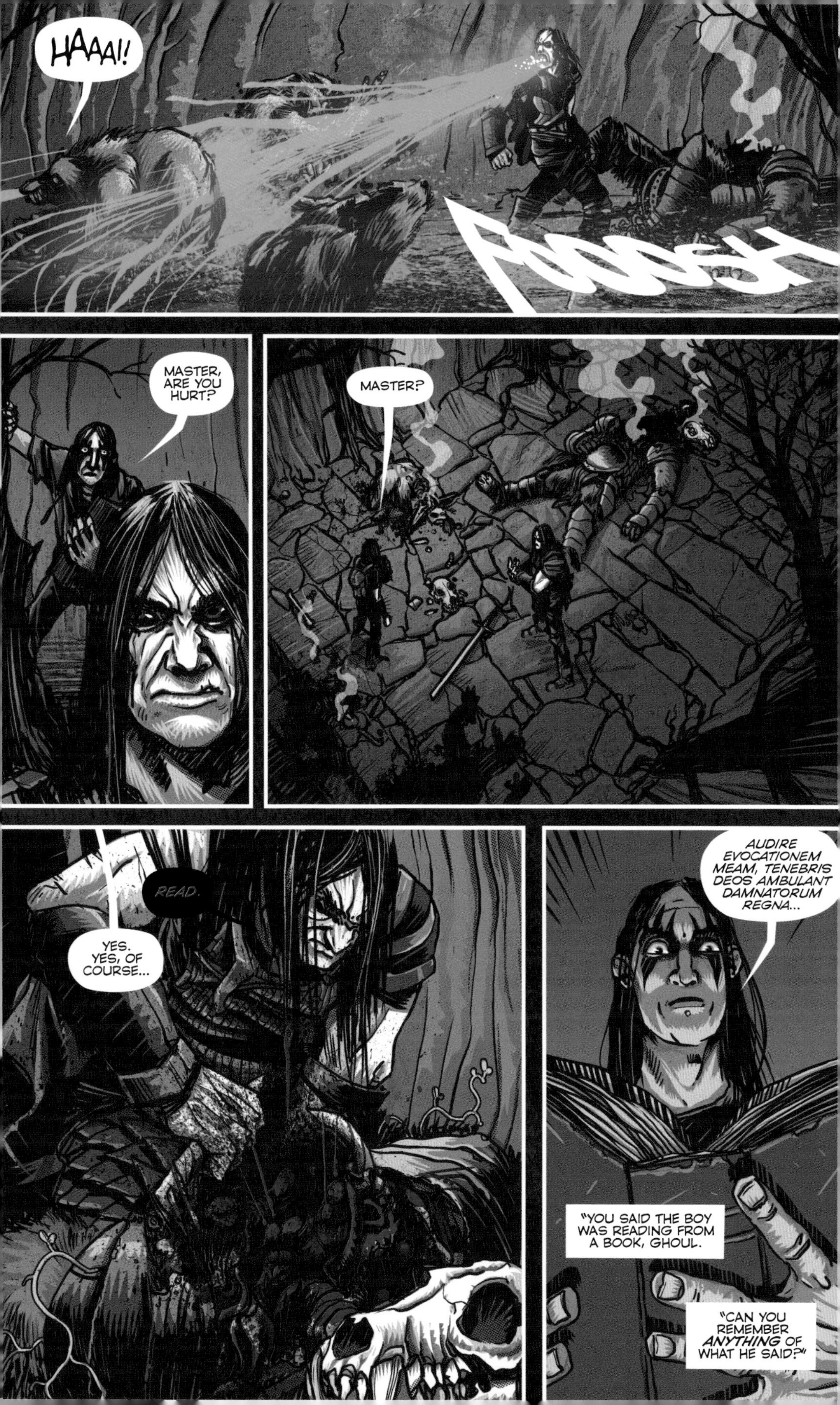
HAAAI!
FOOOSH
MASTER, ARE YOU HURT?
MASTER?
READ.
YES. YES, OF COURSE...
AUDIRE EVOCATIONEM MEAM, TENEBRIS DEOS AMBULANT DAMNATORUM REGNA...
"YOU SAID THE BOY WAS READING FROM A BOOK, GHOUL.
"CAN YOU REMEMBER *ANYTHING* OF WHAT HE SAID?"

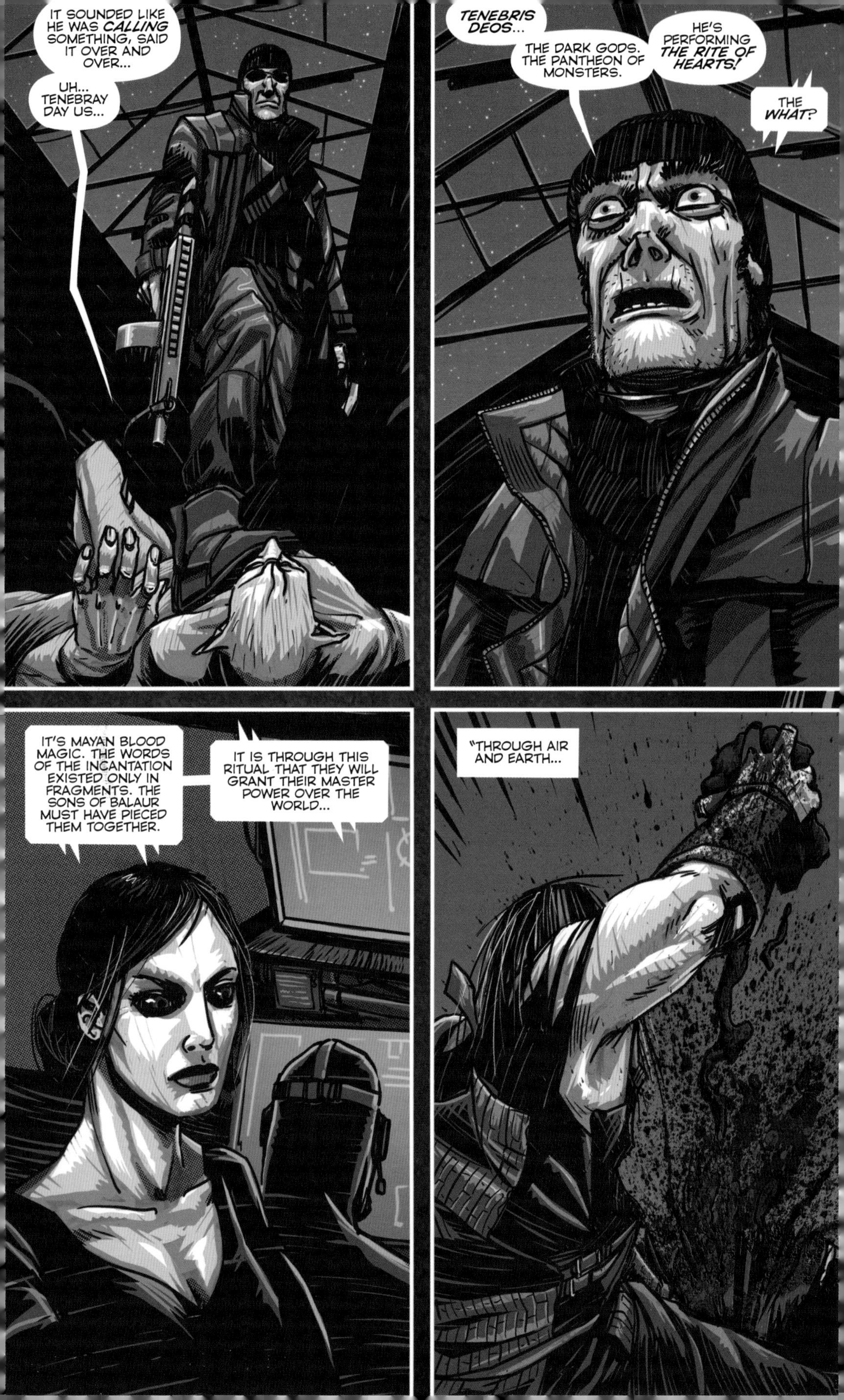
IT SOUNDED LIKE HE WAS CALLING SOMETHING, SAID IT OVER AND OVER...
UH... TENEBRAY DAY US...
TENEBRIS DEOS...
THE DARK GODS. THE PANTHEON OF MONSTERS.
HE'S PERFORMING THE RITE OF HEARTS!
THE WHAT?
IT'S MAYAN BLOOD MAGIC. THE WORDS OF THE INCANTATION EXISTED ONLY IN FRAGMENTS. THE SONS OF BALAUR MUST HAVE PIECED THEM TOGETHER.
IT IS THROUGH THIS RITUAL THAT THEY WILL GRANT THEIR MASTER POWER OVER THE WORLD...
"THROUGH AIR AND EARTH...

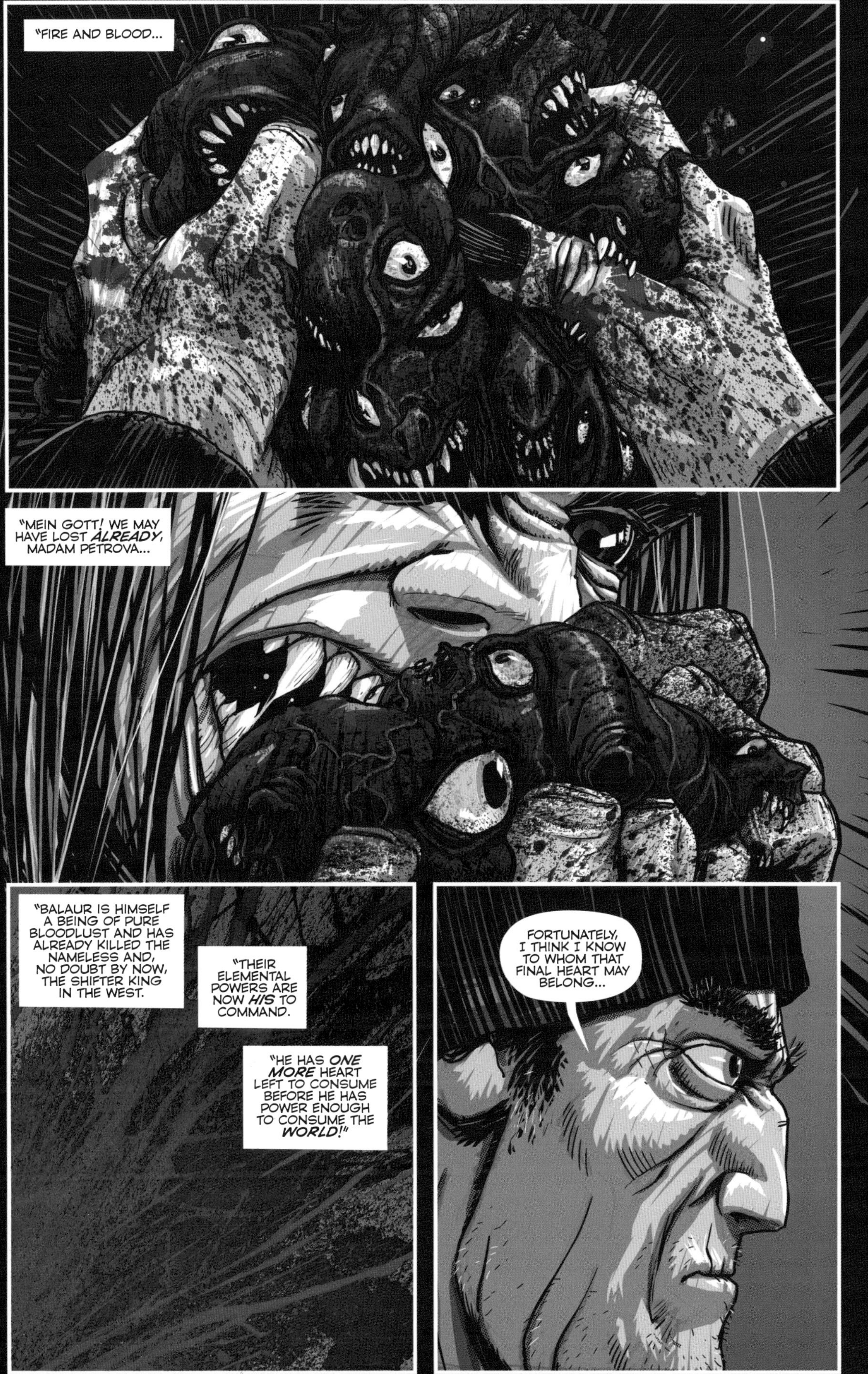
"FIRE AND BLOOD...
"MEIN GOTT! WE MAY HAVE LOST ALREADY, MADAM PETROVA...
"BALAUR IS HIMSELF A BEING OF PURE BLOODLUST AND HAS ALREADY KILLED THE NAMELESS AND, NO DOUBT BY NOW, THE SHIFTER KING IN THE WEST.
"THEIR ELEMENTAL POWERS ARE NOW HIS TO COMMAND.
"HE HAS ONE MORE HEART LEFT TO CONSUME BEFORE HE HAS POWER ENOUGH TO CONSUME THE WORLD!"
FORTUNATELY, I THINK I KNOW TO WHOM THAT FINAL HEART MAY BELONG...

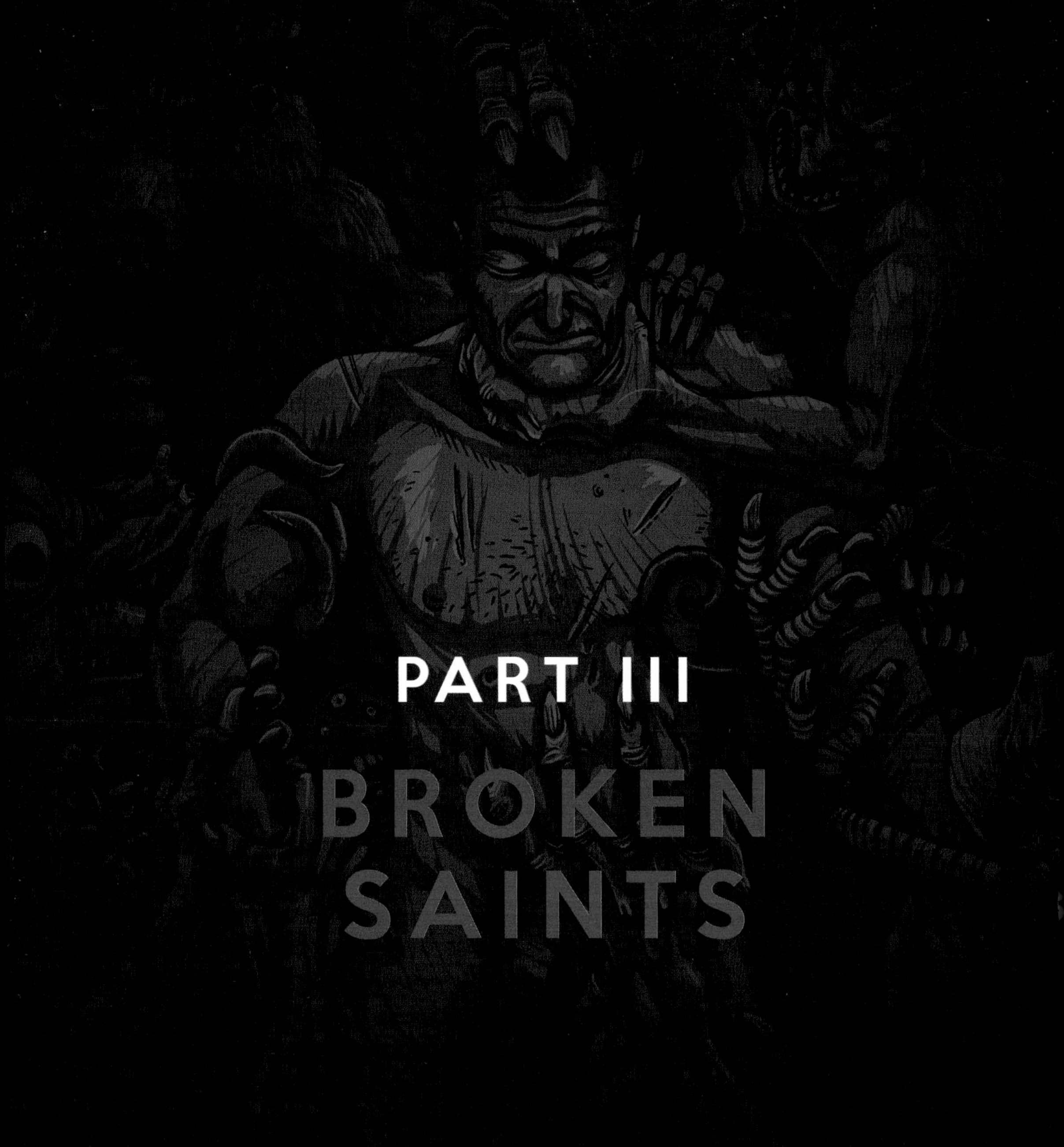

PART III

BROKEN SAINTS

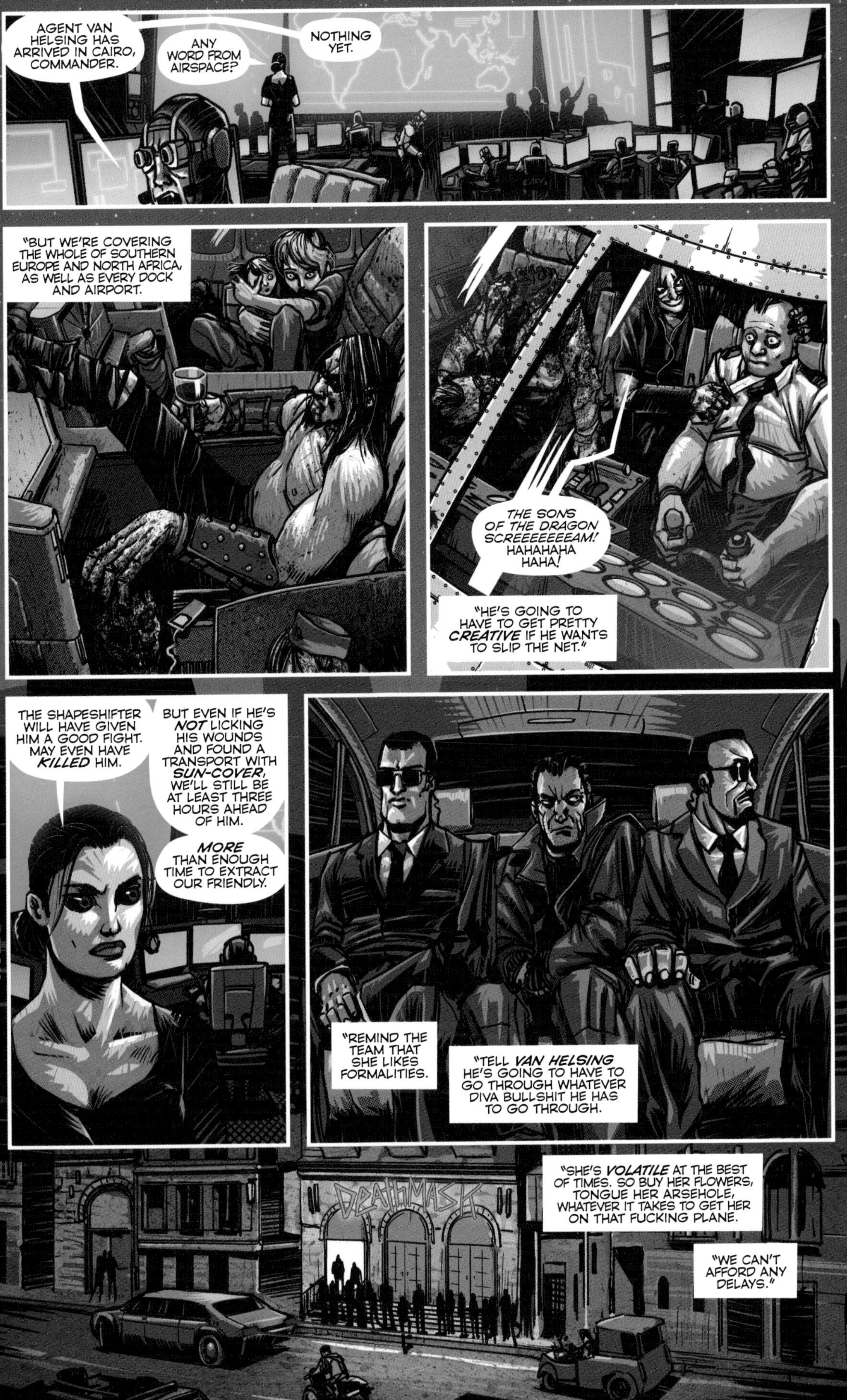
AGENT VAN HELSING HAS ARRIVED IN CAIRO, COMMANDER.
ANY WORD FROM AIRSPACE?
NOTHING YET.
"BUT WE'RE COVERING THE WHOLE OF SOUTHERN EUROPE AND NORTH AFRICA, AS WELL AS EVERY DOCK AND AIRPORT.
THE SONS OF THE DRAGON SCREEEEEEEAM! HAHAHAHA HAHA!
"HE'S GOING TO HAVE TO GET PRETTY CREATIVE IF HE WANTS TO SLIP THE NET."
THE SHAPESHIFTER WILL HAVE GIVEN HIM A GOOD FIGHT. MAY EVEN HAVE KILLED HIM.
BUT EVEN IF HE'S NOT LICKING HIS WOUNDS AND FOUND A TRANSPORT WITH SUN-COVER, WE'LL STILL BE AT LEAST THREE HOURS AHEAD OF HIM.
MORE THAN ENOUGH TIME TO EXTRACT OUR FRIENDLY.
"REMIND THE TEAM THAT SHE LIKES FORMALITIES.
"TELL VAN HELSING HE'S GOING TO HAVE TO GO THROUGH WHATEVER DIVA BULLSHIT HE HAS TO GO THROUGH.
DEATHMASK
"SHE'S VOLATILE AT THE BEST OF TIMES. SO BUY HER FLOWERS, TONGUE HER ARSEHOLE, WHATEVER IT TAKES TO GET HER ON THAT FUCKING PLANE.
"WE CAN'T AFFORD ANY DELAYS."

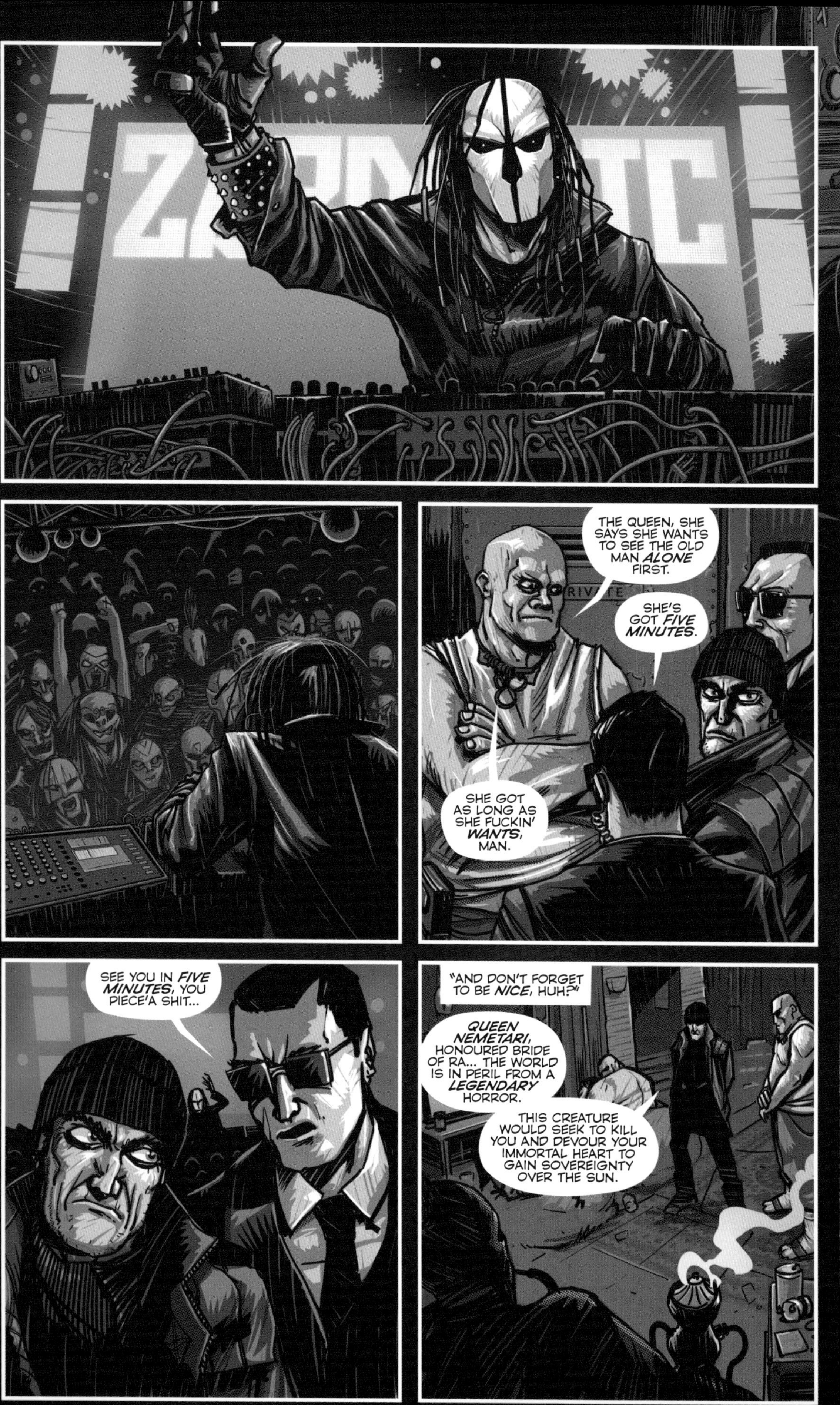

THE QUEEN, SHE SAYS SHE WANTS TO SEE THE OLD MAN *ALONE* FIRST.
SHE'S GOT *FIVE MINUTES*.
SHE GOT AS LONG AS SHE FUCKIN' *WANTS*, MAN.
SEE YOU IN *FIVE MINUTES*, YOU PIECE'A SHIT...
"AND DON'T FORGET TO BE *NICE*, HUH?"
QUEEN NEMETARI, HONOURED BRIDE OF RA... THE WORLD IS IN PERIL FROM A *LEGENDARY* HORROR.
THIS CREATURE WOULD SEEK TO KILL YOU AND DEVOUR YOUR IMMORTAL HEART TO GAIN SOVEREIGNTY OVER THE SUN.

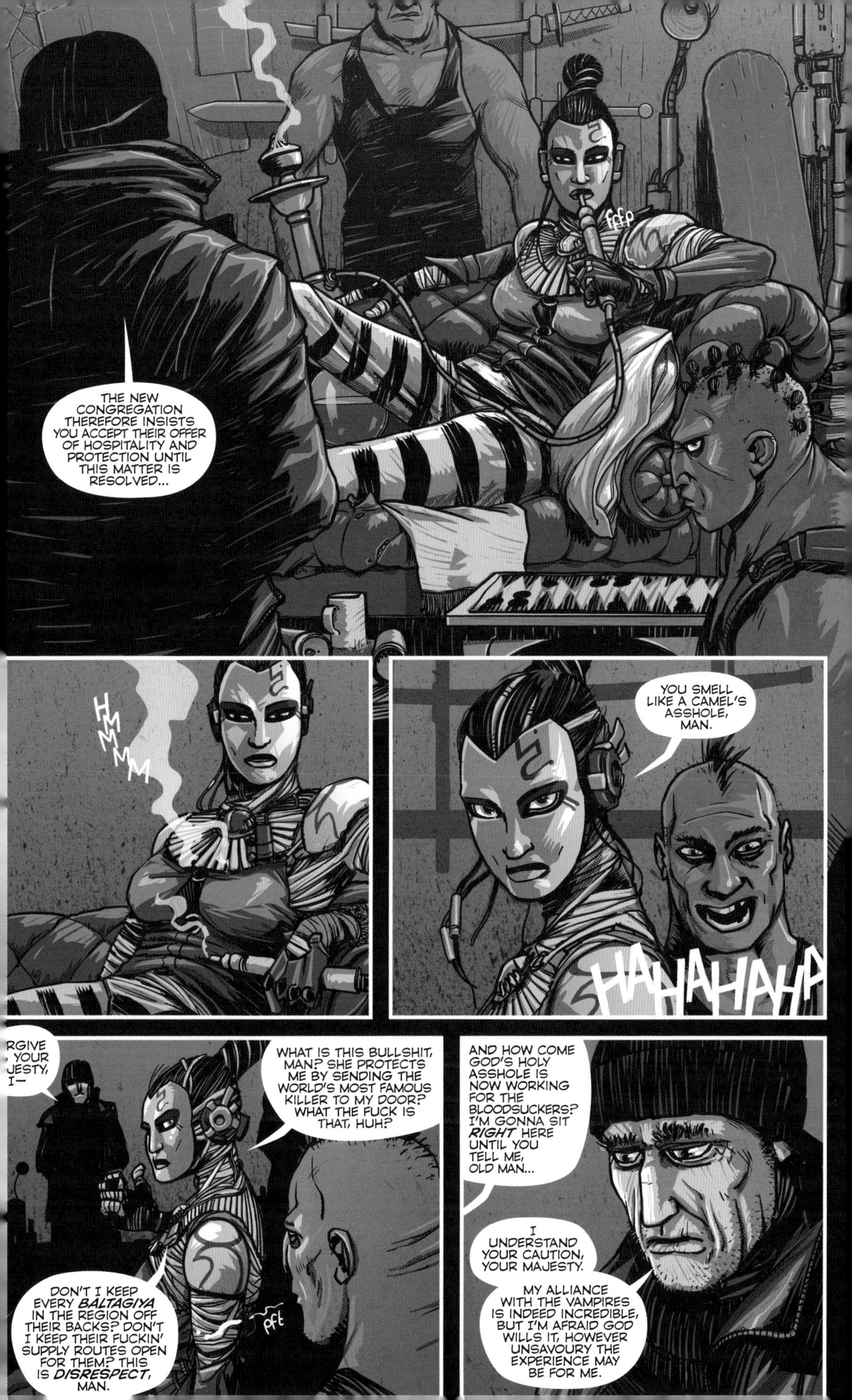

THE NEW CONGREGATION THEREFORE INSISTS YOU ACCEPT THEIR OFFER OF HOSPITALITY AND PROTECTION UNTIL THIS MATTER IS RESOLVED...
FFFP
HMMMM
YOU SMELL LIKE A CAMEL'S ASSHOLE, MAN.
HAHAHAHP
RGIVE YOUR JESTY, I—
WHAT IS THIS BULLSHIT, MAN? SHE PROTECTS ME BY SENDING THE WORLD'S MOST FAMOUS KILLER TO MY DOOR? WHAT THE FUCK IS THAT, HUH?
DON'T I KEEP EVERY *BALTAGIYA* IN THE REGION OFF THEIR BACKS? DON'T I KEEP THEIR FUCKIN' SUPPLY ROUTES OPEN FOR THEM? THIS IS *DISRESPECT*, MAN.
PFT
AND HOW COME GOD'S HOLY ASSHOLE IS NOW WORKING FOR THE BLOODSUCKERS? I'M GONNA SIT *RIGHT* HERE UNTIL YOU TELL ME, OLD MAN...
I UNDERSTAND YOUR CAUTION, YOUR MAJESTY.
MY ALLIANCE WITH THE VAMPIRES IS INDEED INCREDIBLE, BUT I'M AFRAID GOD WILLS IT, HOWEVER UNSAVOURY THE EXPERIENCE MAY BE FOR ME.

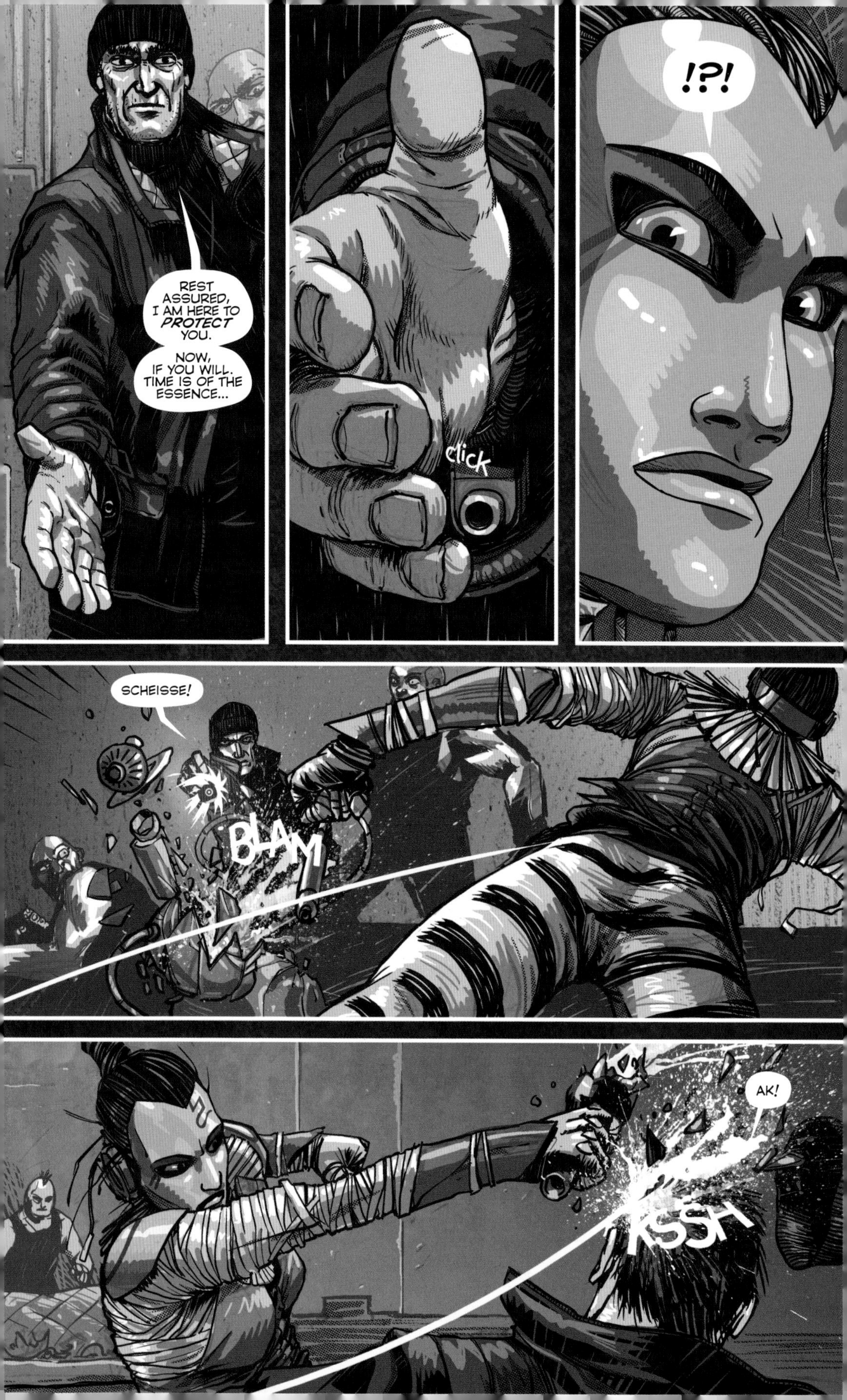
REST ASSURED, I AM HERE TO *PROTECT* YOU.
NOW, IF YOU WILL. TIME IS OF THE ESSENCE...
CLICK
!?!
SCHEISSE!
BLAM
AK!
KSSH

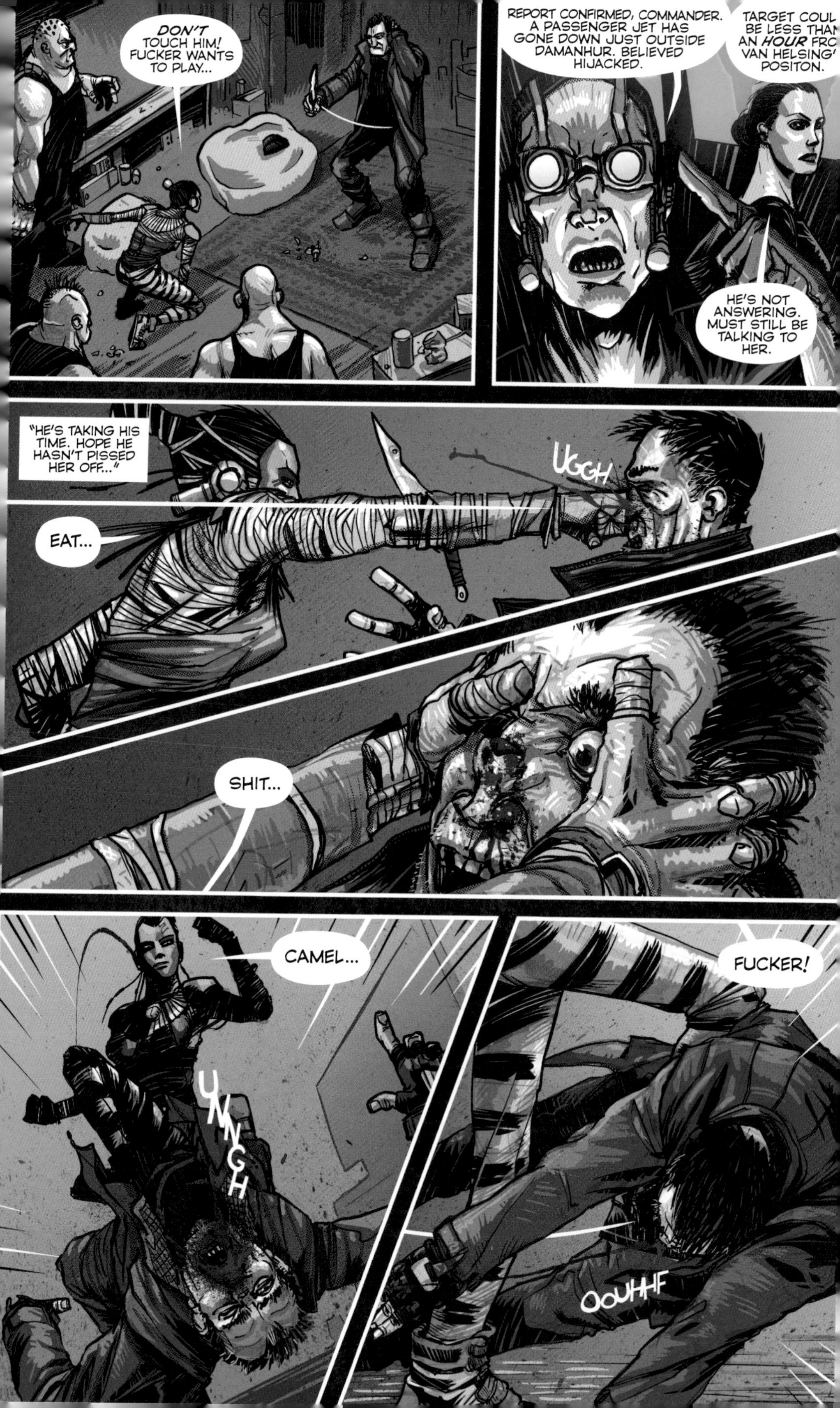
DON'T TOUCH HIM! FUCKER WANTS TO PLAY...
REPORT CONFIRMED, COMMANDER. A PASSENGER JET HAS GONE DOWN JUST OUTSIDE DAMANHUR. BELIEVED HIJACKED.
TARGET COUL BE LESS THAN AN HOUR FRO VAN HELSING' POSITON.
HE'S NOT ANSWERING. MUST STILL BE TALKING TO HER.
"HE'S TAKING HIS TIME. HOPE HE HASN'T PISSED HER OFF..."
UGGH
EAT...
SHIT...
CAMEL...
UNNGH
FUCKER!
OOUHHF

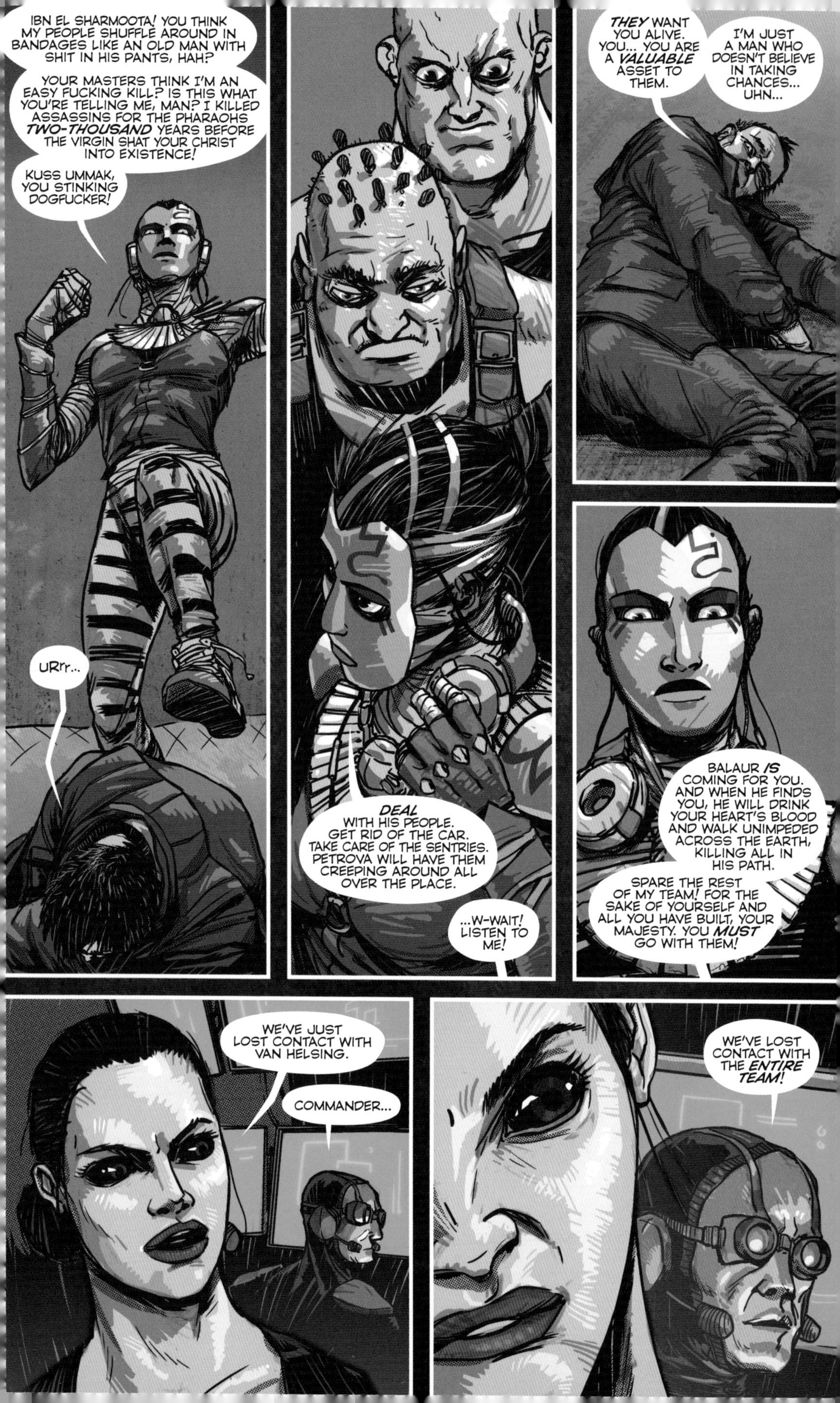
IBN EL SHARMOOTA! YOU THINK MY PEOPLE SHUFFLE AROUND IN BANDAGES LIKE AN OLD MAN WITH SHIT IN HIS PANTS, HAH?
YOUR MASTERS THINK I'M AN EASY FUCKING KILL? IS THIS WHAT YOU'RE TELLING ME, MAN? I KILLED ASSASSINS FOR THE PHARAOHS TWO-THOUSAND YEARS BEFORE THE VIRGIN SHAT YOUR CHRIST INTO EXISTENCE!
KUSS UMMAK, YOU STINKING DOGFUCKER!
URrr...
DEAL WITH HIS PEOPLE. GET RID OF THE CAR. TAKE CARE OF THE SENTRIES. PETROVA WILL HAVE THEM CREEPING AROUND ALL OVER THE PLACE.
...W-WAIT! LISTEN TO ME!
THEY WANT YOU ALIVE. YOU... YOU ARE A VALUABLE ASSET TO THEM.
I'M JUST A MAN WHO DOESN'T BELIEVE IN TAKING CHANCES... UHN...
BALAUR IS COMING FOR YOU. AND WHEN HE FINDS YOU, HE WILL DRINK YOUR HEART'S BLOOD AND WALK UNIMPEDED ACROSS THE EARTH, KILLING ALL IN HIS PATH.
SPARE THE REST OF MY TEAM! FOR THE SAKE OF YOURSELF AND ALL YOU HAVE BUILT, YOUR MAJESTY. YOU MUST GO WITH THEM!
WE'VE JUST LOST CONTACT WITH VAN HELSING.
COMMANDER...
WE'VE LOST CONTACT WITH THE ENTIRE TEAM!

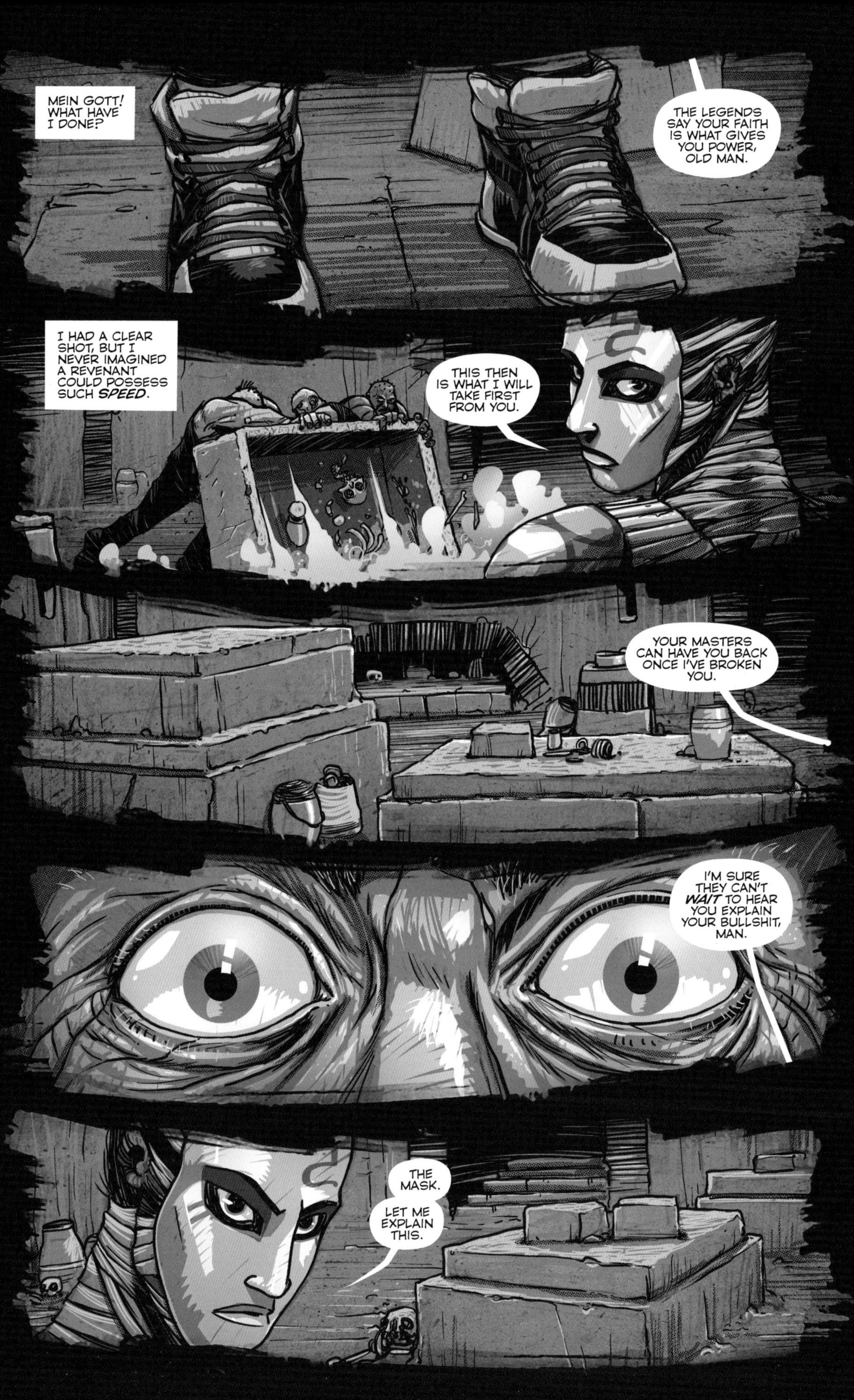
MEIN GOTT! WHAT HAVE I DONE?
THE LEGENDS SAY YOUR FAITH IS WHAT GIVES YOU POWER, OLD MAN.
I HAD A CLEAR SHOT, BUT I NEVER IMAGINED A REVENANT COULD POSSESS SUCH SPEED.
THIS THEN IS WHAT I WILL TAKE FIRST FROM YOU.
YOUR MASTERS CAN HAVE YOU BACK ONCE I'VE BROKEN YOU.
I'M SURE THEY CAN'T WAIT TO HEAR YOU EXPLAIN YOUR BULLSHIT, MAN.
THE MASK.
LET ME EXPLAIN THIS.

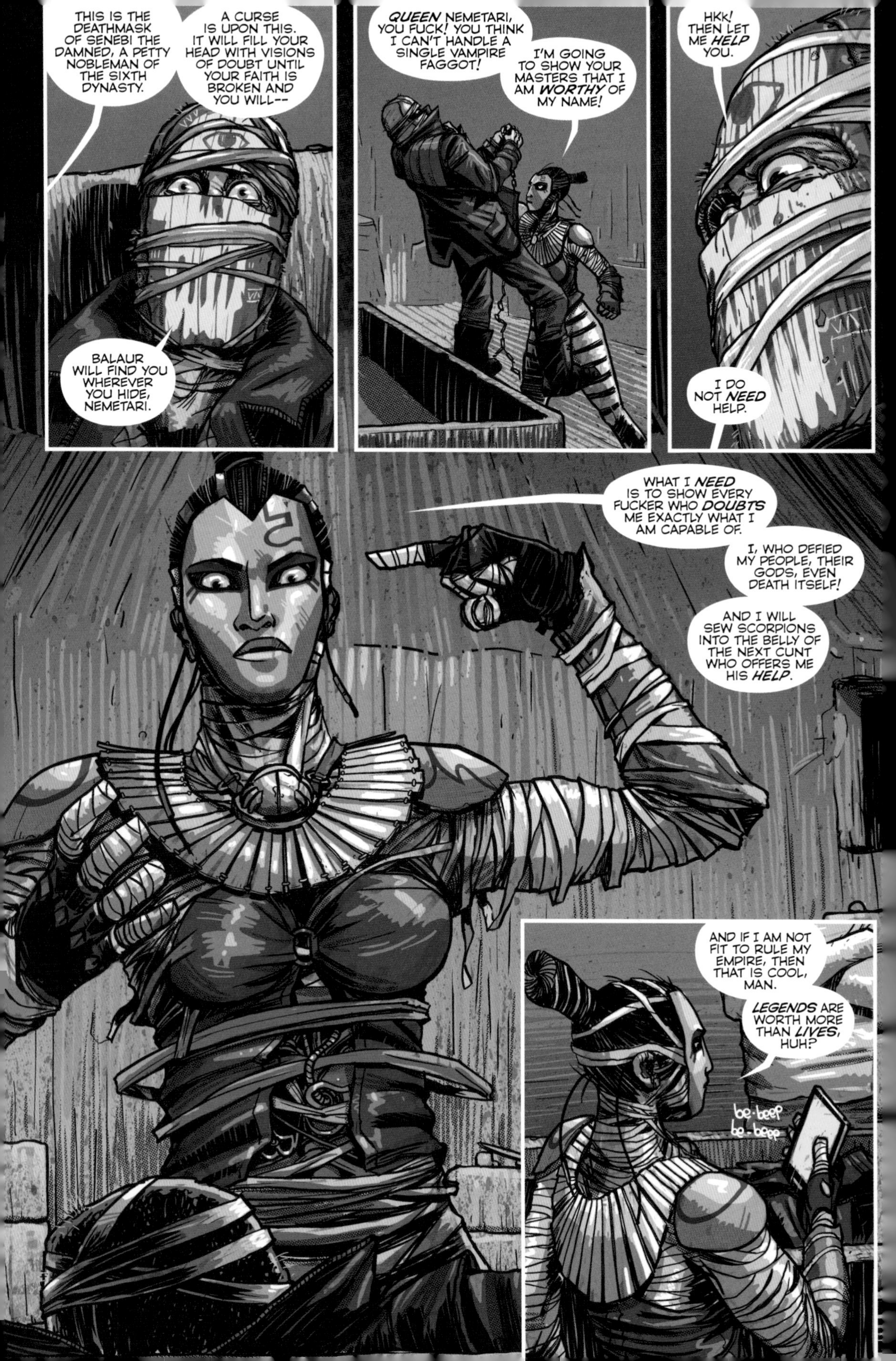
THIS IS THE DEATHMASK OF SENEBI THE DAMNED, A PETTY NOBLEMAN OF THE SIXTH DYNASTY.
A CURSE IS UPON THIS. IT WILL FILL YOUR HEAD WITH VISIONS OF DOUBT UNTIL YOUR FAITH IS BROKEN AND YOU WILL--
BALAUR WILL FIND YOU WHEREVER YOU HIDE, NEMETARI.
QUEEN NEMETARI, YOU FUCK! YOU THINK I CAN'T HANDLE A SINGLE VAMPIRE FAGGOT!
I'M GOING TO SHOW YOUR MASTERS THAT I AM WORTHY OF MY NAME!
HKK! THEN LET ME HELP YOU.
I DO NOT NEED HELP.
WHAT I NEED IS TO SHOW EVERY FUCKER WHO DOUBTS ME EXACTLY WHAT I AM CAPABLE OF.
I, WHO DEFIED MY PEOPLE, THEIR GODS, EVEN DEATH ITSELF!
AND I WILL SEW SCORPIONS INTO THE BELLY OF THE NEXT CUNT WHO OFFERS ME HIS HELP.
AND IF I AM NOT FIT TO RULE MY EMPIRE, THEN THAT IS COOL, MAN.
LEGENDS ARE WORTH MORE THAN LIVES, HUH?
be-beep
be-beep

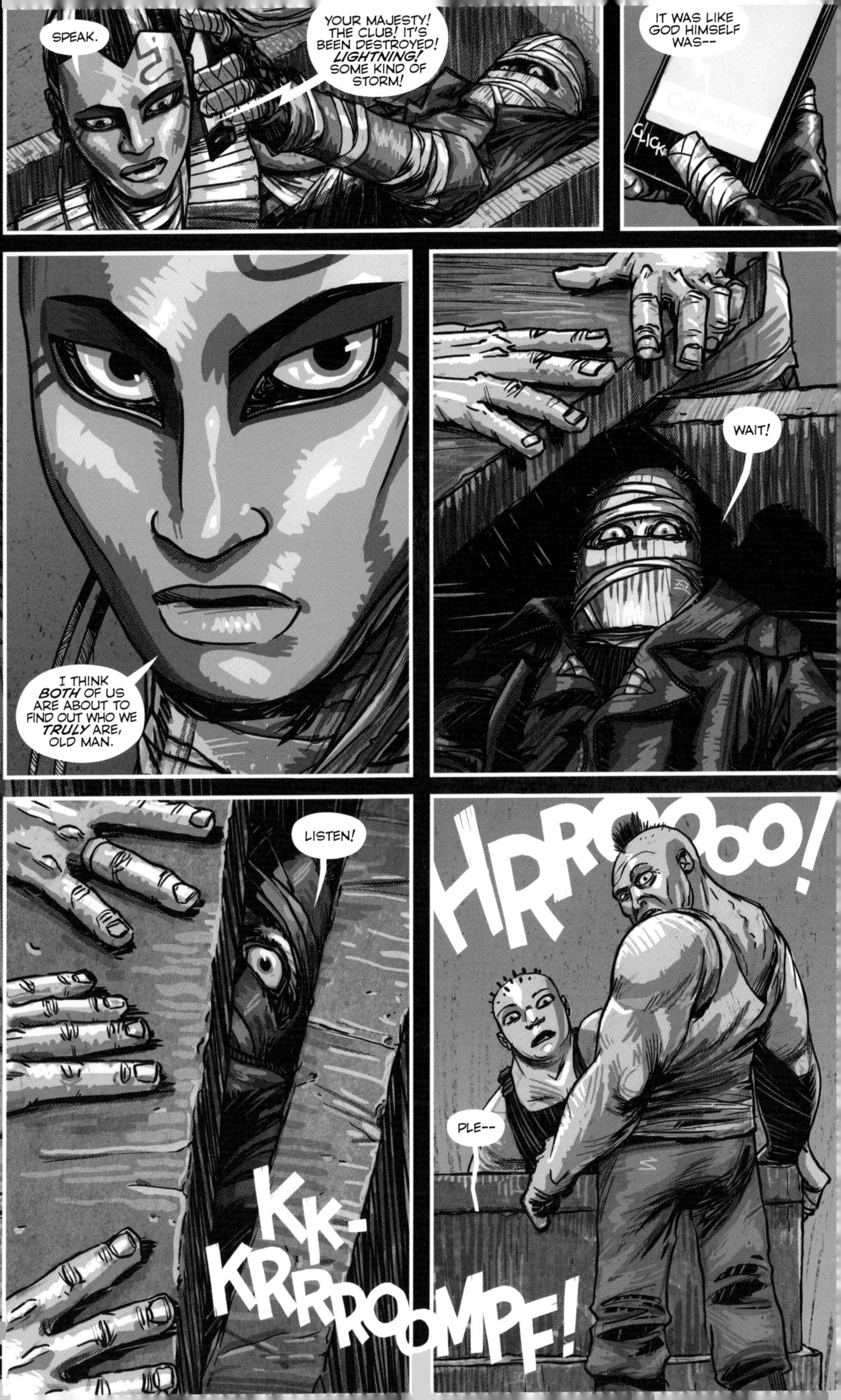
SPEAK.
YOUR MAJESTY! THE CLUB! IT'S BEEN DESTROYED! LIGHTNING! SOME KIND OF STORM!
IT WAS LIKE GOD HIMSELF WAS--
Call ended
CLICK
I THINK BOTH OF US ARE ABOUT TO FIND OUT WHO WE TRULY ARE, OLD MAN.
WAIT!
LISTEN!
KK-KRRRROOMPF!
HRROOOOO!
PLE--

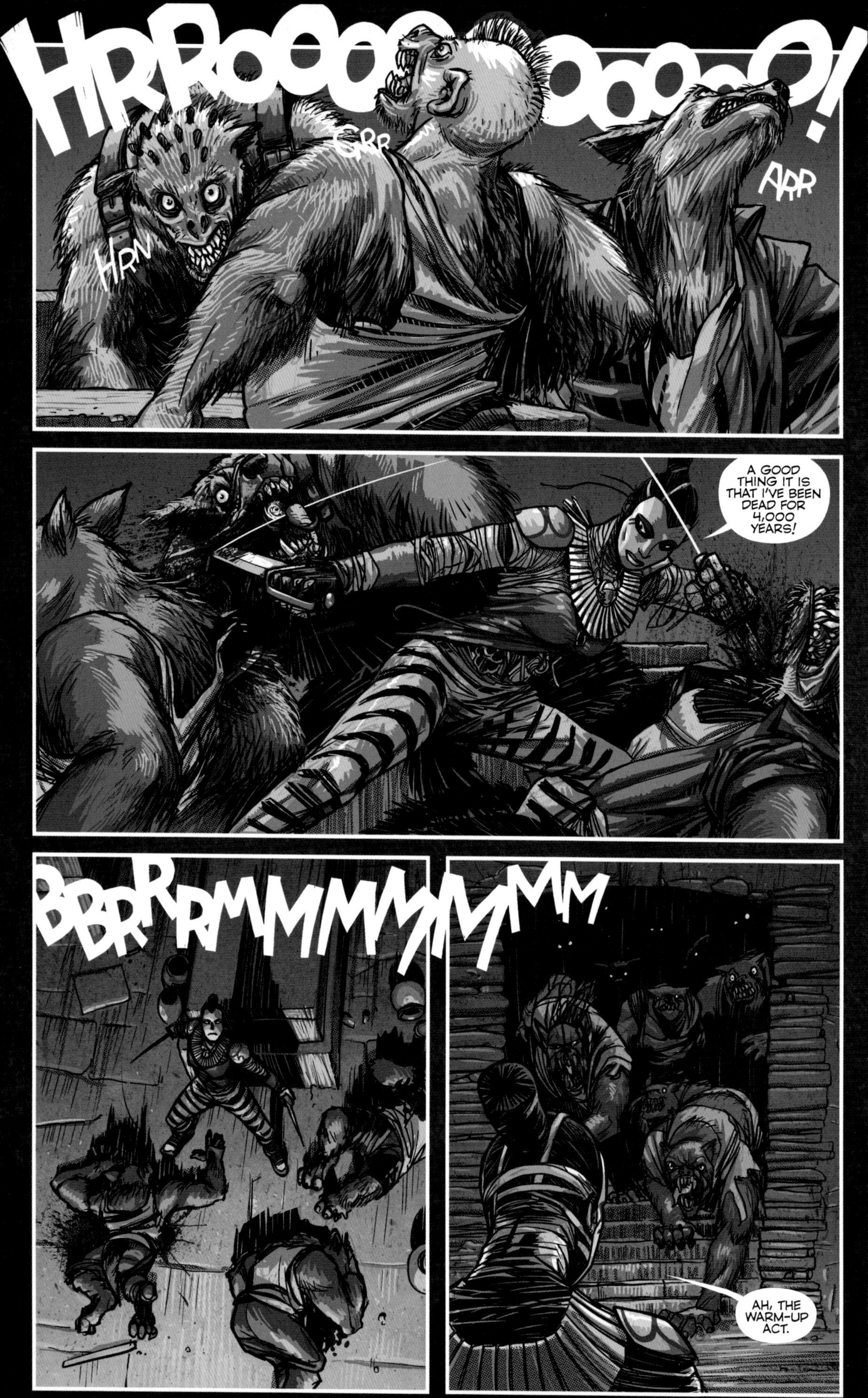
HRROOOOOOOOOOOO!
HRN
GRR
ARR
A GOOD THING IT IS THAT I'VE BEEN DEAD FOR 4,000 YEARS!
BBRRRMMMMMMMM
AH, THE WARM-UP ACT.

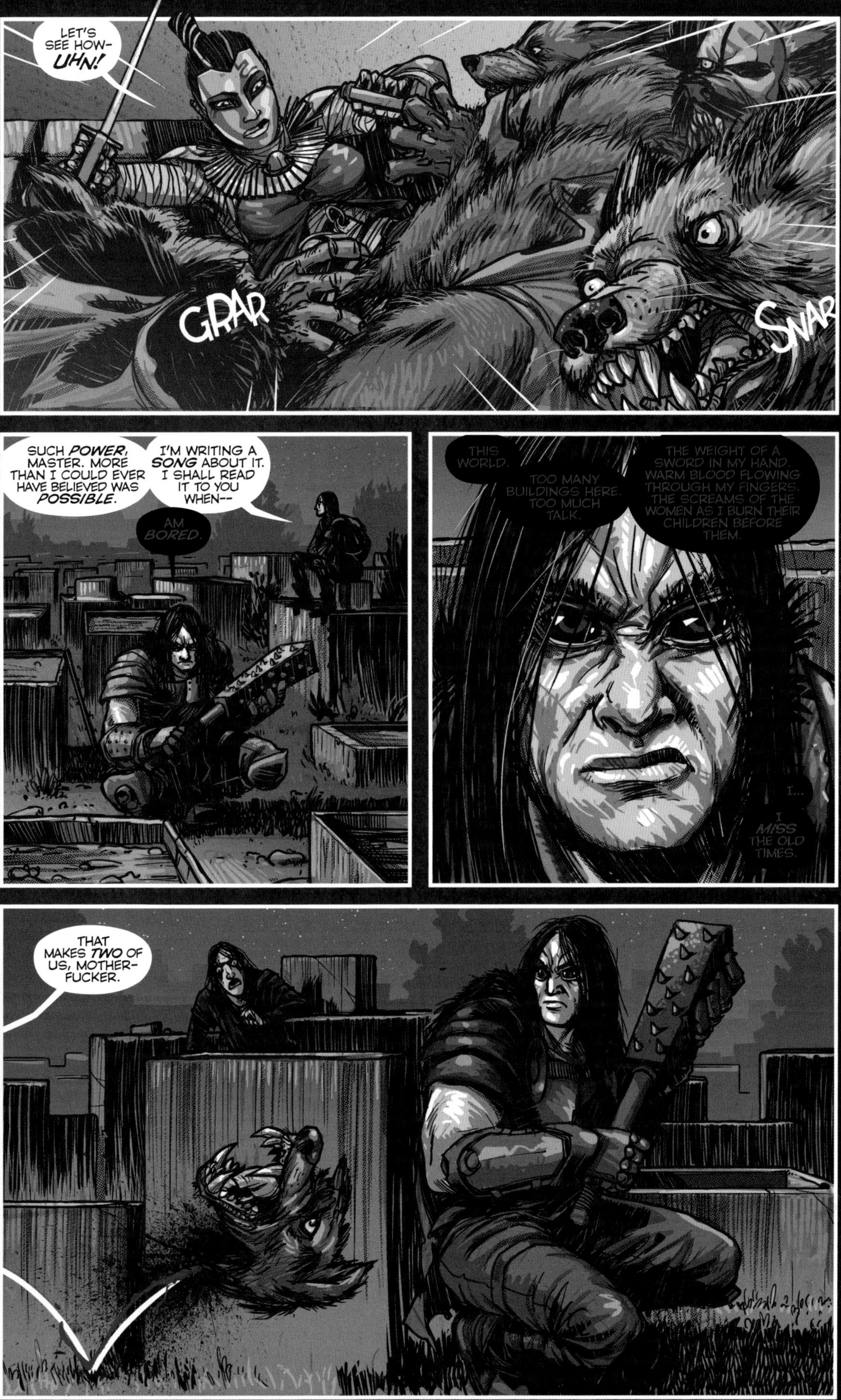
LET'S SEE HOW- UHN!
GRAR
SNAR
SUCH POWER, MASTER. MORE THAN I COULD EVER HAVE BELIEVED WAS POSSIBLE.
I'M WRITING A SONG ABOUT IT. I SHALL READ IT TO YOU WHEN--
AM BORED.
THIS WORLD.
TOO MANY BUILDINGS HERE. TOO MUCH TALK.
THE WEIGHT OF A SWORD IN MY HAND. WARM BLOOD FLOWING THROUGH MY FINGERS. THE SCREAMS OF THE WOMEN AS I BURN THEIR CHILDREN BEFORE THEM.
I...
I MISS THE OLD TIMES.
THAT MAKES TWO OF US, MOTHER-FUCKER.

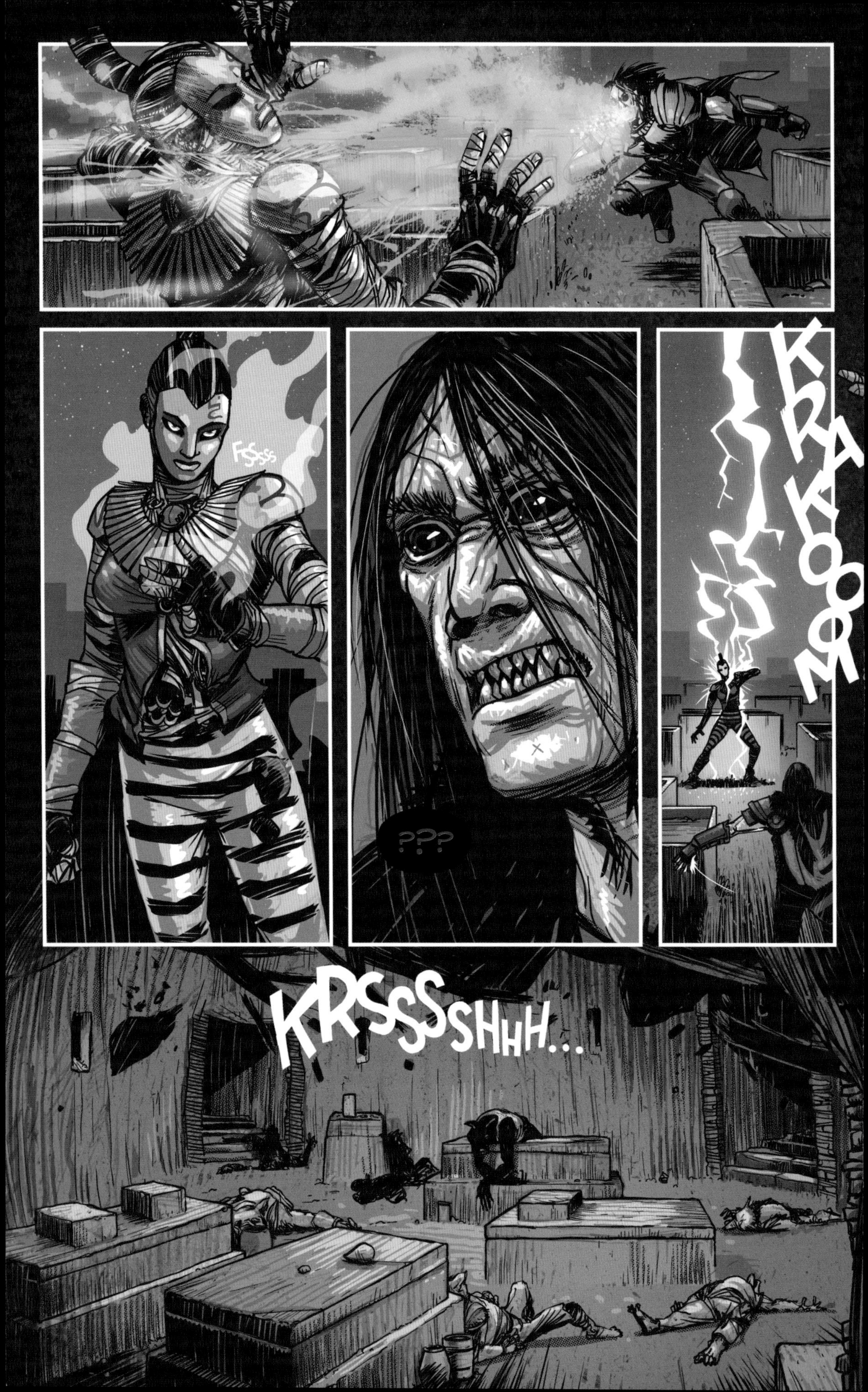
FSSSSS
???
KRAKOOOM
KRSSSSHHH...

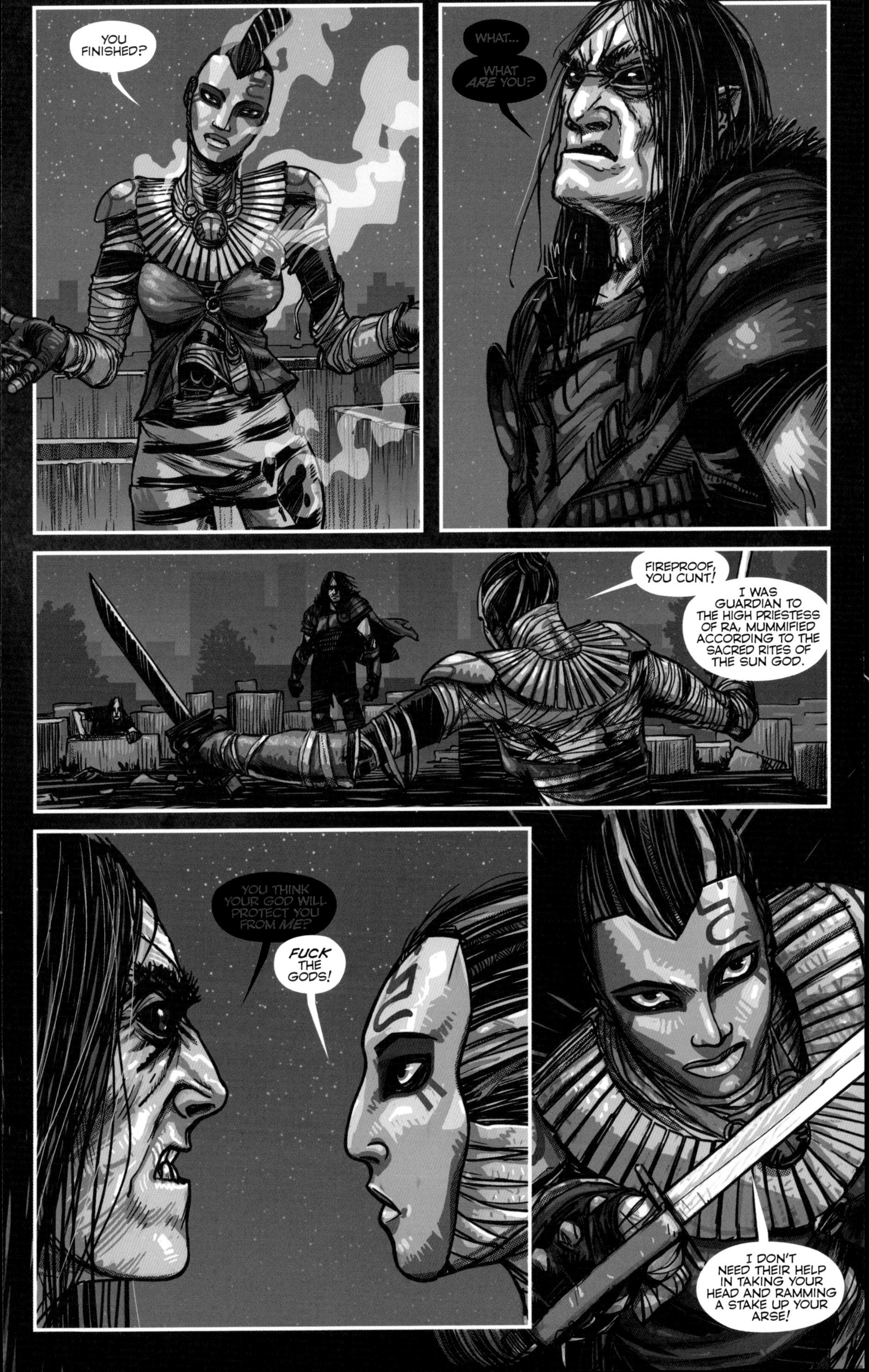
YOU FINISHED?
WHAT...
WHAT *ARE* YOU?
FIREPROOF, YOU CUNT!
I WAS GUARDIAN TO THE HIGH PRIESTESS OF RA, MUMMIFIED ACCORDING TO THE SACRED RITES OF THE SUN GOD.
YOU THINK YOUR GOD WILL PROTECT YOU FROM *ME*?
FUCK THE GODS!
I DON'T NEED THEIR HELP IN TAKING YOUR HEAD AND RAMMING A STAKE UP YOUR ARSE!

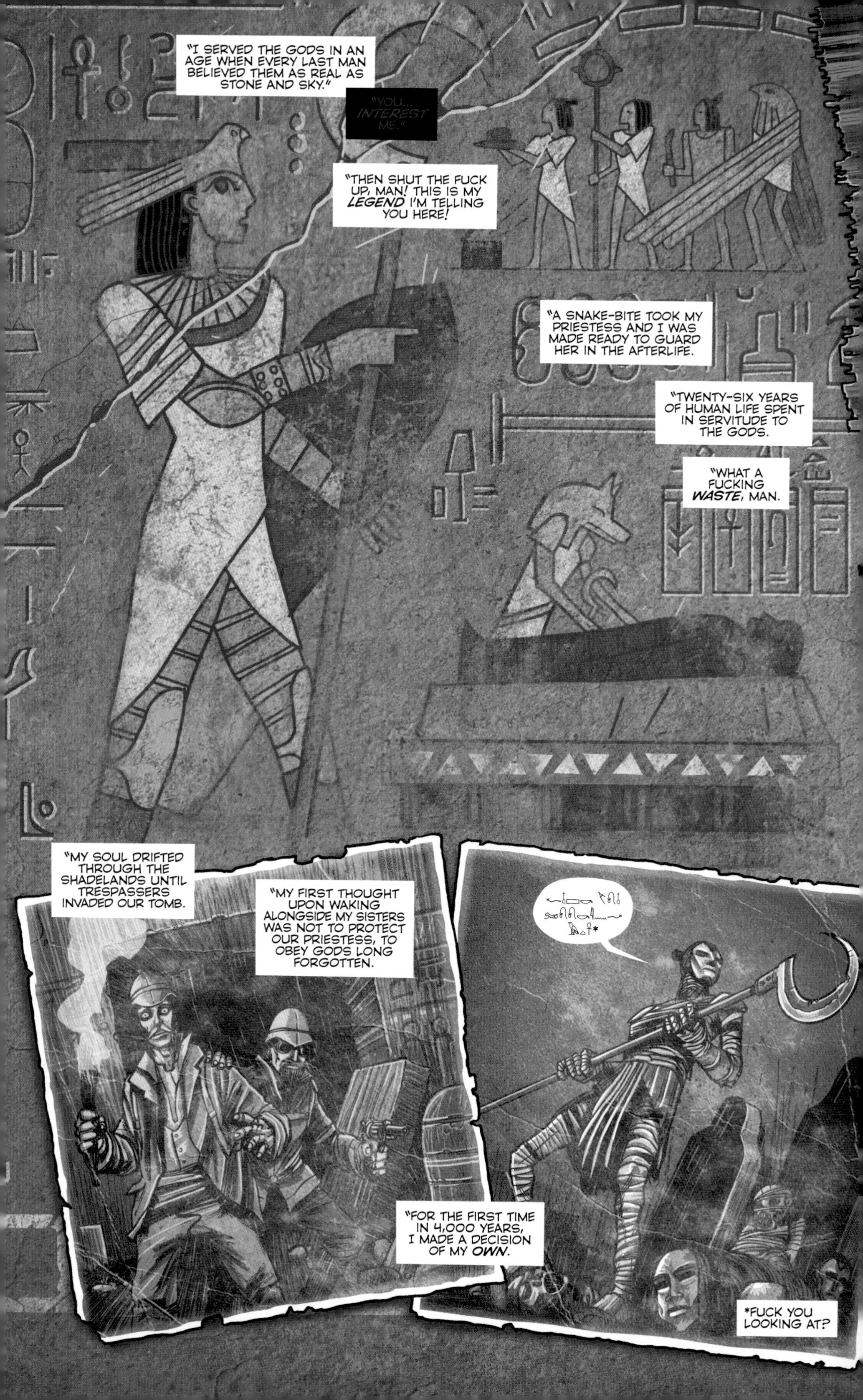
"I SERVED THE GODS IN AN AGE WHEN EVERY LAST MAN BELIEVED THEM AS REAL AS STONE AND SKY."
"YOU... INTEREST ME."
"THEN SHUT THE FUCK UP, MAN! THIS IS MY LEGEND I'M TELLING YOU HERE!
"A SNAKE-BITE TOOK MY PRIESTESS AND I WAS MADE READY TO GUARD HER IN THE AFTERLIFE.
"TWENTY-SIX YEARS OF HUMAN LIFE SPENT IN SERVITUDE TO THE GODS.
"WHAT A FUCKING WASTE, MAN.
"MY SOUL DRIFTED THROUGH THE SHADELANDS UNTIL TRESPASSERS INVADED OUR TOMB.
"MY FIRST THOUGHT UPON WAKING ALONGSIDE MY SISTERS WAS NOT TO PROTECT OUR PRIESTESS, TO OBEY GODS LONG FORGOTTEN.
"FOR THE FIRST TIME IN 4,000 YEARS, I MADE A DECISION OF MY OWN.
*FUCK YOU LOOKING AT?

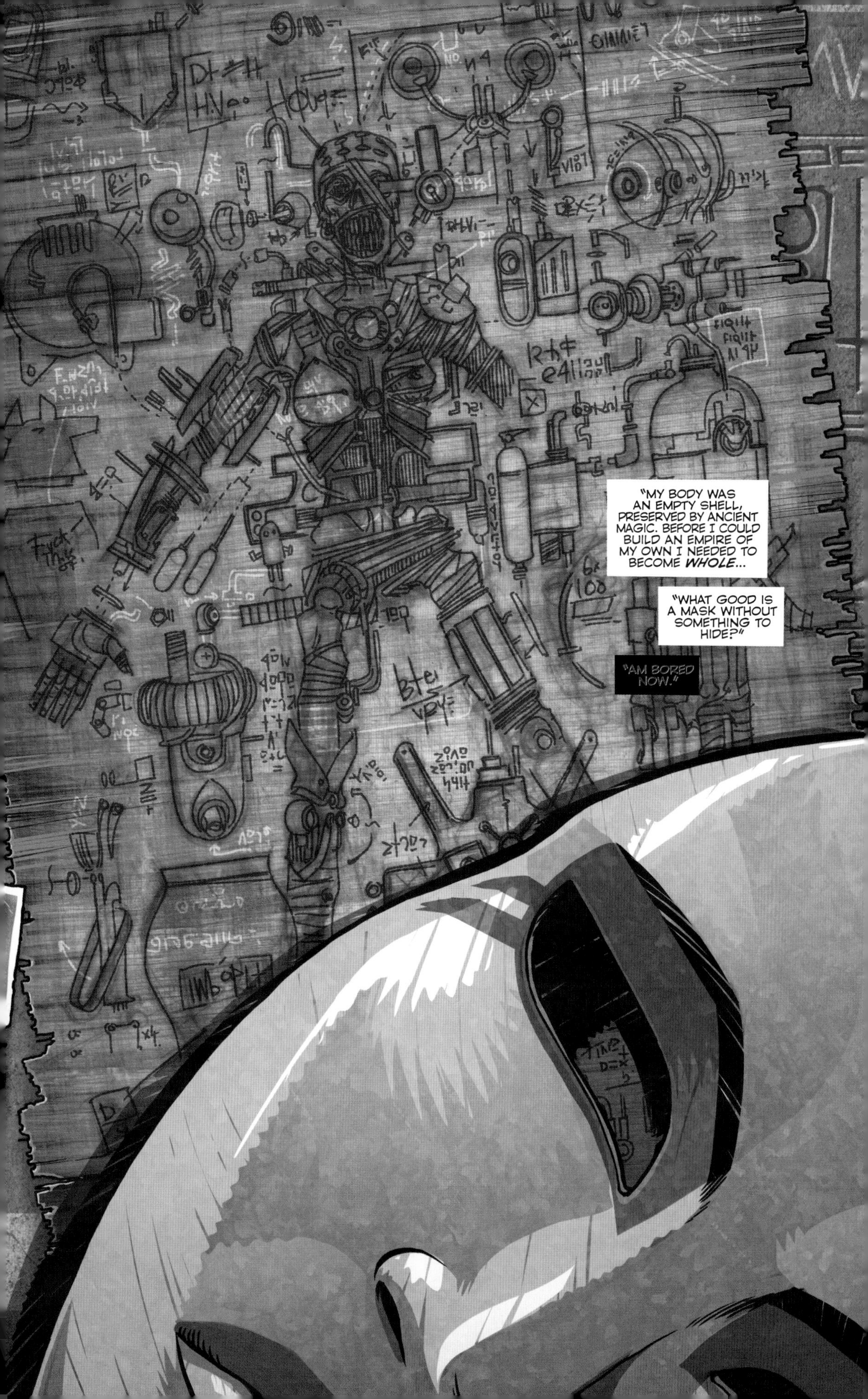
"MY BODY WAS AN EMPTY SHELL, PRESERVED BY ANCIENT MAGIC. BEFORE I COULD BUILD AN EMPIRE OF MY OWN I NEEDED TO BECOME *WHOLE*...
"WHAT GOOD IS A MASK WITHOUT SOMETHING TO HIDE?"
"AM BORED NOW."

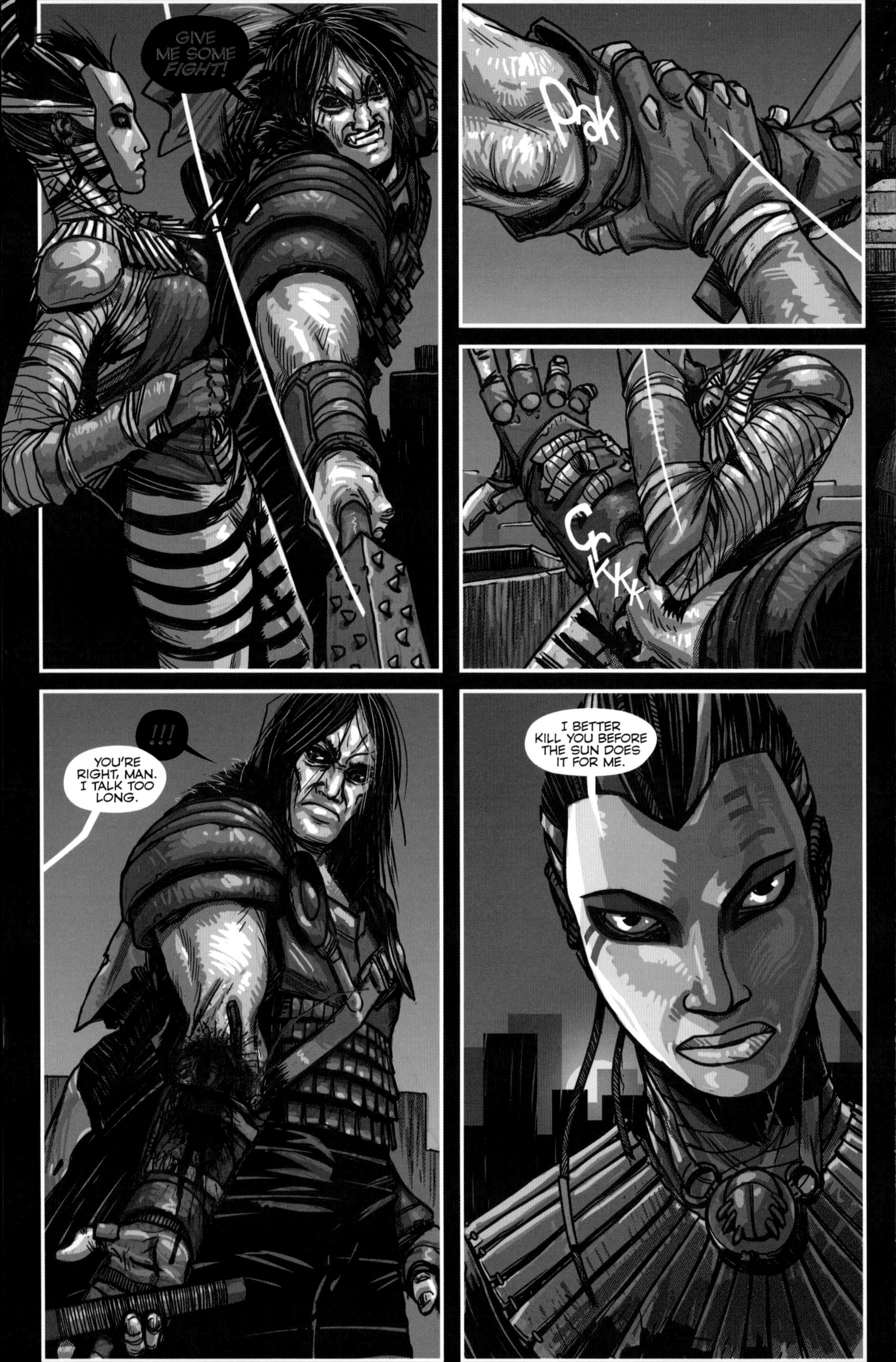
GIVE ME SOME FIGHT!
Pdak
Crkkkk
!!!
YOU'RE RIGHT, MAN. I TALK TOO LONG.
I BETTER KILL YOU BEFORE THE SUN DOES IT FOR ME.

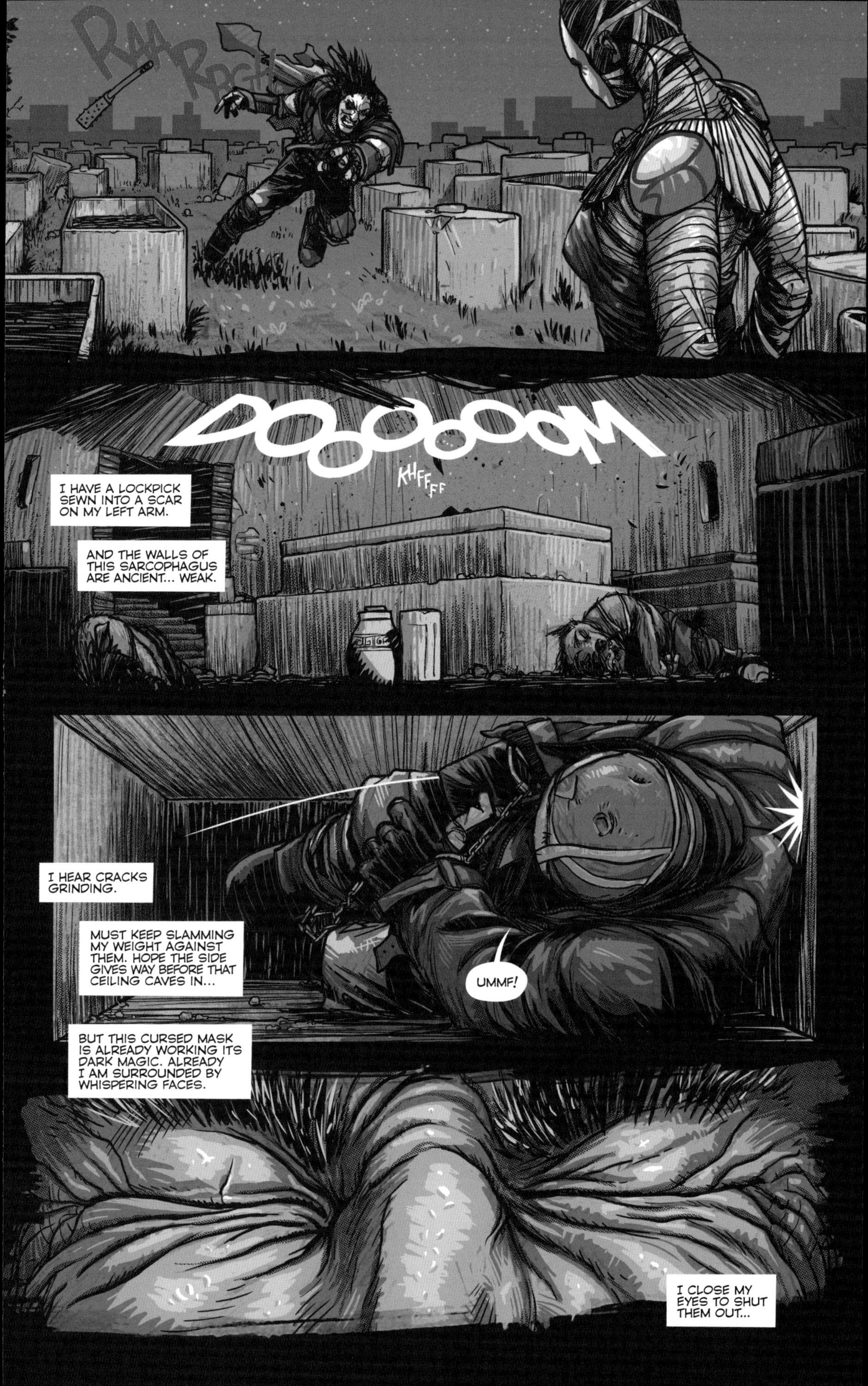
RAARRGH!
DOOOOOOOM
KHFFFFF
I HAVE A LOCKPICK SEWN INTO A SCAR ON MY LEFT ARM.
AND THE WALLS OF THIS SARCOPHAGUS ARE ANCIENT... WEAK.
I HEAR CRACKS GRINDING.
MUST KEEP SLAMMING MY WEIGHT AGAINST THEM. HOPE THE SIDE GIVES WAY BEFORE THAT CEILING CAVES IN...
UMMF!
BUT THIS CURSED MASK IS ALREADY WORKING ITS DARK MAGIC. ALREADY I AM SURROUNDED BY WHISPERING FACES.
I CLOSE MY EYES TO SHUT THEM OUT...

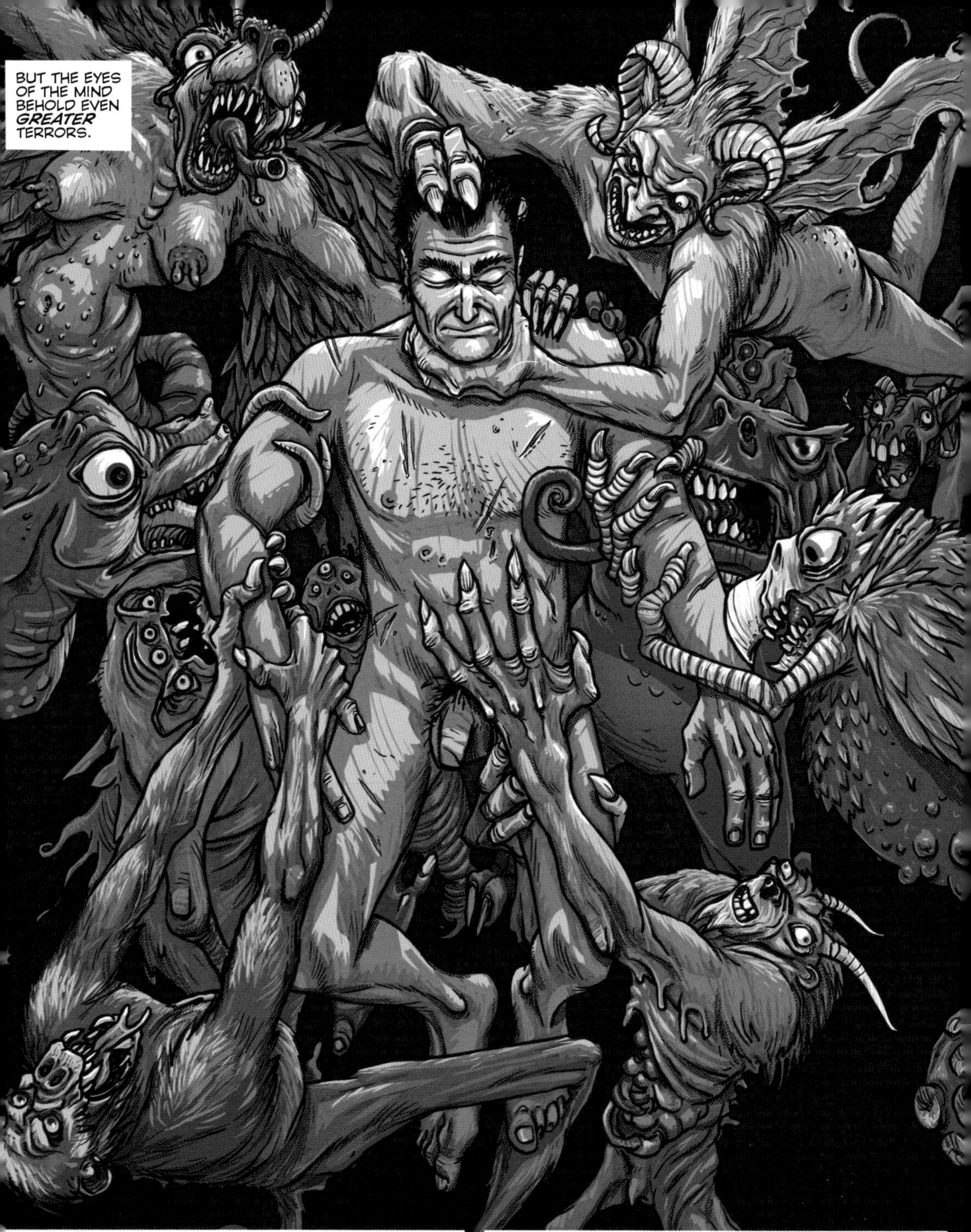
BUT THE EYES OF THE MIND BEHOLD EVEN **GREATER** TERRORS.

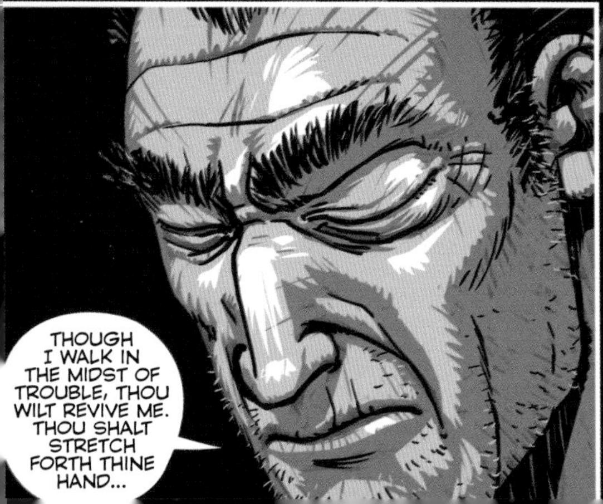
THOUGH I WALK IN THE MIDST OF TROUBLE, THOU WILT REVIVE ME. THOU SHALT STRETCH FORTH THINE HAND...

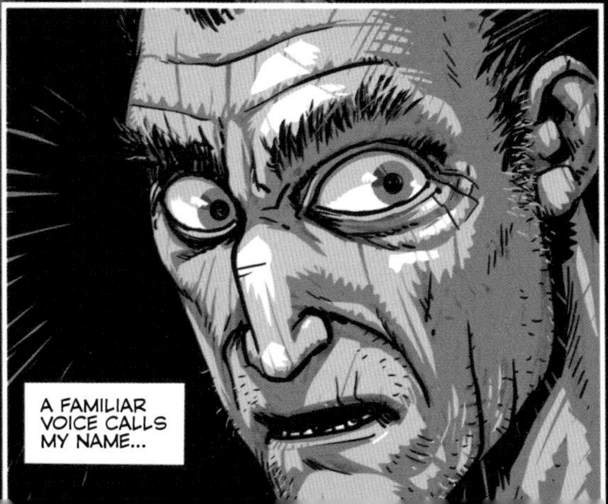
A FAMILIAR VOICE CALLS MY NAME...

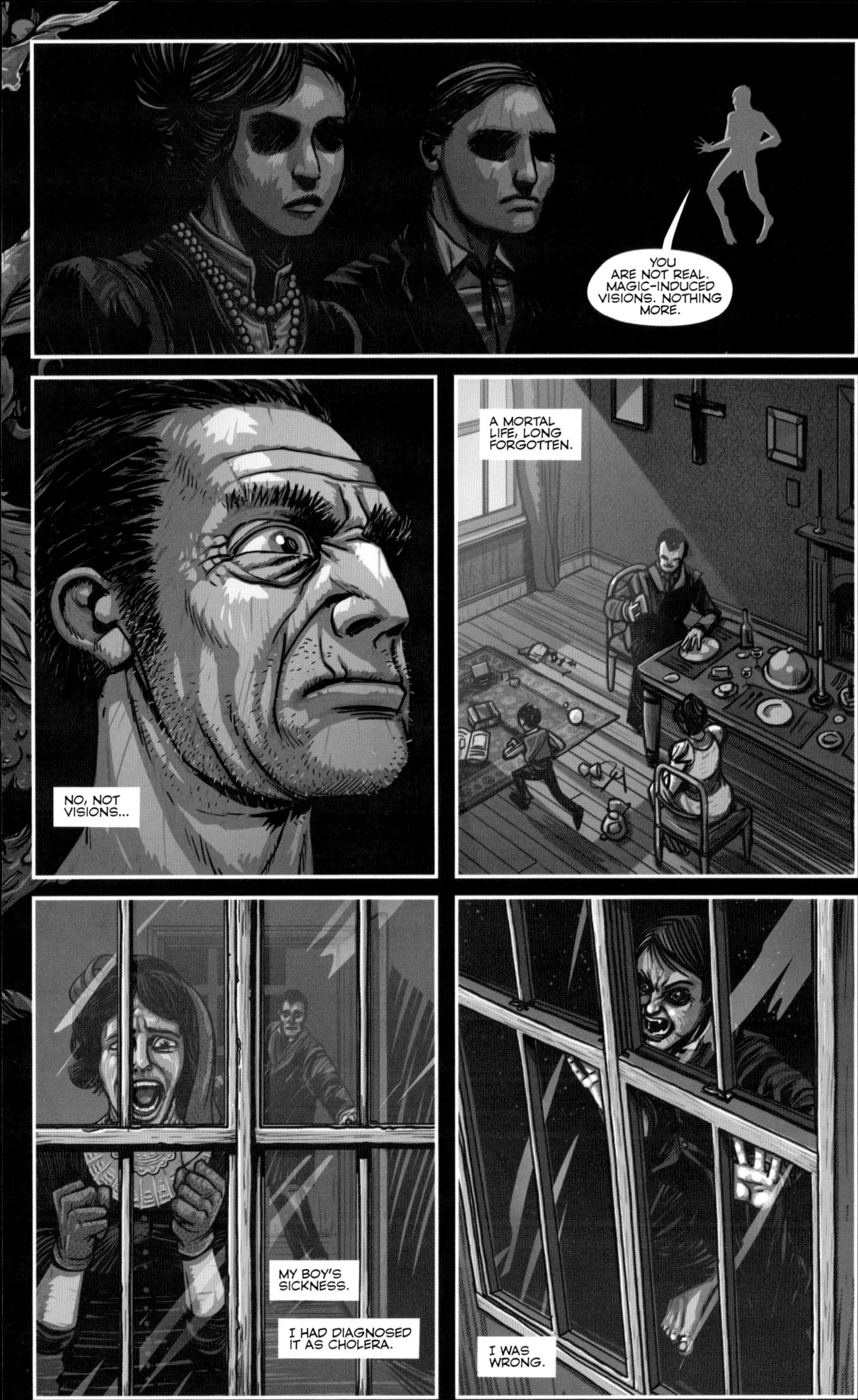
YOU ARE NOT REAL. MAGIC-INDUCED VISIONS. NOTHING MORE.
NO, NOT VISIONS...
A MORTAL LIFE, LONG FORGOTTEN.
MY BOY'S SICKNESS.
I HAD DIAGNOSED IT AS CHOLERA.
I WAS WRONG.

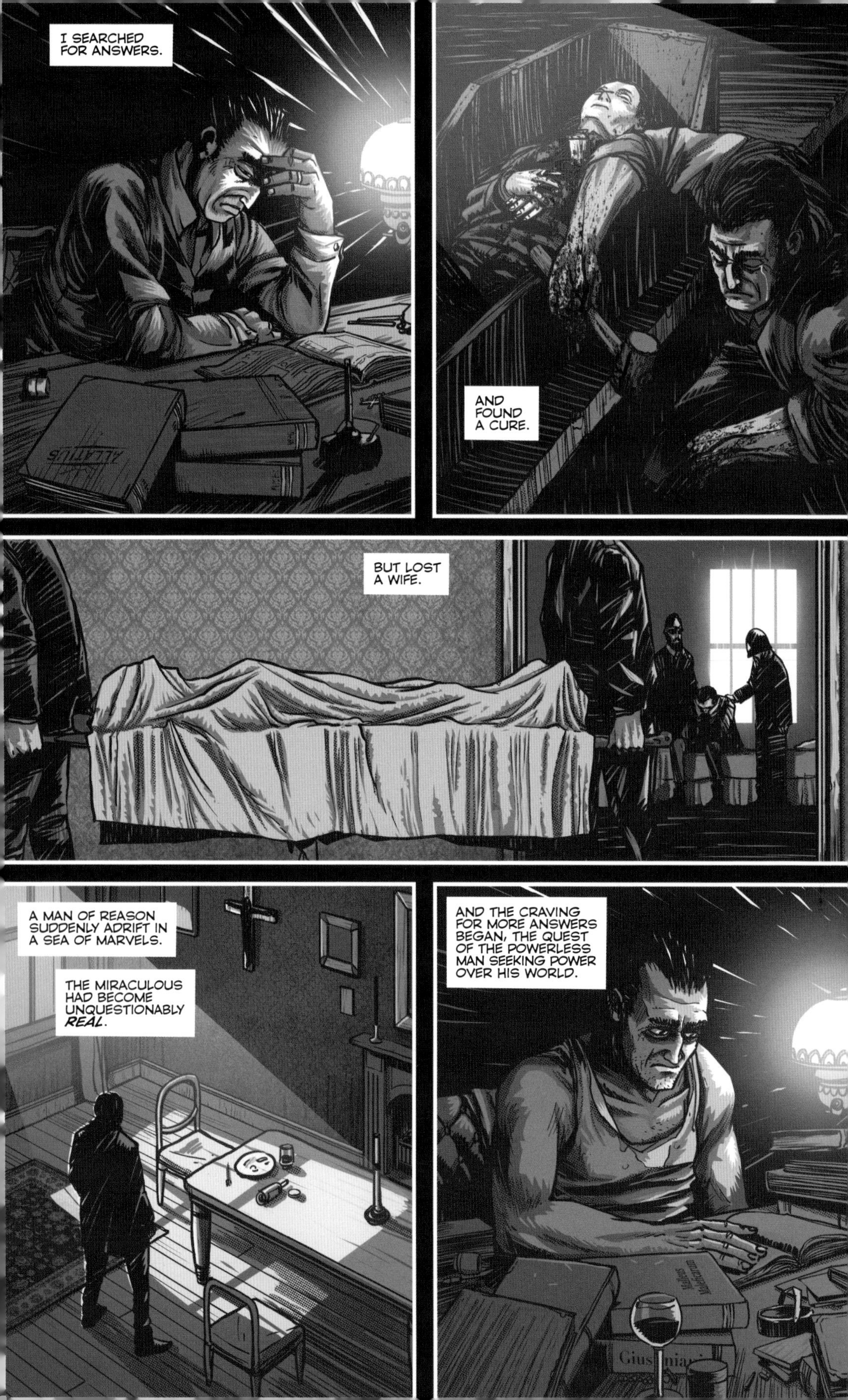
I SEARCHED FOR ANSWERS.
AND FOUND A CURE.
BUT LOST A WIFE.
A MAN OF REASON SUDDENLY ADRIFT IN A SEA OF MARVELS.
THE MIRACULOUS HAD BECOME UNQUESTIONABLY *REAL*.
AND THE CRAVING FOR MORE ANSWERS BEGAN, THE QUEST OF THE POWERLESS MAN SEEKING POWER OVER HIS WORLD.

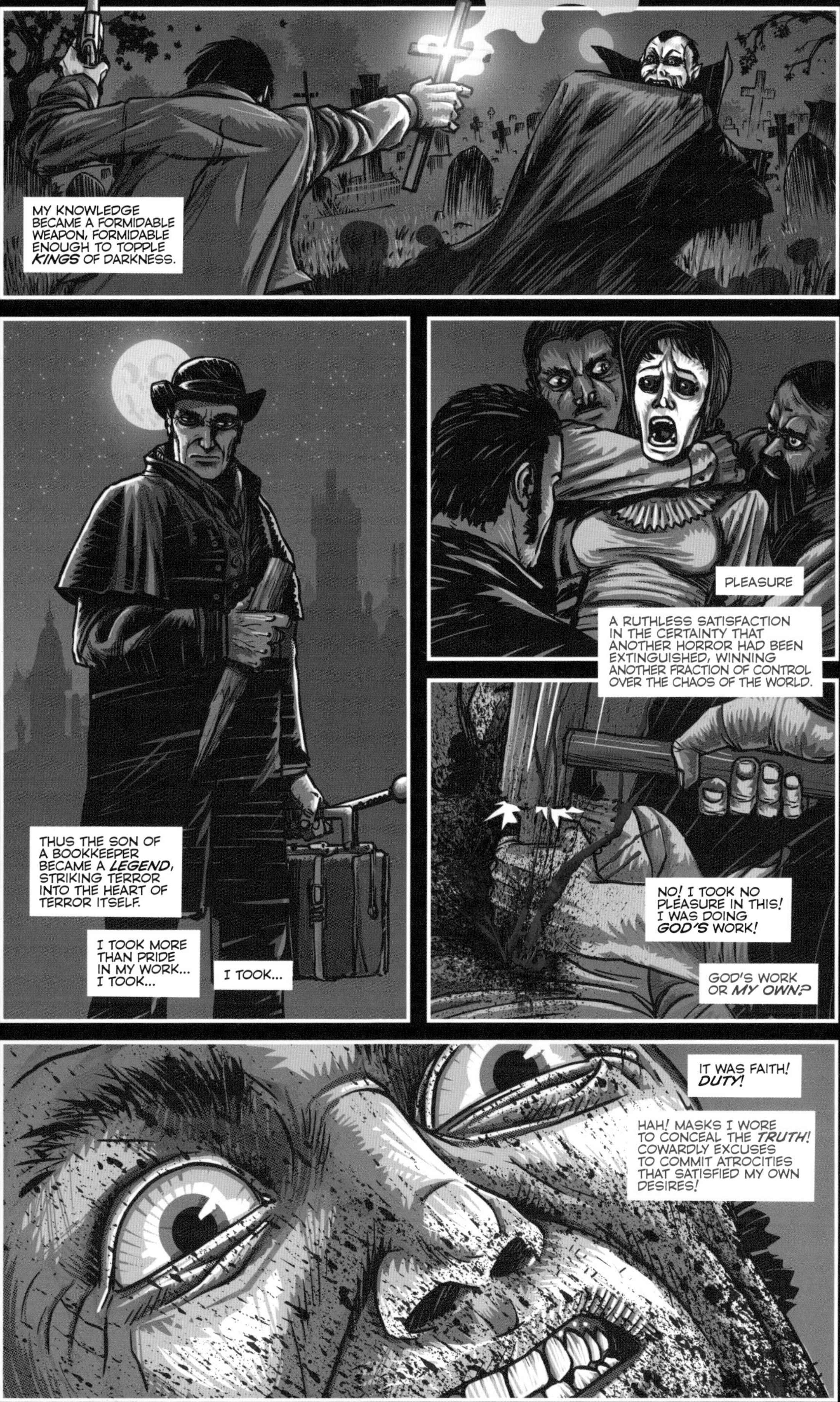

MY KNOWLEDGE BECAME A FORMIDABLE WEAPON, FORMIDABLE ENOUGH TO TOPPLE *KINGS* OF DARKNESS.
THUS THE SON OF A BOOKKEEPER BECAME A *LEGEND*, STRIKING TERROR INTO THE HEART OF TERROR ITSELF.
I TOOK MORE THAN PRIDE IN MY WORK... I TOOK...
I TOOK...
PLEASURE
A RUTHLESS SATISFACTION IN THE CERTAINTY THAT ANOTHER HORROR HAD BEEN EXTINGUISHED, WINNING ANOTHER FRACTION OF CONTROL OVER THE CHAOS OF THE WORLD.
NO! I TOOK NO PLEASURE IN THIS! I WAS DOING *GOD'S* WORK!
GOD'S WORK OR *MY OWN?*
IT WAS FAITH! *DUTY!*
HAH! MASKS I WORE TO CONCEAL THE *TRUTH!* COWARDLY EXCUSES TO COMMIT ATROCITIES THAT SATISFIED MY OWN DESIRES!

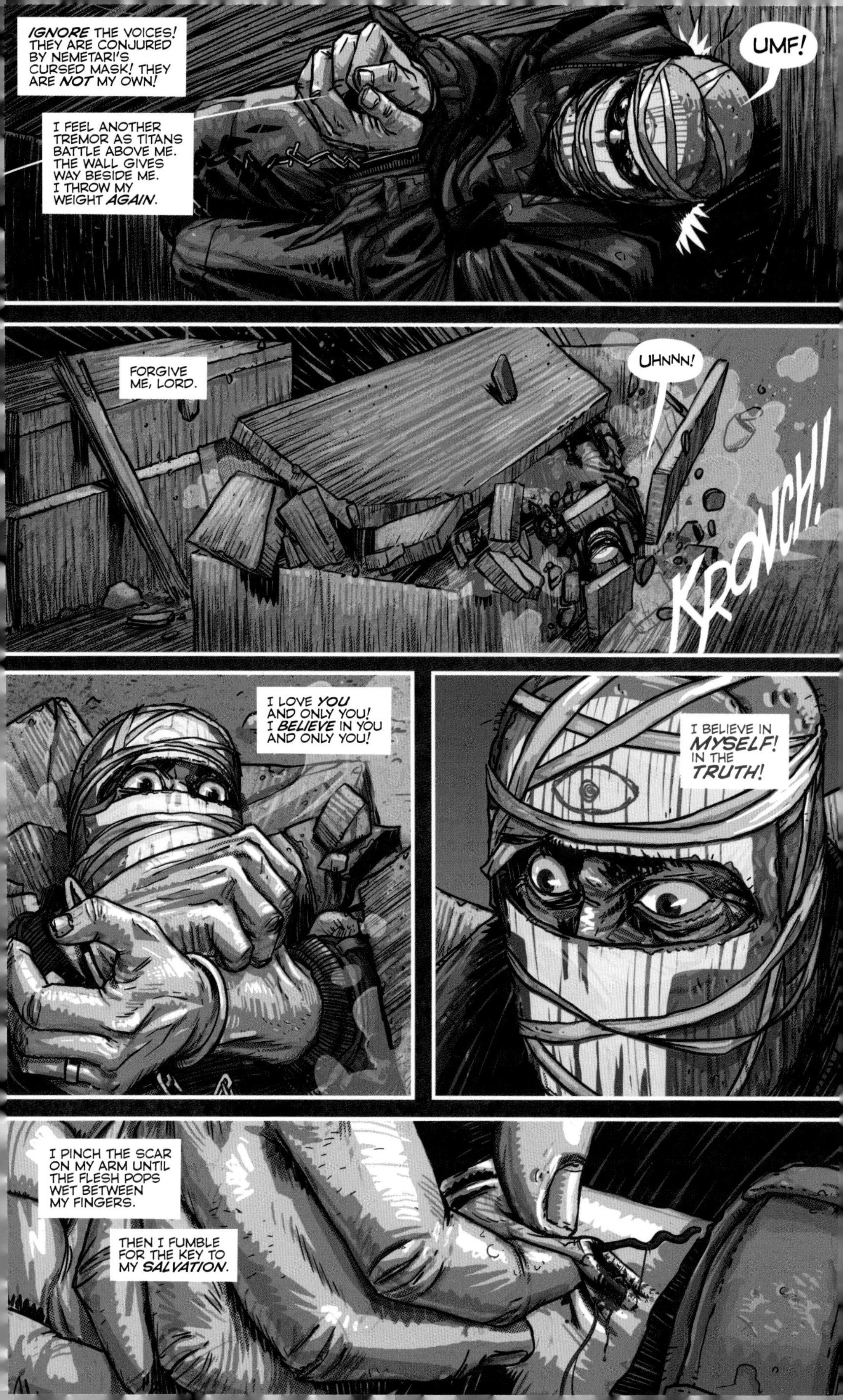
IGNORE THE VOICES! THEY ARE CONJURED BY NEMETARI'S CURSED MASK! THEY ARE NOT MY OWN!
UMF!
I FEEL ANOTHER TREMOR AS TITANS BATTLE ABOVE ME. THE WALL GIVES WAY BESIDE ME. I THROW MY WEIGHT AGAIN.
FORGIVE ME, LORD.
UHNNN!
KRONCH!
I LOVE YOU AND ONLY YOU! I BELIEVE IN YOU AND ONLY YOU!
I BELIEVE IN MYSELF! IN THE TRUTH!
I PINCH THE SCAR ON MY ARM UNTIL THE FLESH POPS WET BETWEEN MY FINGERS.
THEN I FUMBLE FOR THE KEY TO MY SALVATION.

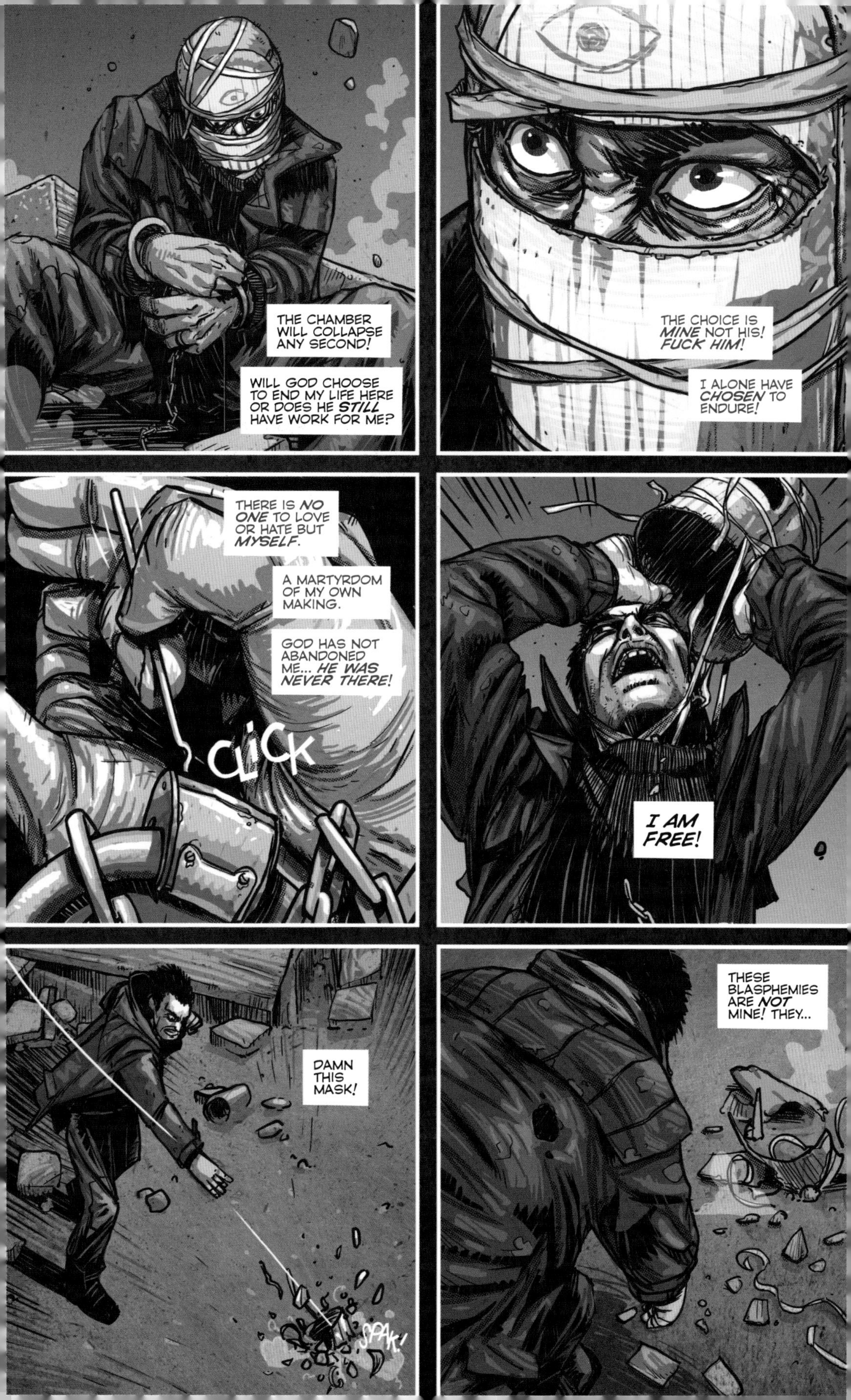
THE CHAMBER WILL COLLAPSE ANY SECOND!
WILL GOD CHOOSE TO END MY LIFE HERE OR DOES HE STILL HAVE WORK FOR ME?
THE CHOICE IS MINE NOT HIS! FUCK HIM!
I ALONE HAVE CHOSEN TO ENDURE!
THERE IS NO ONE TO LOVE OR HATE BUT MYSELF.
A MARTYRDOM OF MY OWN MAKING.
GOD HAS NOT ABANDONED ME... HE WAS NEVER THERE!
CLICK
I AM FREE!
DAMN THIS MASK!
SPAK!
THESE BLASPHEMIES ARE NOT MINE! THEY...

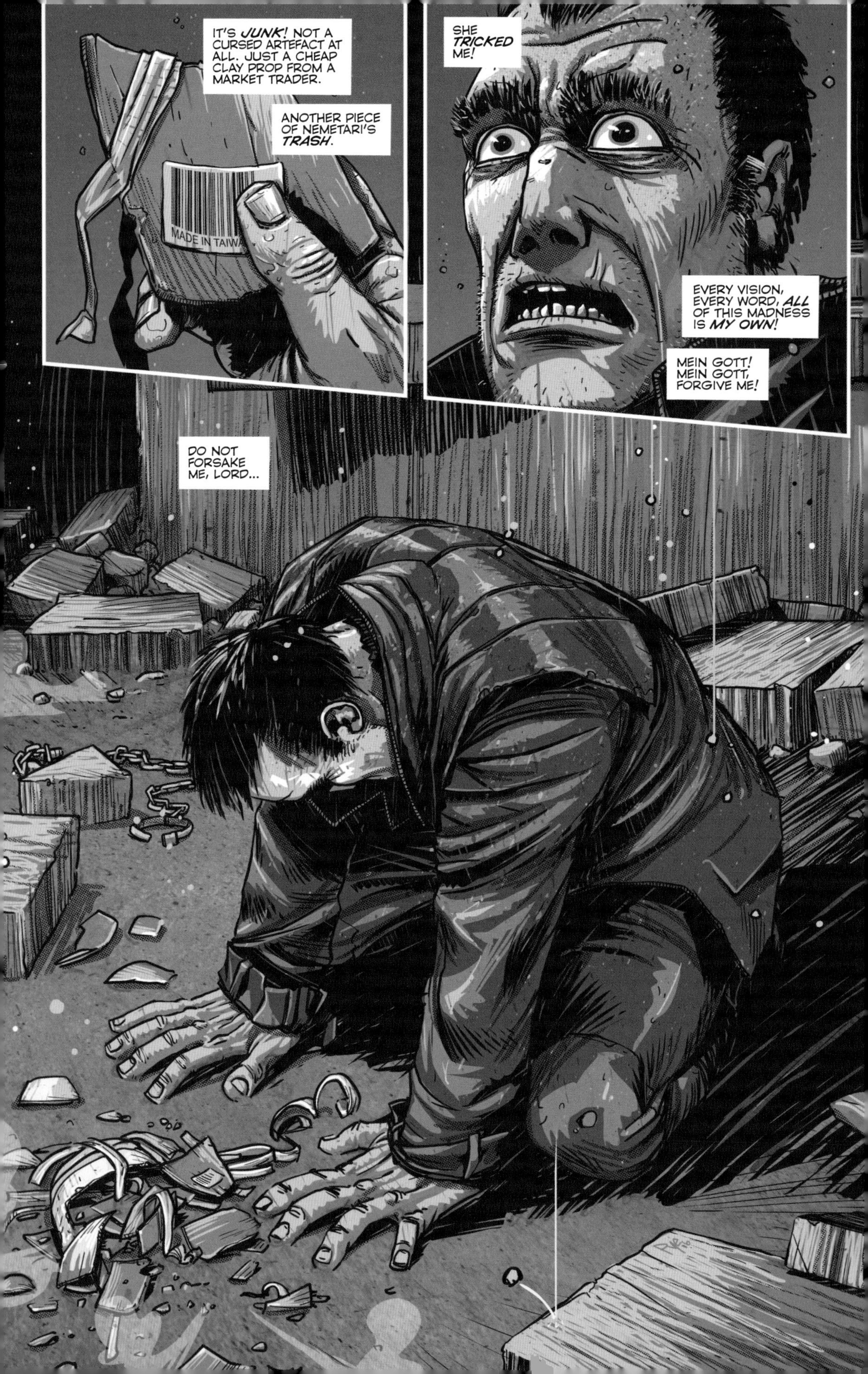
IT'S JUNK! NOT A CURSED ARTEFACT AT ALL. JUST A CHEAP CLAY PROP FROM A MARKET TRADER.
ANOTHER PIECE OF NEMETARI'S TRASH.
MADE IN TAIWA
SHE TRICKED ME!
EVERY VISION, EVERY WORD, ALL OF THIS MADNESS IS MY OWN!
MEIN GOTT! MEIN GOTT, FORGIVE ME!
DO NOT FORSAKE ME, LORD...

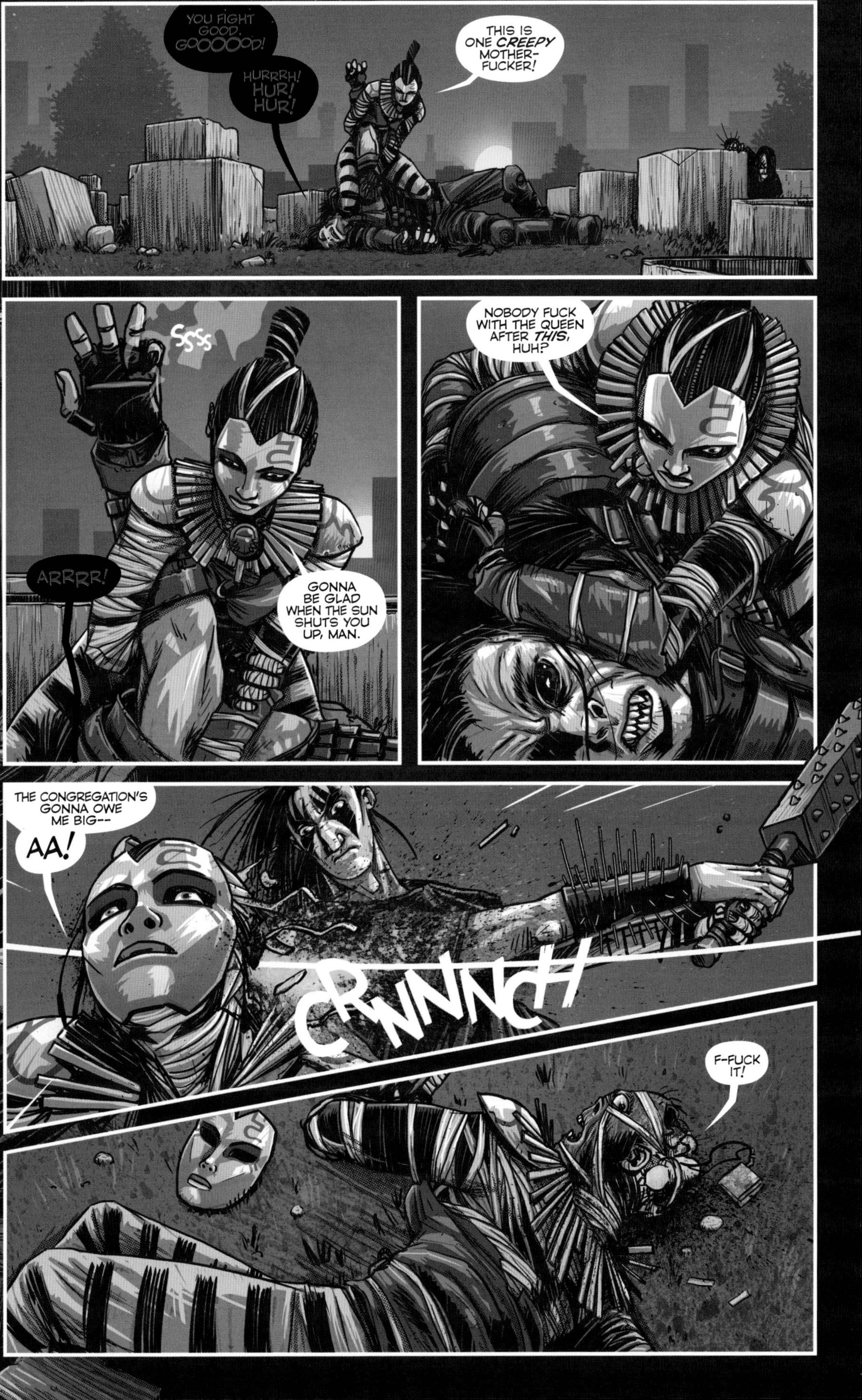
YOU FIGHT GOOD. GOOOOOD!
HURRRH! HUR! HUR!
THIS IS ONE CREEPY MOTHER-FUCKER!
SSSS
ARRRR!
GONNA BE GLAD WHEN THE SUN SHUTS YOU UP, MAN.
NOBODY FUCK WITH THE QUEEN AFTER THIS, HUH?
THE CONGREGATION'S GONNA OWE ME BIG--
AA!
CRWNNCH
F-FUCK IT!

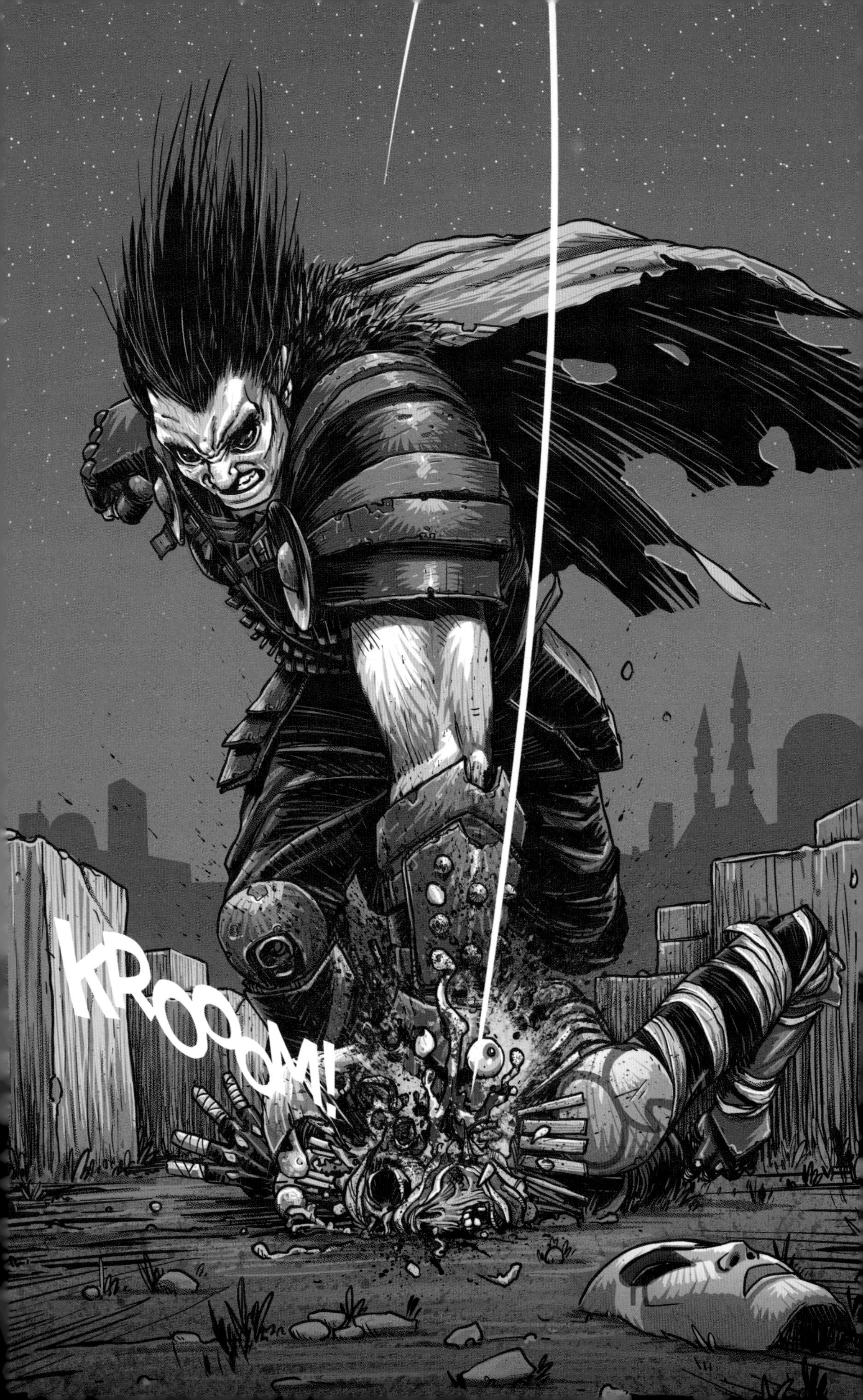
KROOOM!

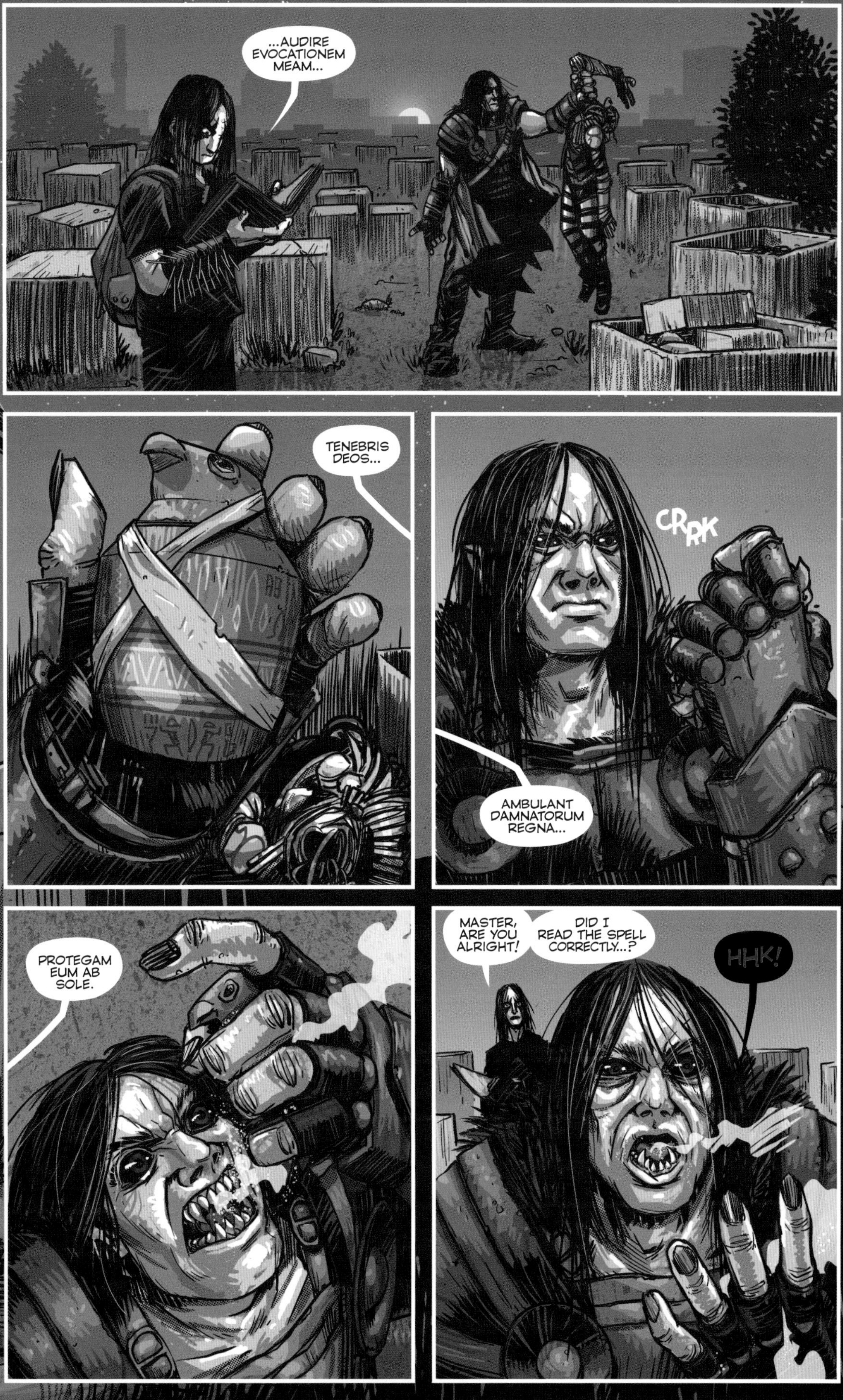
...AUDIRE EVOCATIONEM MEAM...
TENEBRIS DEOS...
CRRK
AMBULANT DAMNATORUM REGNA...
PROTEGAM EUM AB SOLE.
MASTER, ARE YOU ALRIGHT!
DID I READ THE SPELL CORRECTLY...?
HHK!

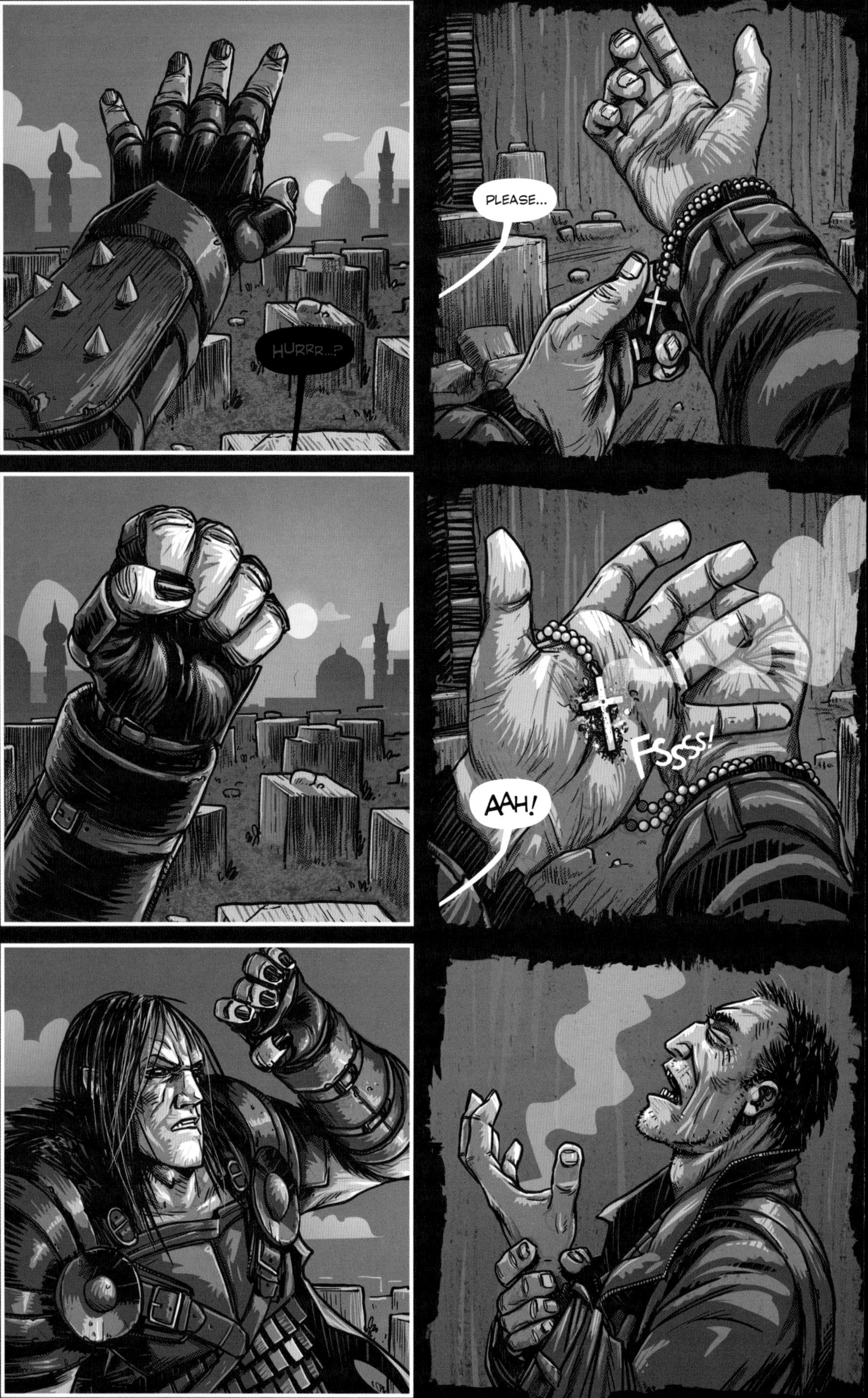
HURRR...?
PLEASE...
FSSSS!
AAH!

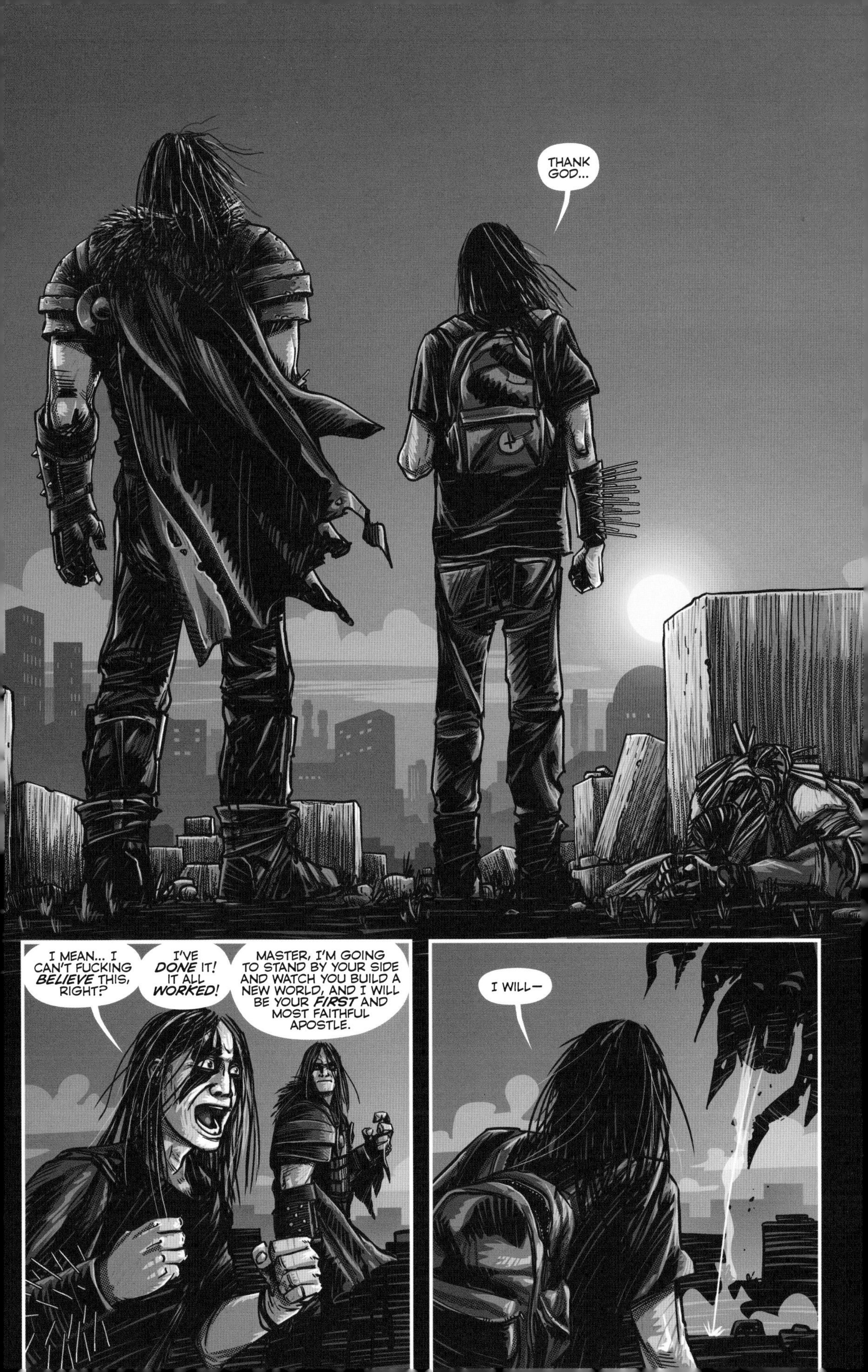
THANK GOD...
I MEAN... I CAN'T FUCKING *BELIEVE* THIS, RIGHT?
I'VE *DONE* IT! IT ALL *WORKED*!
MASTER, I'M GOING TO STAND BY YOUR SIDE AND WATCH YOU BUILD A NEW WORLD, AND I WILL BE YOUR *FIRST* AND MOST FAITHFUL APOSTLE.
I WILL—

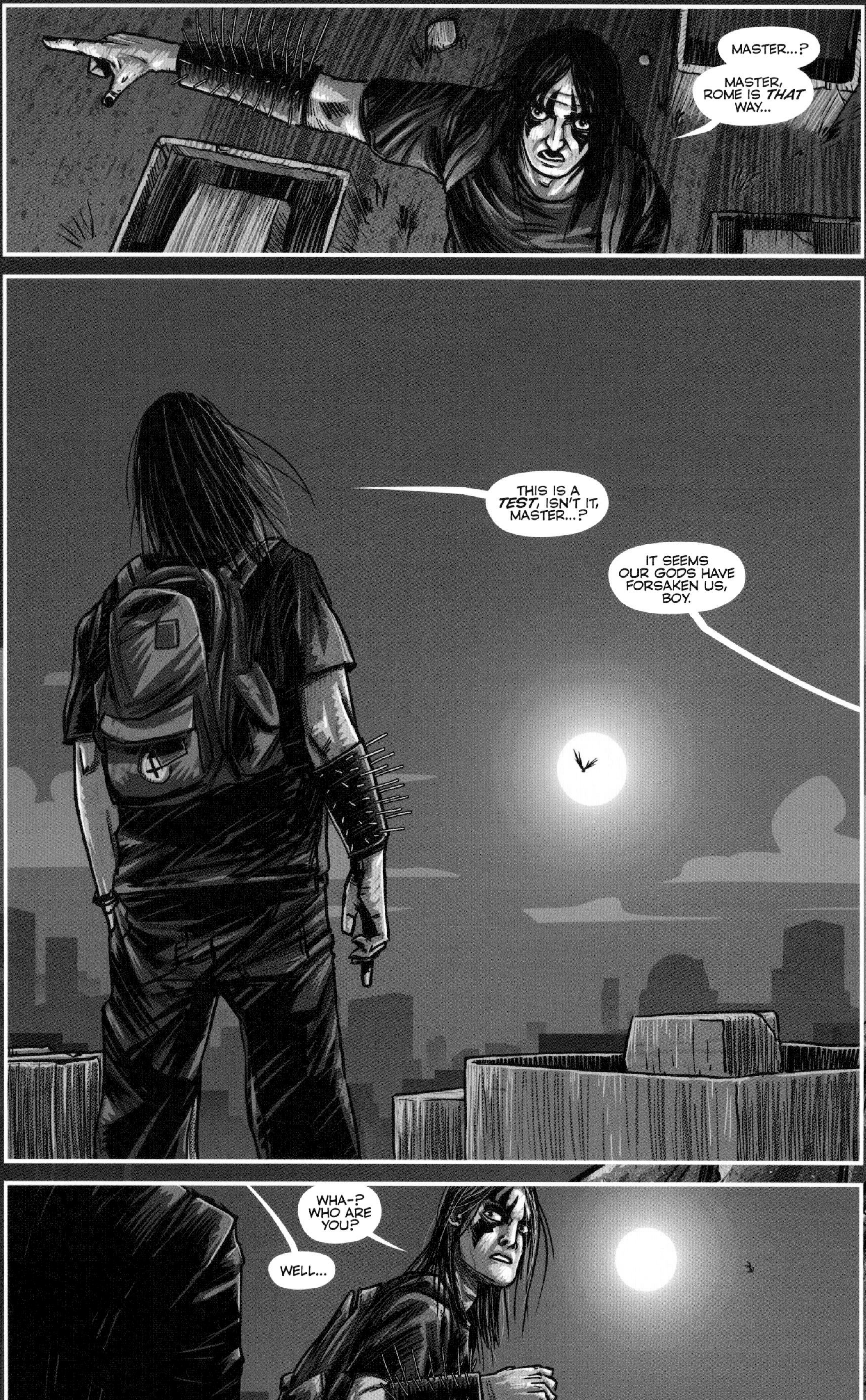
MASTER...?
MASTER, ROME IS *THAT* WAY...
THIS IS A *TEST*, ISN'T IT, MASTER...?
IT SEEMS OUR GODS HAVE FORSAKEN US, BOY.
WHA-? WHO ARE YOU?
WELL...

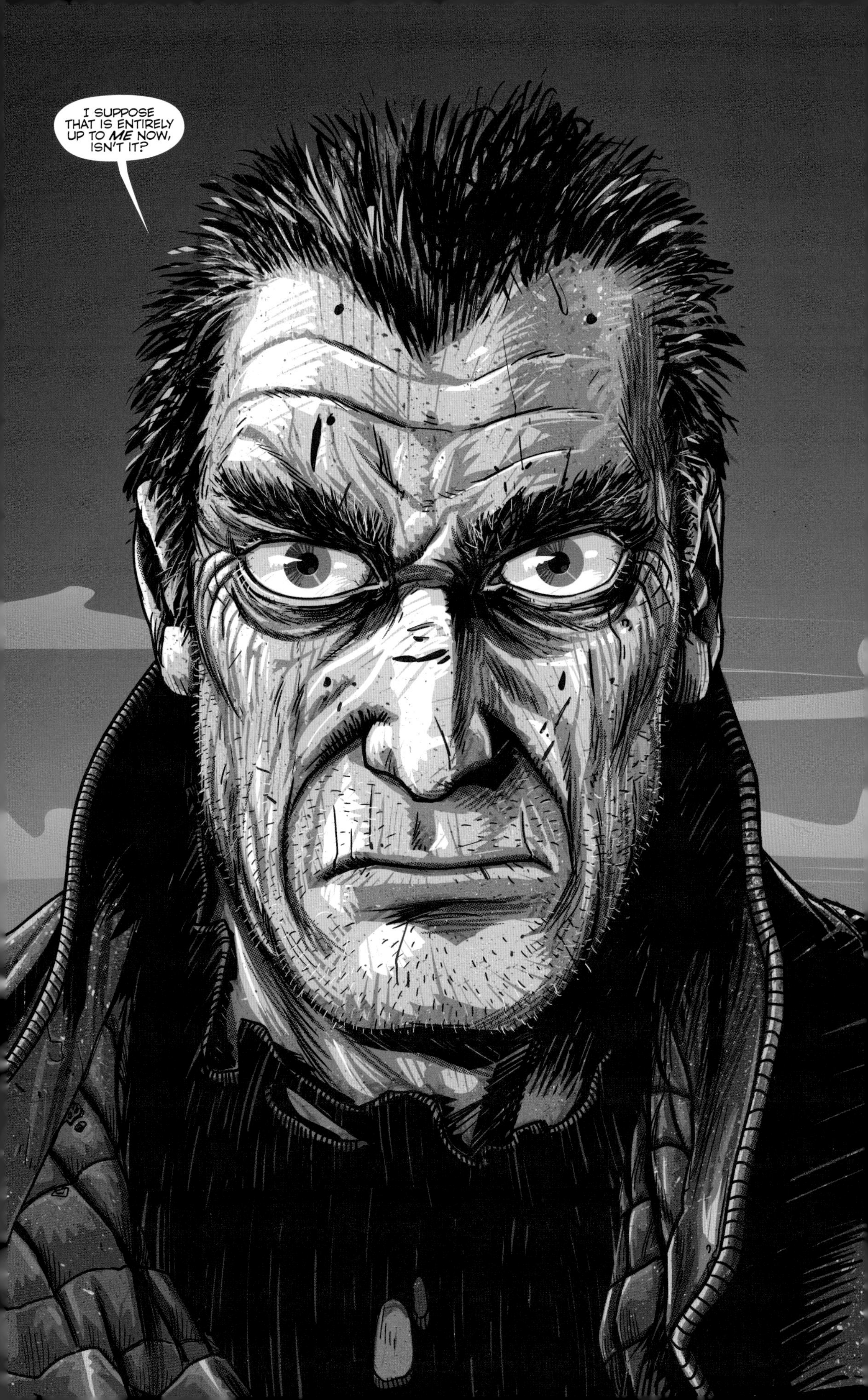
I SUPPOSE THAT IS ENTIRELY UP TO *ME* NOW, ISN'T IT?

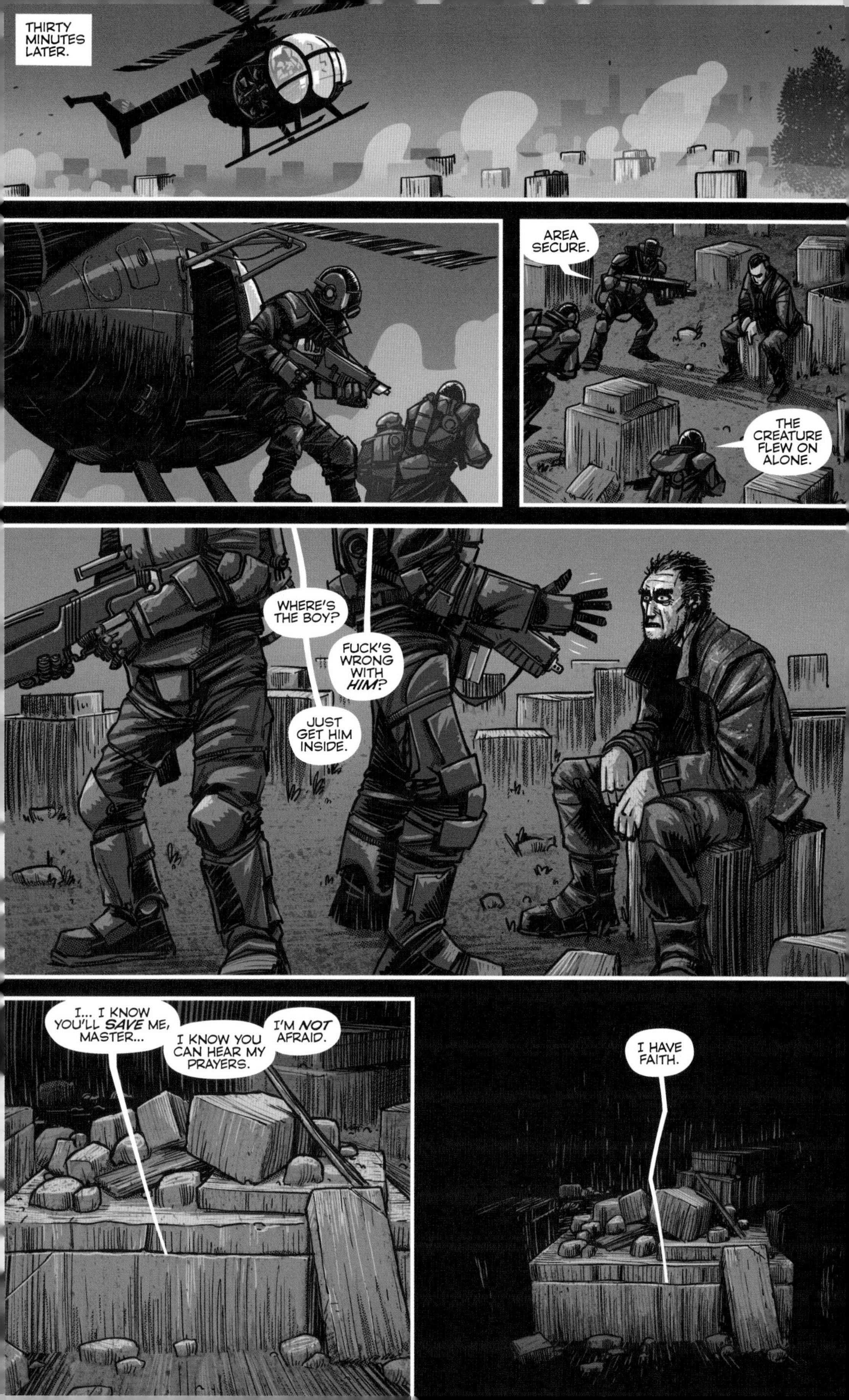
THIRTY MINUTES LATER.
AREA SECURE.
THE CREATURE FLEW ON ALONE.
WHERE'S THE BOY?
FUCK'S WRONG WITH *HIM*?
JUST GET HIM INSIDE.
I... I KNOW YOU'LL *SAVE* ME, MASTER...
I KNOW YOU CAN HEAR MY PRAYERS.
I'M *NOT* AFRAID.
I HAVE FAITH.

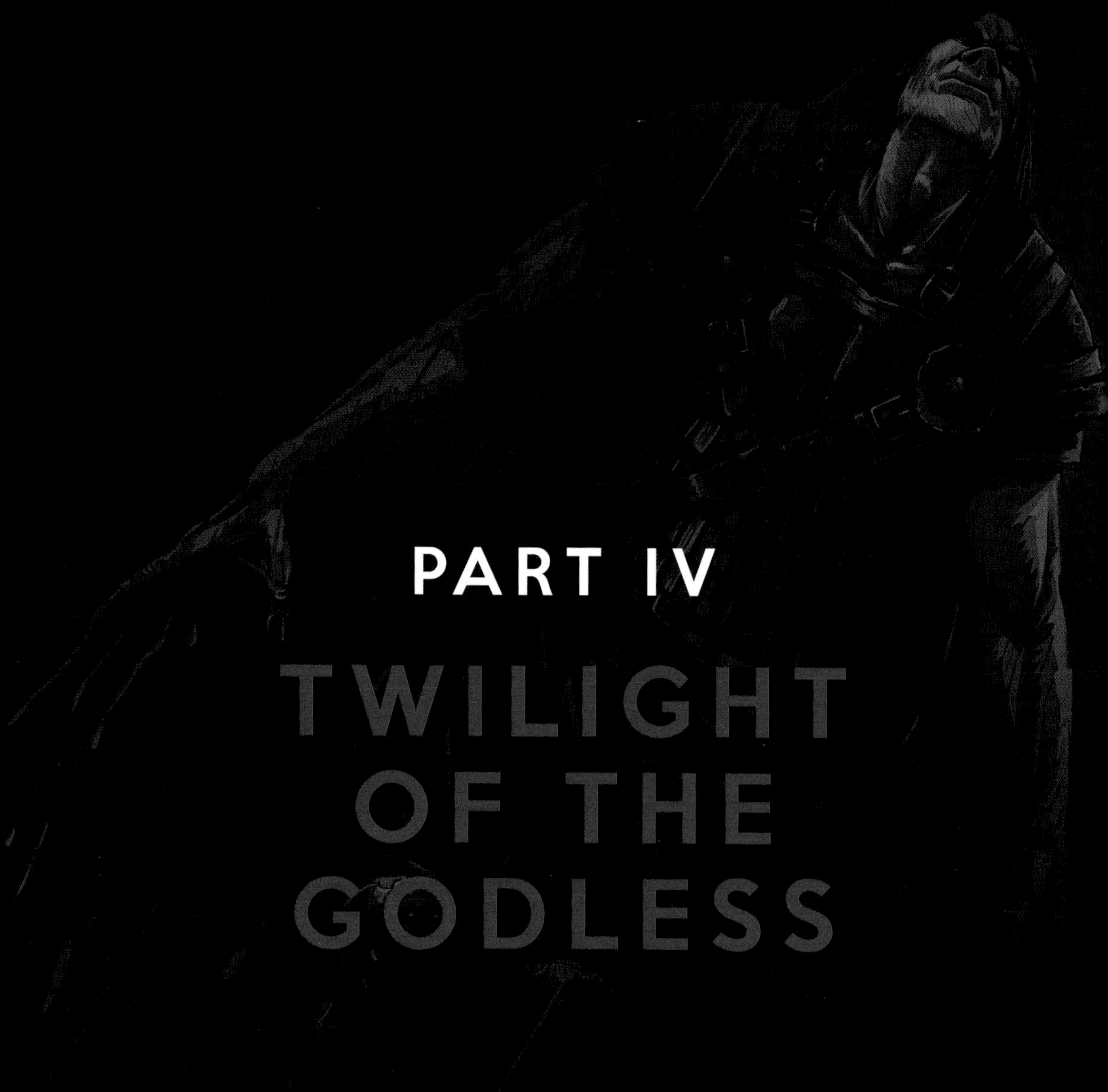

PART IV

TWILIGHT OF THE GODLESS

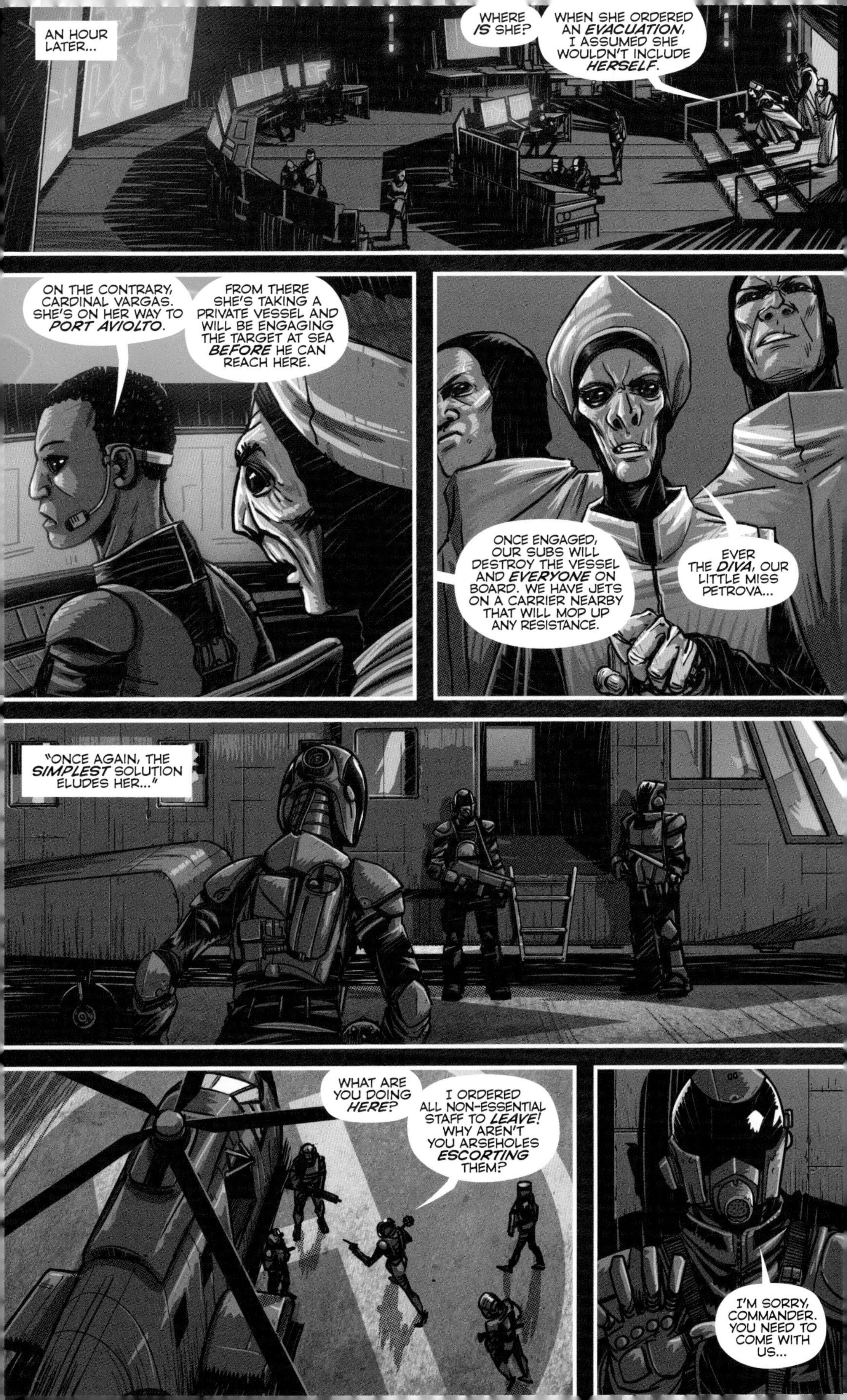
AN HOUR LATER...
WHERE IS SHE?
WHEN SHE ORDERED AN EVACUATION, I ASSUMED SHE WOULDN'T INCLUDE HERSELF.
ON THE CONTRARY, CARDINAL VARGAS. SHE'S ON HER WAY TO PORT AVIOLTO.
FROM THERE SHE'S TAKING A PRIVATE VESSEL AND WILL BE ENGAGING THE TARGET AT SEA BEFORE HE CAN REACH HERE.
EVER THE DIVA, OUR LITTLE MISS PETROVA...
ONCE ENGAGED, OUR SUBS WILL DESTROY THE VESSEL AND EVERYONE ON BOARD. WE HAVE JETS ON A CARRIER NEARBY THAT WILL MOP UP ANY RESISTANCE.
"ONCE AGAIN, THE SIMPLEST SOLUTION ELUDES HER..."
WHAT ARE YOU DOING HERE?
I ORDERED ALL NON-ESSENTIAL STAFF TO LEAVE! WHY AREN'T YOU ARSEHOLES ESCORTING THEM?
I'M SORRY, COMMANDER. YOU NEED TO COME WITH US...

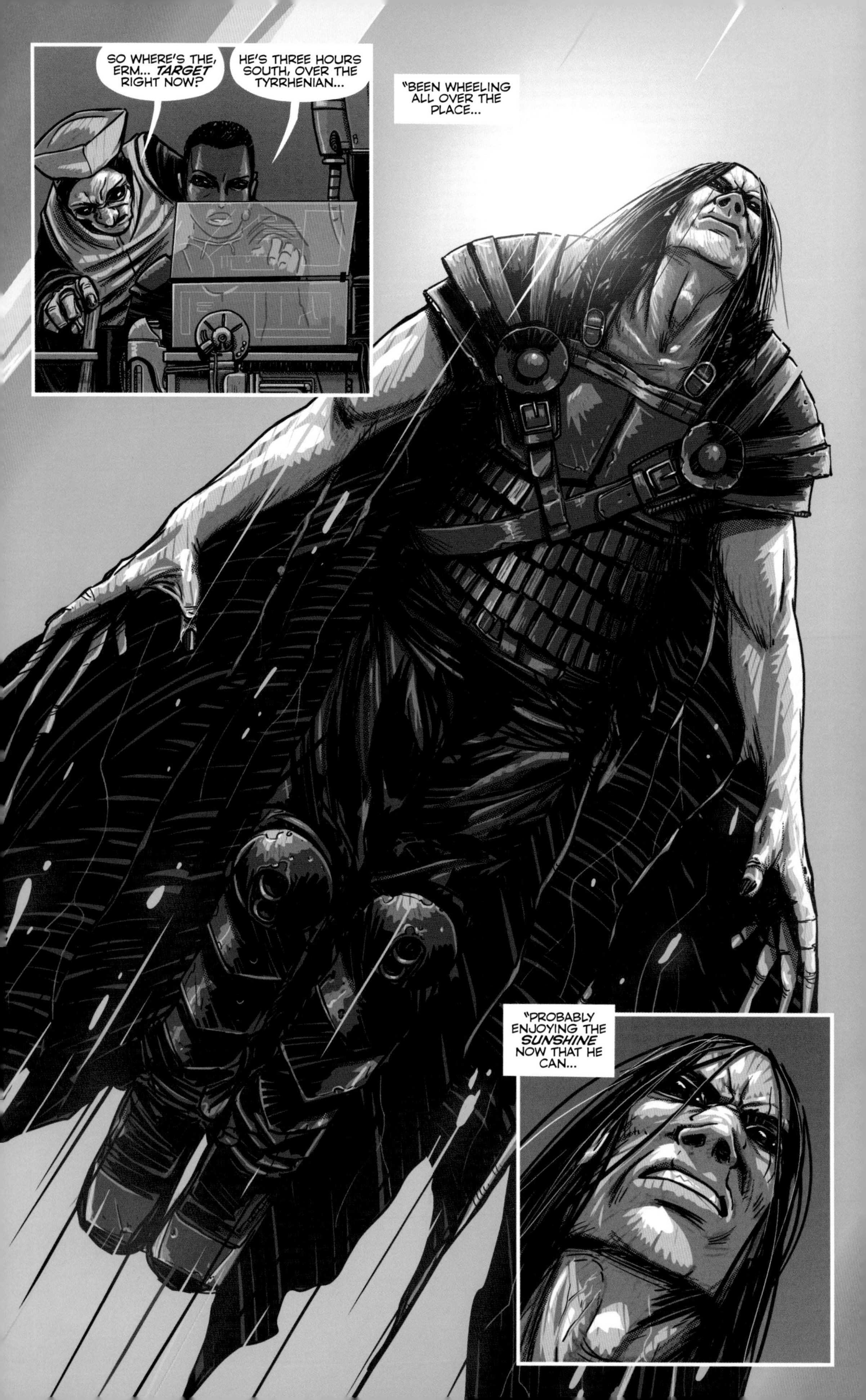
SO WHERE'S THE, ERM... *TARGET* RIGHT NOW?
HE'S THREE HOURS SOUTH, OVER THE TYRRHENIAN...
"BEEN WHEELING ALL OVER THE PLACE...
"PROBABLY ENJOYING THE *SUNSHINE* NOW THAT HE CAN...

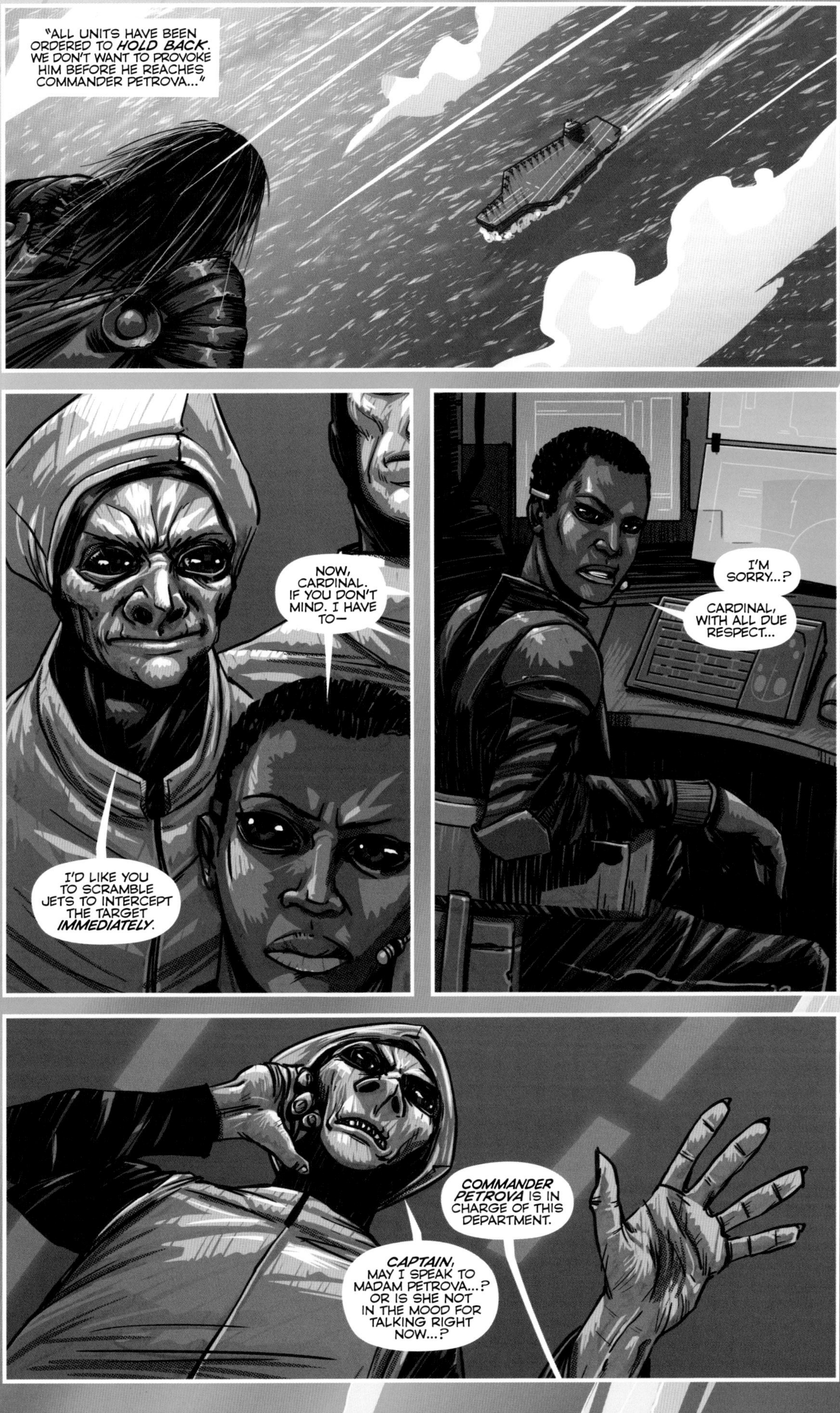
"ALL UNITS HAVE BEEN ORDERED TO *HOLD BACK*. WE DON'T WANT TO PROVOKE HIM BEFORE HE REACHES COMMANDER PETROVA..."
NOW, CARDINAL. IF YOU DON'T MIND. I HAVE TO—
I'D LIKE YOU TO SCRAMBLE JETS TO INTERCEPT THE TARGET *IMMEDIATELY*.
I'M SORRY...?
CARDINAL, WITH ALL DUE RESPECT...
COMMANDER PETROVA IS IN CHARGE OF THIS DEPARTMENT.
CAPTAIN, MAY I SPEAK TO MADAM PETROVA...? OR IS SHE NOT IN THE MOOD FOR TALKING RIGHT NOW...?

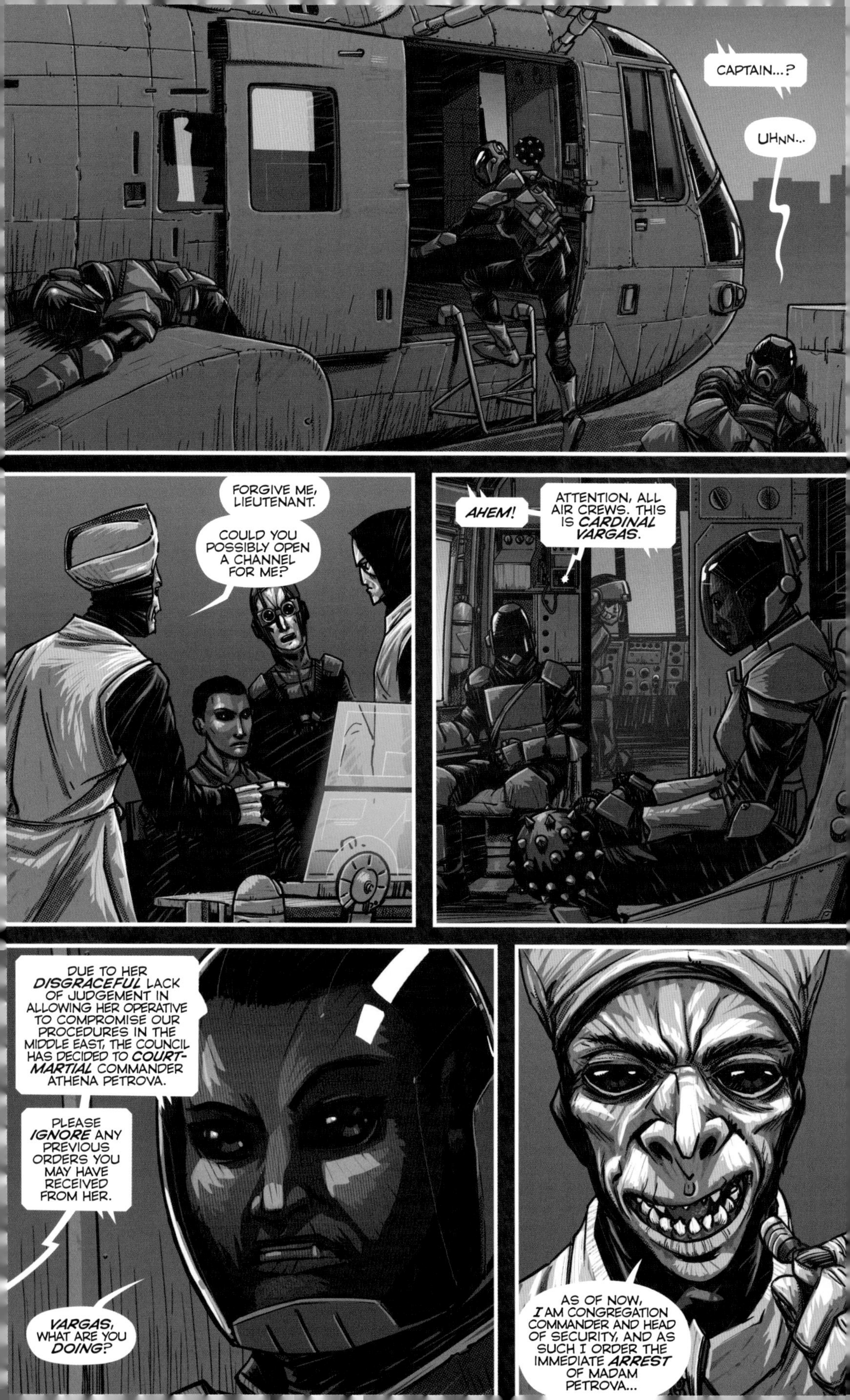
CAPTAIN...?
UHNN...
FORGIVE ME, LIEUTENANT.
COULD YOU POSSIBLY OPEN A CHANNEL FOR ME?
AHEM!
ATTENTION, ALL AIR CREWS. THIS IS CARDINAL VARGAS.
DUE TO HER DISGRACEFUL LACK OF JUDGEMENT IN ALLOWING HER OPERATIVE TO COMPROMISE OUR PROCEDURES IN THE MIDDLE EAST, THE COUNCIL HAS DECIDED TO COURT-MARTIAL COMMANDER ATHENA PETROVA.
PLEASE IGNORE ANY PREVIOUS ORDERS YOU MAY HAVE RECEIVED FROM HER.
VARGAS, WHAT ARE YOU DOING?
AS OF NOW, I AM CONGREGATION COMMANDER AND HEAD OF SECURITY, AND AS SUCH I ORDER THE IMMEDIATE ARREST OF MADAM PETROVA...

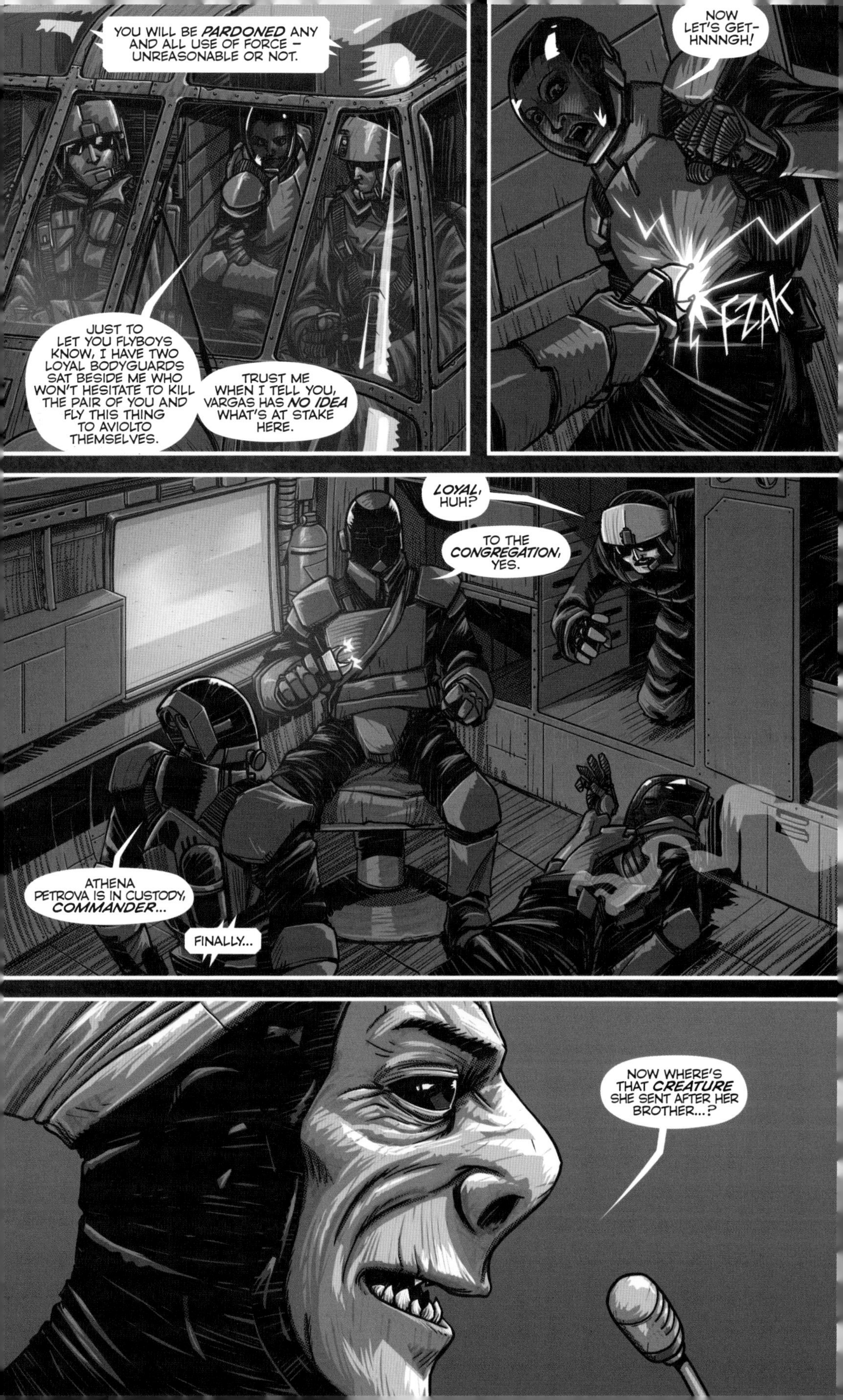
YOU WILL BE *PARDONED* ANY AND ALL USE OF FORCE – UNREASONABLE OR NOT.
JUST TO LET YOU FLYBOYS KNOW, I HAVE TWO LOYAL BODYGUARDS SAT BESIDE ME WHO WON'T HESITATE TO KILL THE PAIR OF YOU AND FLY THIS THING TO AVIOLTO THEMSELVES.
TRUST ME WHEN I TELL YOU, VARGAS HAS *NO IDEA* WHAT'S AT STAKE HERE.
NOW LET'S GET– HNNNGH!
FZAK
LOYAL, HUH?
TO THE *CONGREGATION*, YES.
ATHENA PETROVA IS IN CUSTODY, *COMMANDER*...
FINALLY...
NOW WHERE'S THAT *CREATURE* SHE SENT AFTER HER BROTHER...?

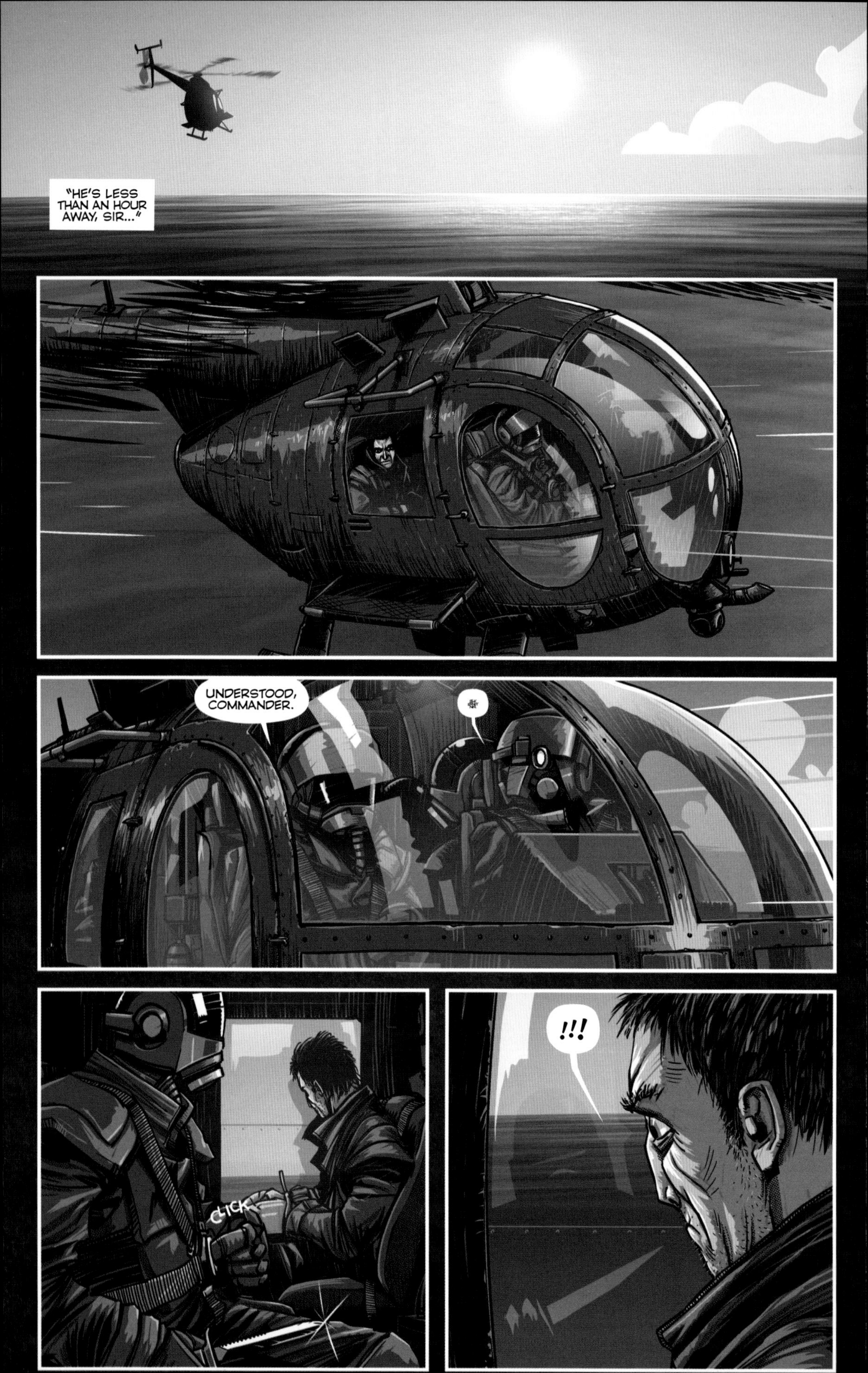
"HE'S LESS THAN AN HOUR AWAY, SIR..."
UNDERSTOOD, COMMANDER.
CLICK
!!!

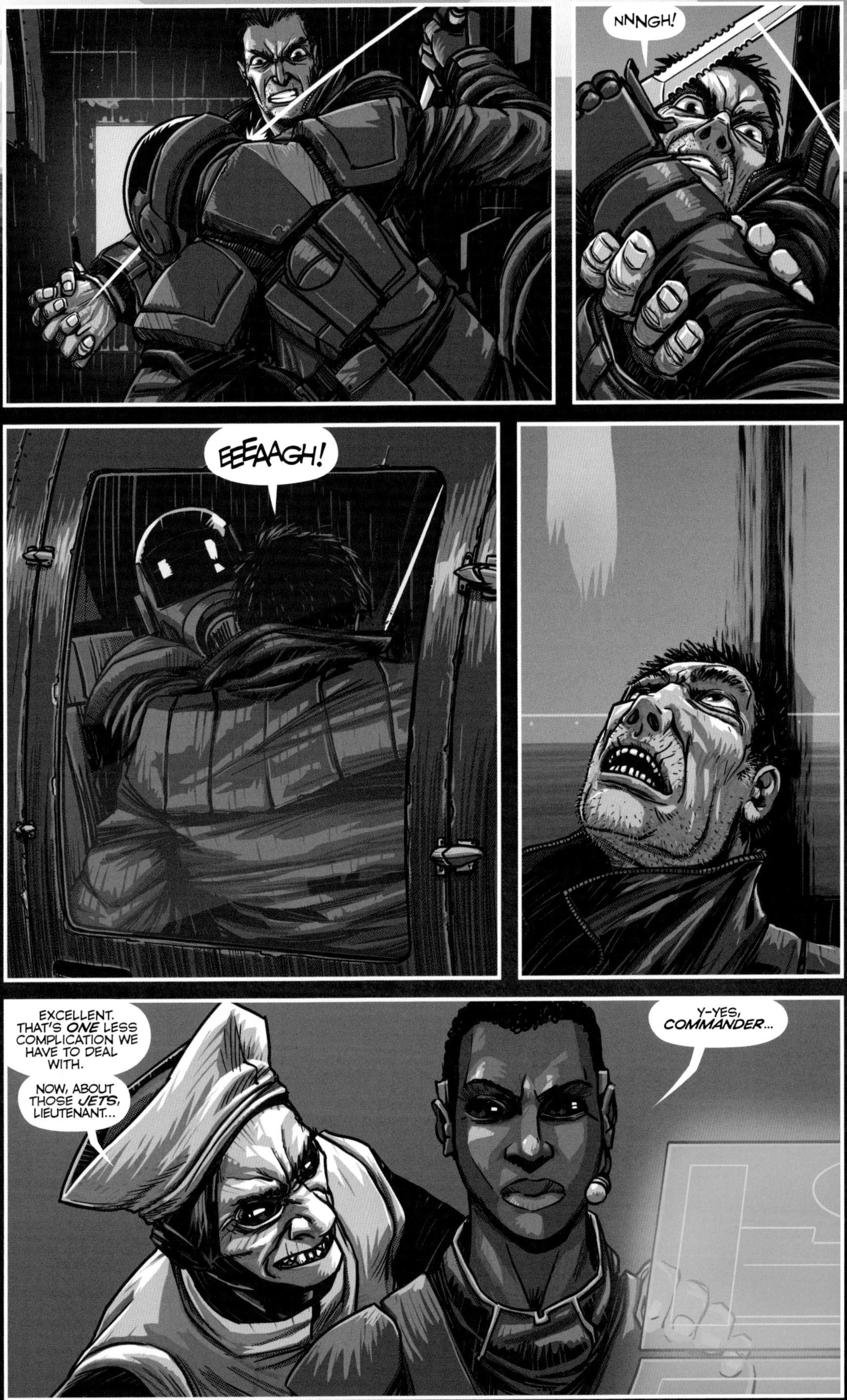
NNNGH!
EEEAAGH!
EXCELLENT. THAT'S ONE LESS COMPLICATION WE HAVE TO DEAL WITH.
NOW, ABOUT THOSE JETS, LIEUTENANT...
Y-YES, COMMANDER...

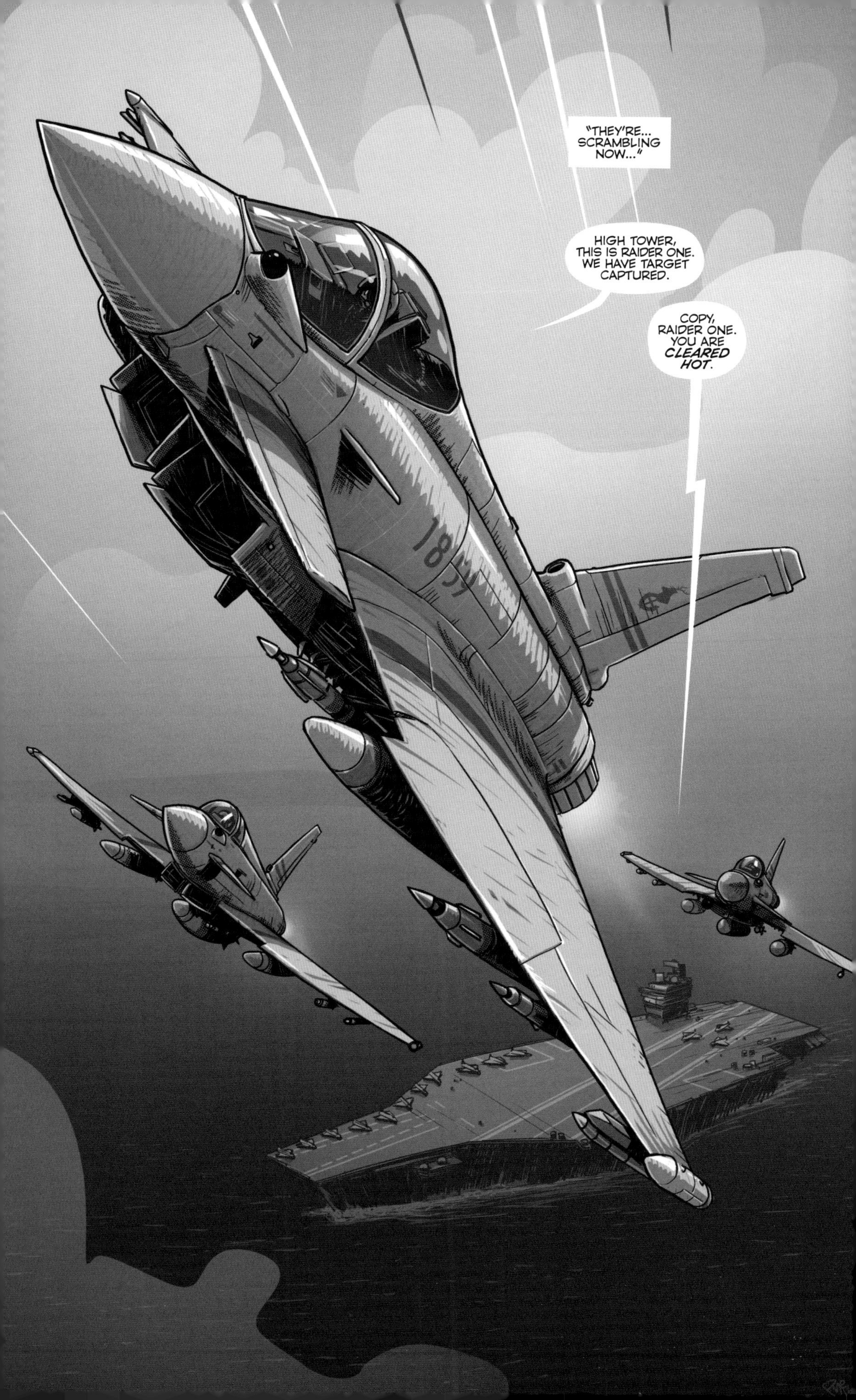
"THEY'RE... SCRAMBLING NOW..."
HIGH TOWER, THIS IS RAIDER ONE. WE HAVE TARGET CAPTURED.
COPY, RAIDER ONE. YOU ARE *CLEARED HOT*.

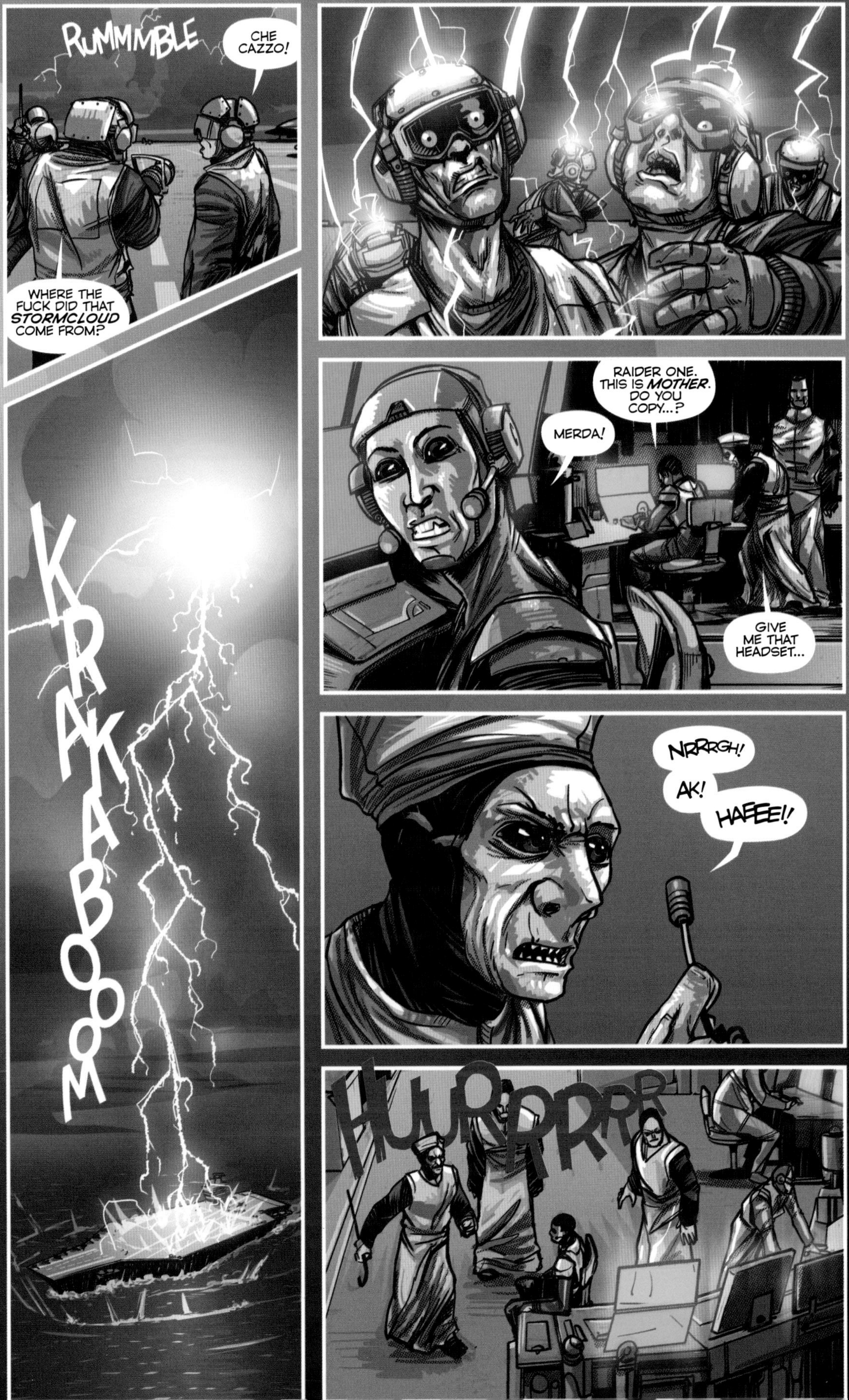
RUMMMBLE
CHE CAZZO!
WHERE THE FUCK DID THAT ***STORMCLOUD*** COME FROM?
KRAKABOOOM
RAIDER ONE. THIS IS ***MOTHER***. DO YOU COPY...?
MERDA!
GIVE ME THAT HEADSET...
NRRRGH!
AK!
HAEEE!!
HUURRRRR

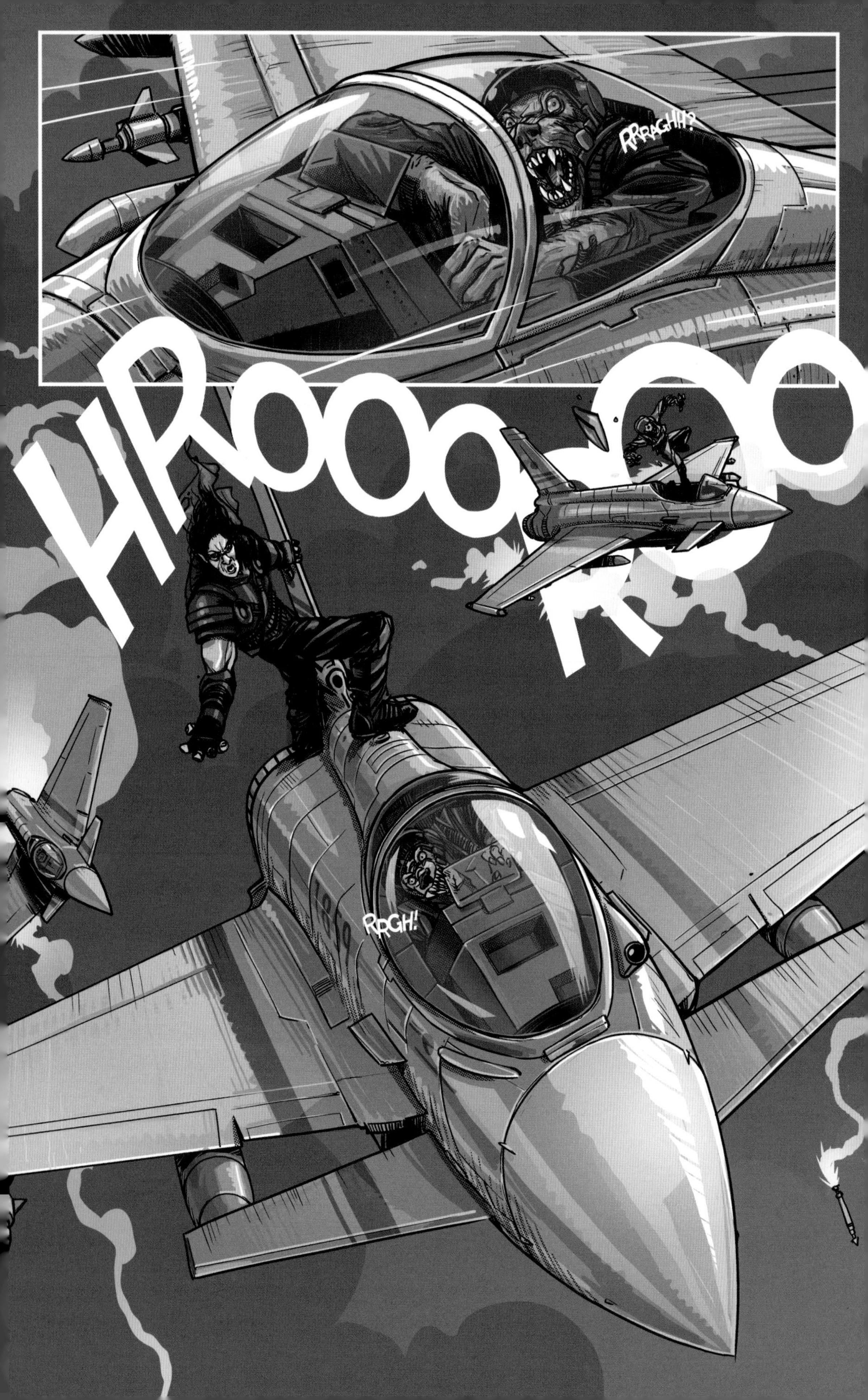
RRRAGHH?
HROOAROOR
RRGH!

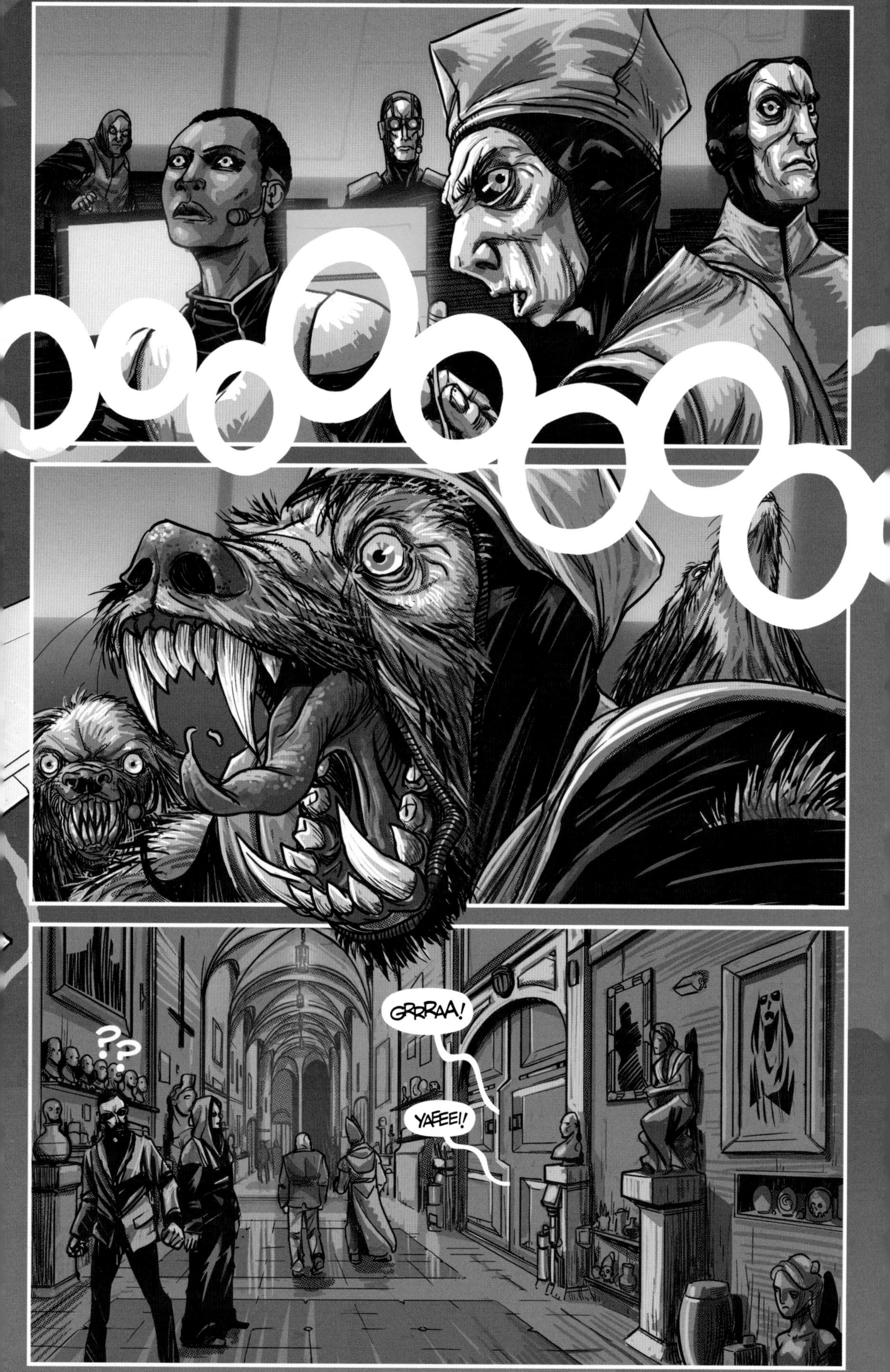
OOOOOOOOO
??
GRRRAA!
YAFEEI!

RAARARGH!

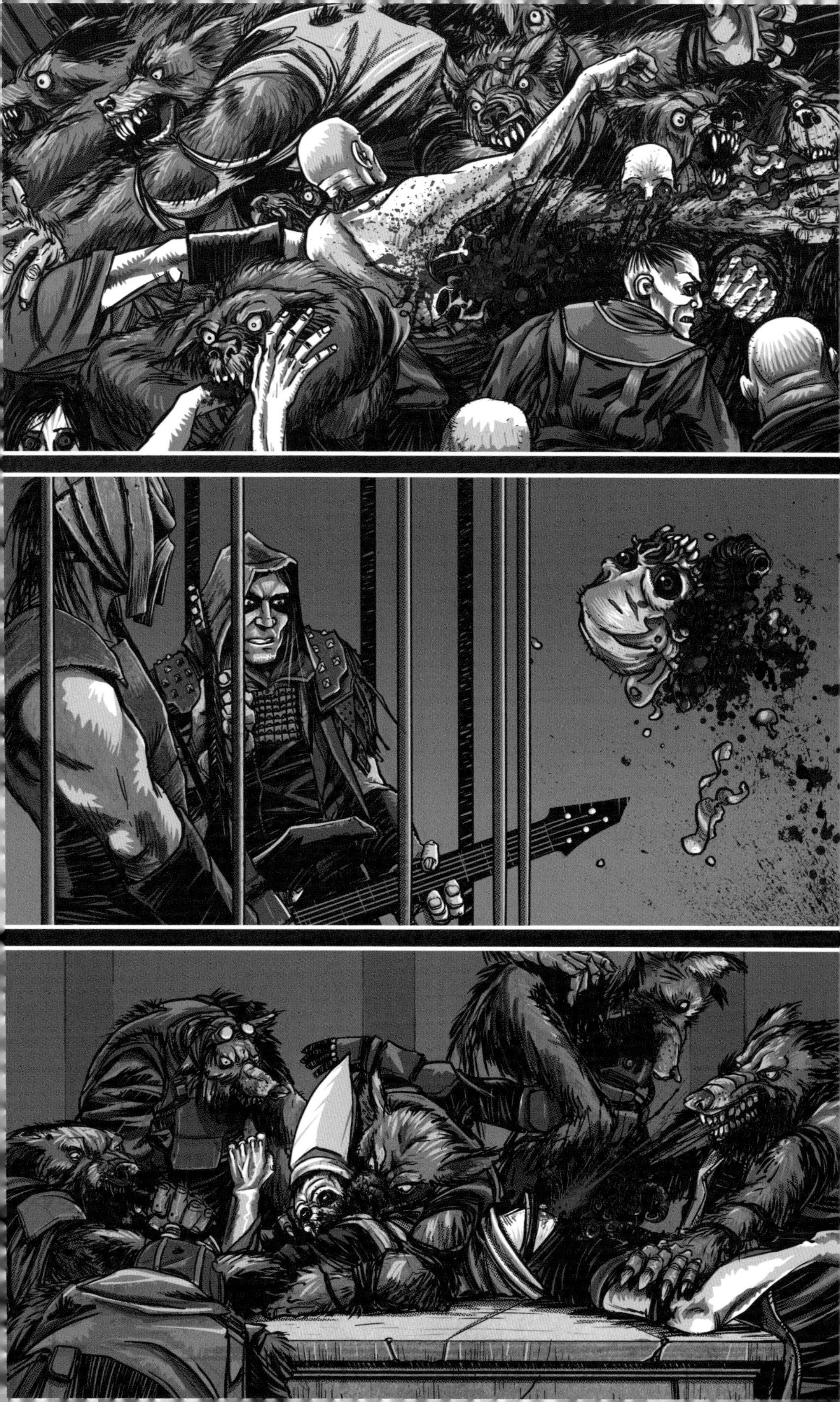

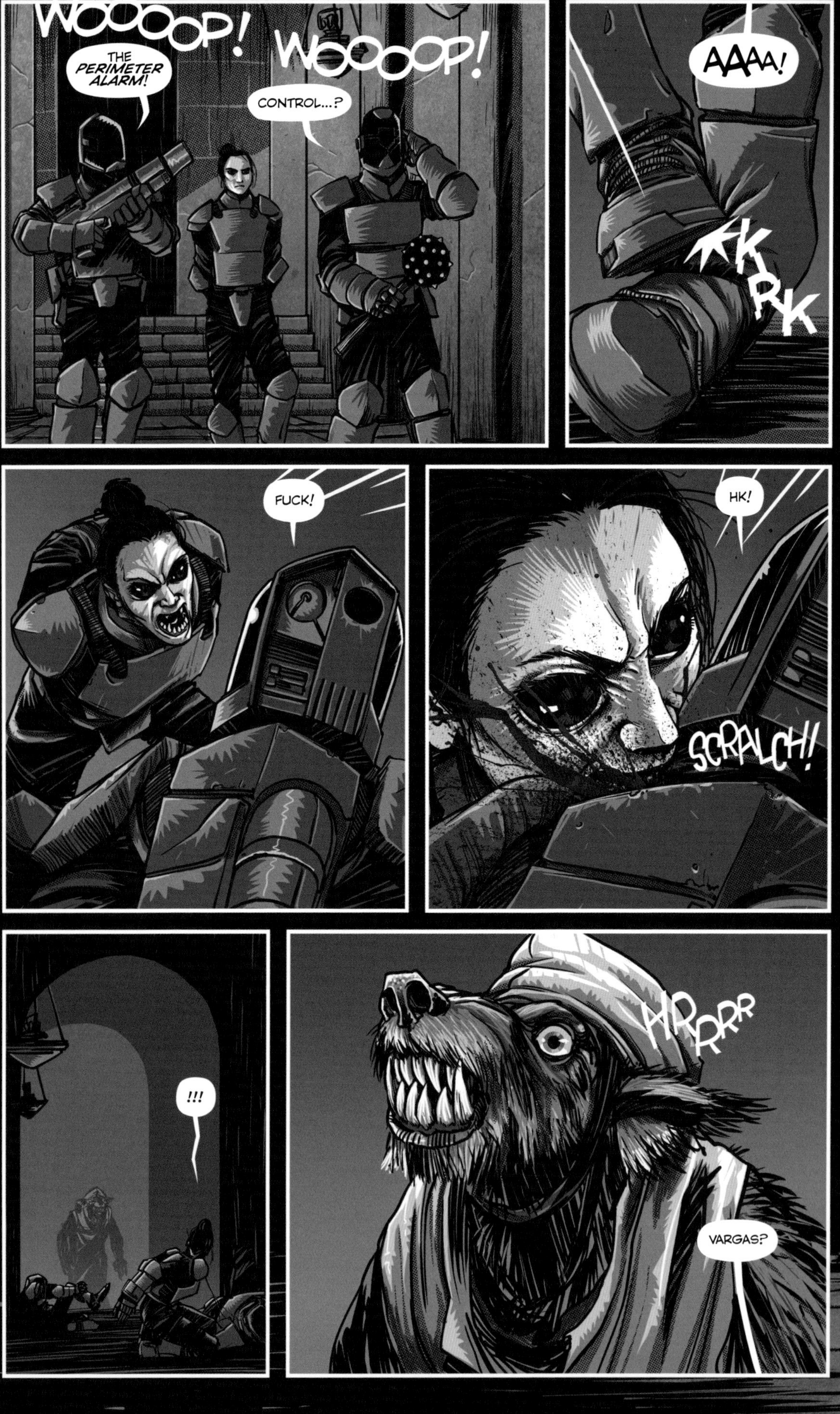
WOOOOP!
THE PERIMETER ALARM!
WOOOOP!
CONTROL...?
AAAA!
KKRK
FUCK!
HK!
SCRALCH!
!!!
HRRRR
VARGAS?

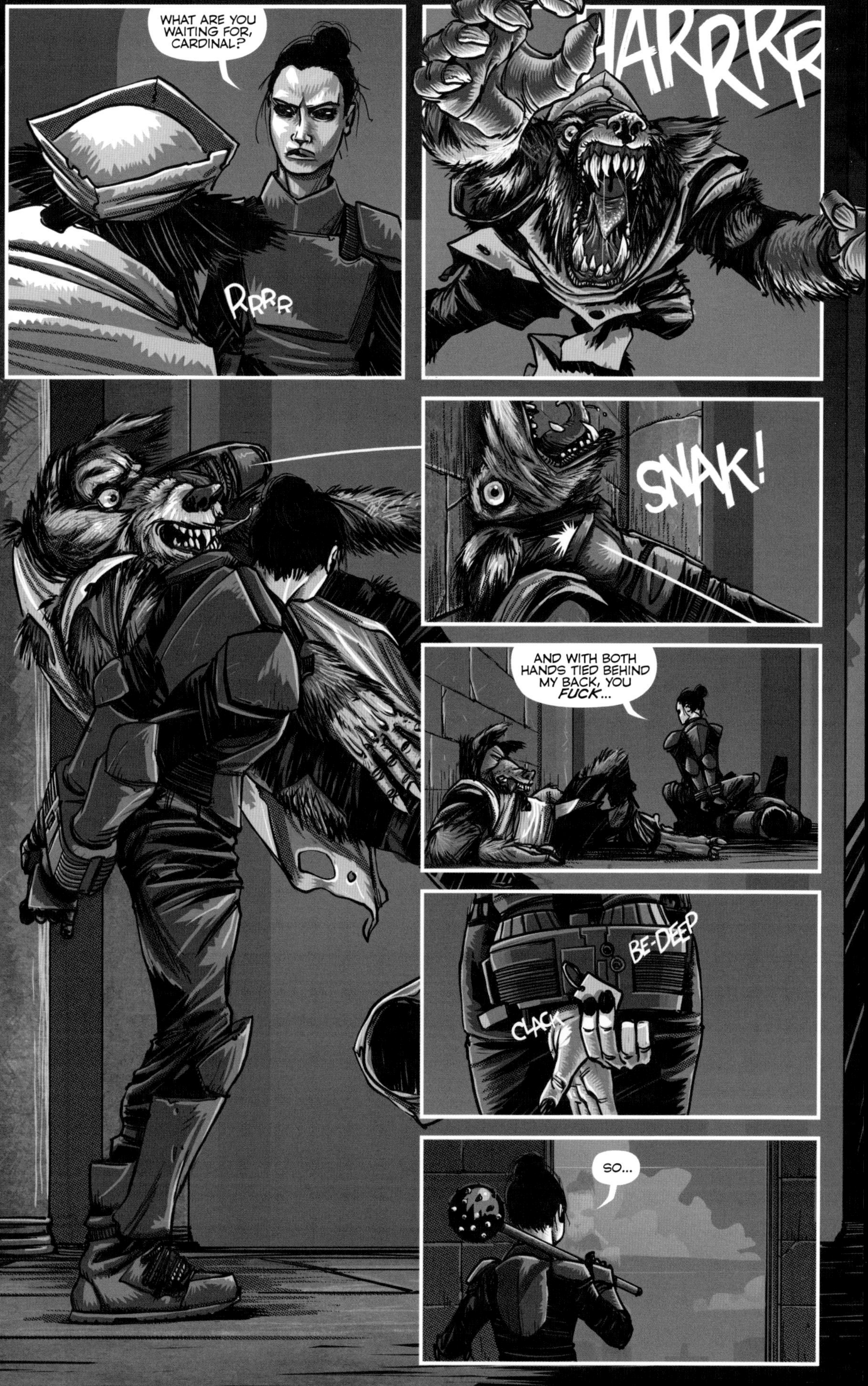
WHAT ARE YOU WAITING FOR, CARDINAL?
RRRR
HARRRR
SNAK!
AND WITH BOTH HANDS TIED BEHIND MY BACK, YOU *FUCK*...
BE-DEEP
CLACK
SO...

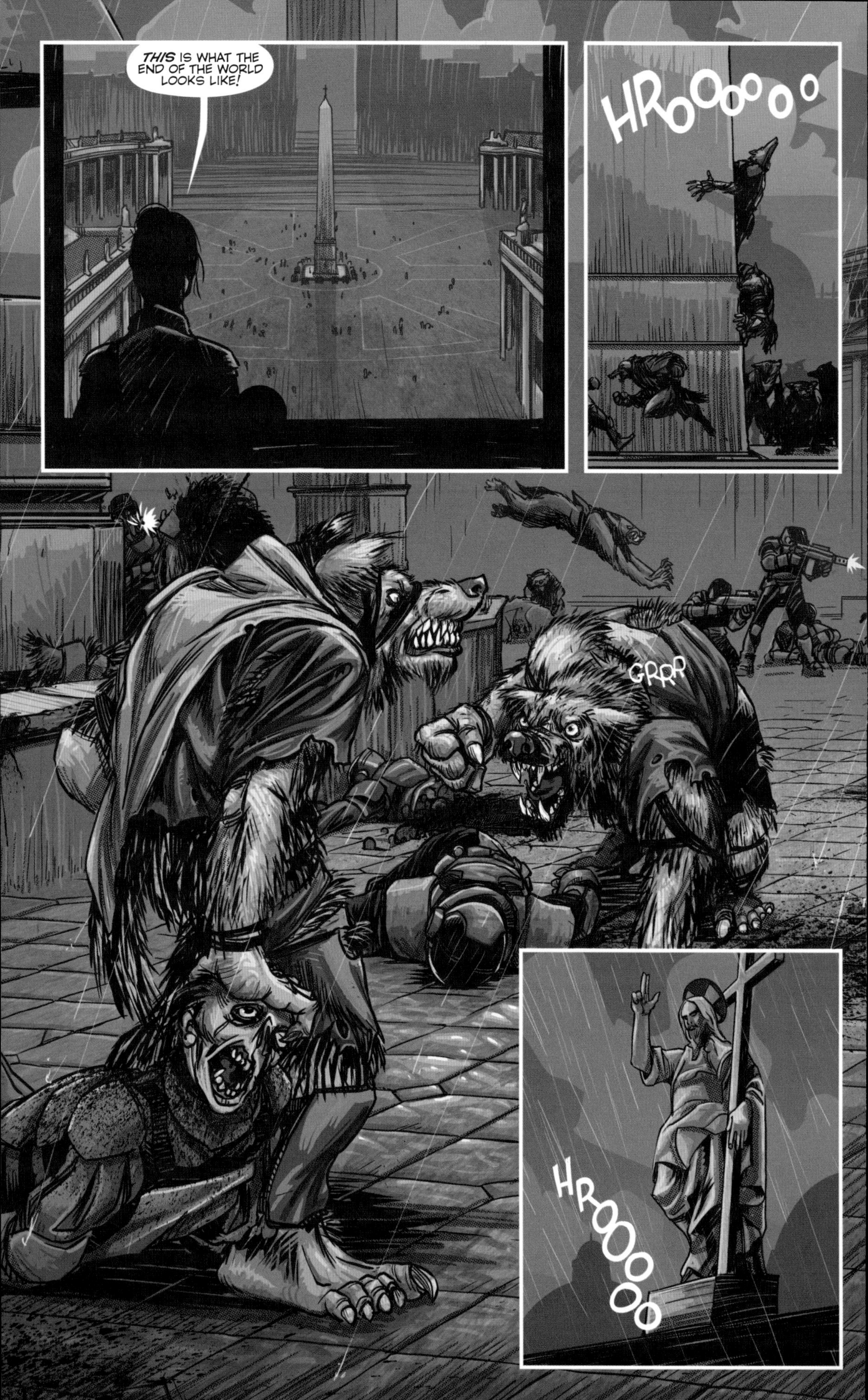

THIS IS WHAT THE END OF THE WORLD LOOKS LIKE!
HROOOOOO
GRRR
HROOOOOO

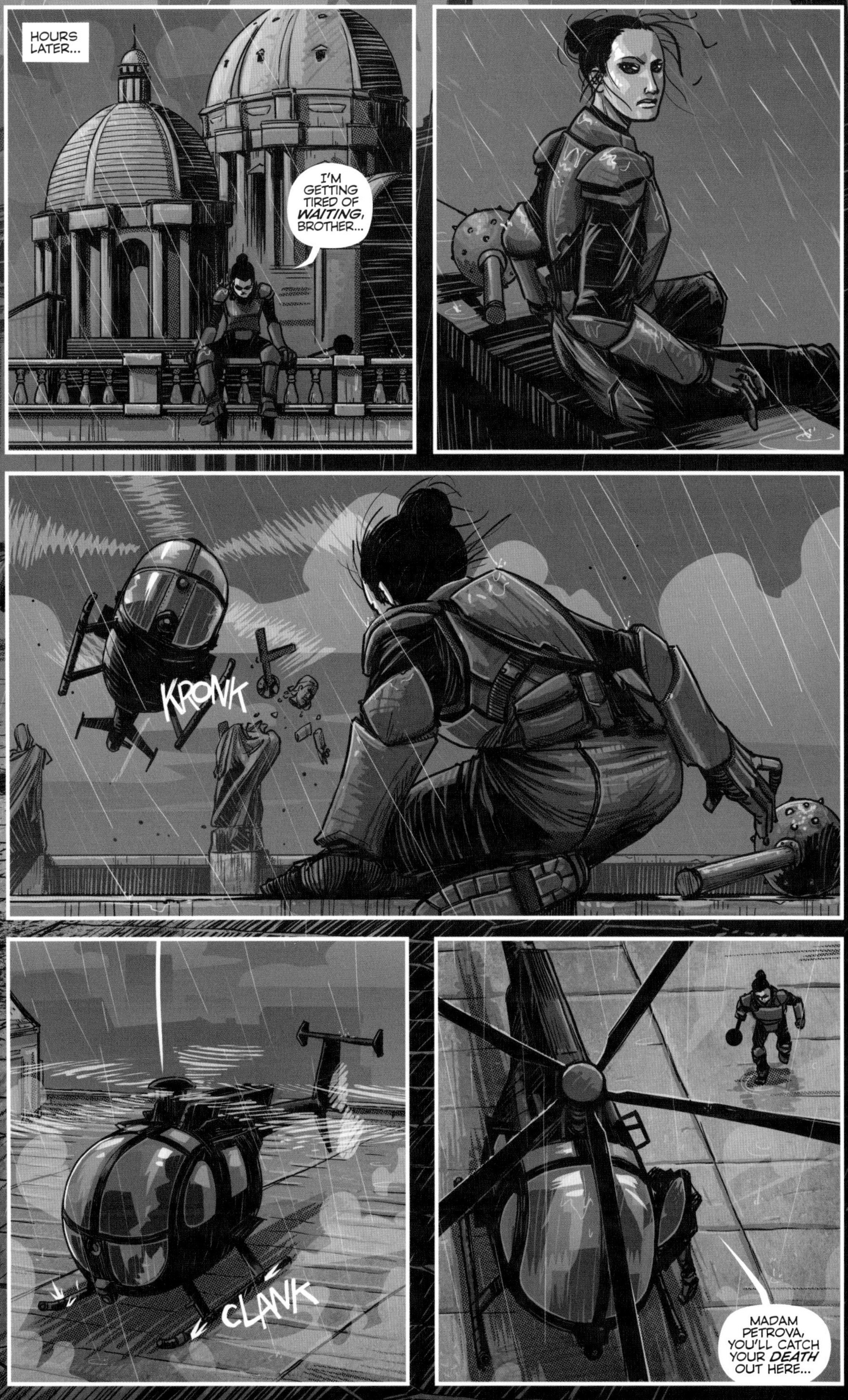
HOURS LATER...
I'M GETTING TIRED OF WAITING, BROTHER...
KRONK
CLANK
MADAM PETROVA, YOU'LL CATCH YOUR DEATH OUT HERE...

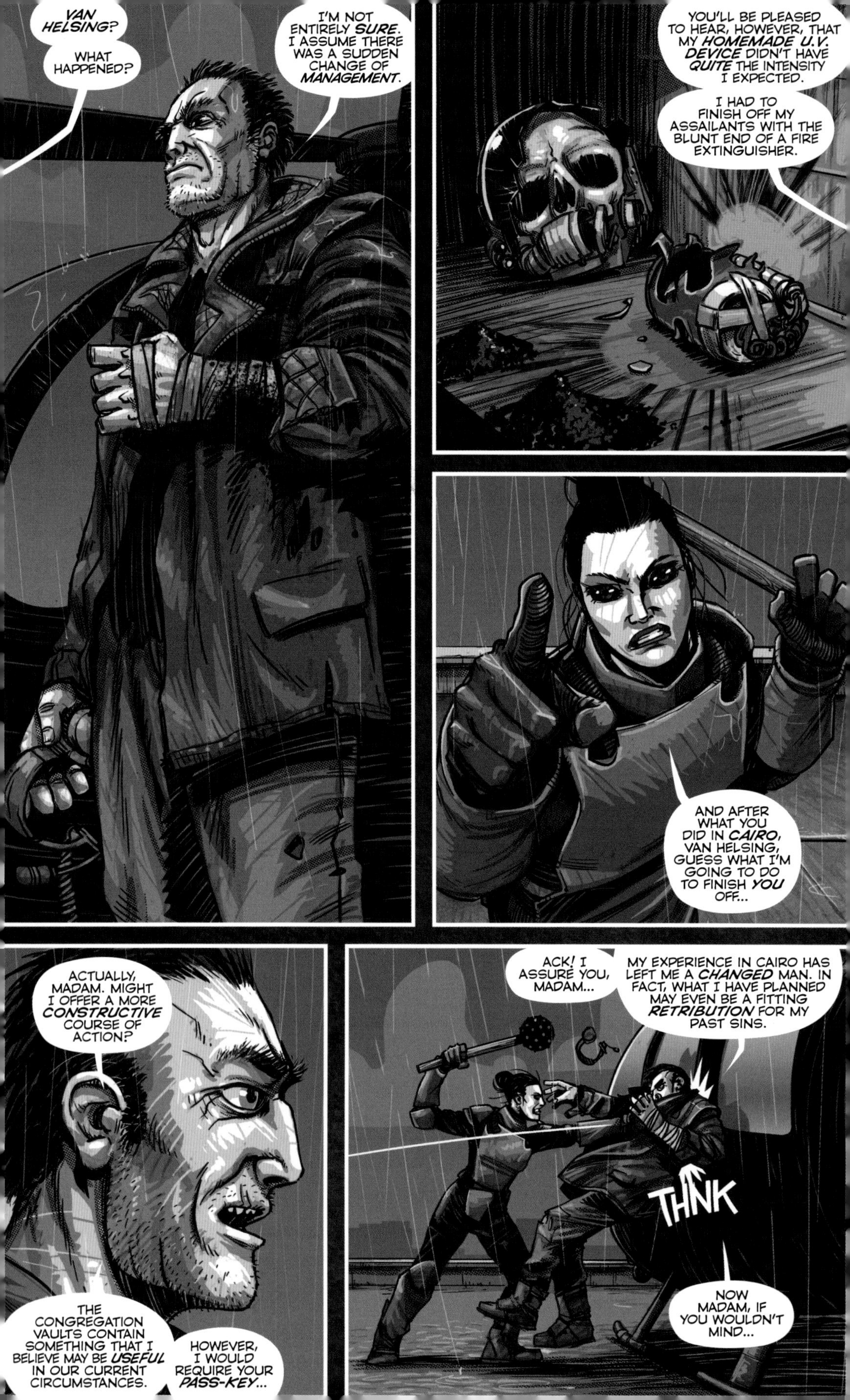
VAN HELSING?
WHAT HAPPENED?
I'M NOT ENTIRELY SURE. I ASSUME THERE WAS A SUDDEN CHANGE OF MANAGEMENT.
YOU'LL BE PLEASED TO HEAR, HOWEVER, THAT MY HOMEMADE U.V. DEVICE DIDN'T HAVE QUITE THE INTENSITY I EXPECTED.
I HAD TO FINISH OFF MY ASSAILANTS WITH THE BLUNT END OF A FIRE EXTINGUISHER.
AND AFTER WHAT YOU DID IN CAIRO, VAN HELSING, GUESS WHAT I'M GOING TO DO TO FINISH YOU OFF...
ACTUALLY, MADAM. MIGHT I OFFER A MORE CONSTRUCTIVE COURSE OF ACTION?
THE CONGREGATION VAULTS CONTAIN SOMETHING THAT I BELIEVE MAY BE USEFUL IN OUR CURRENT CIRCUMSTANCES.
HOWEVER, I WOULD REQUIRE YOUR PASS-KEY...
ACK! I ASSURE YOU, MADAM...
MY EXPERIENCE IN CAIRO HAS LEFT ME A CHANGED MAN. IN FACT, WHAT I HAVE PLANNED MAY EVEN BE A FITTING RETRIBUTION FOR MY PAST SINS.
THNK
NOW MADAM, IF YOU WOULDN'T MIND...

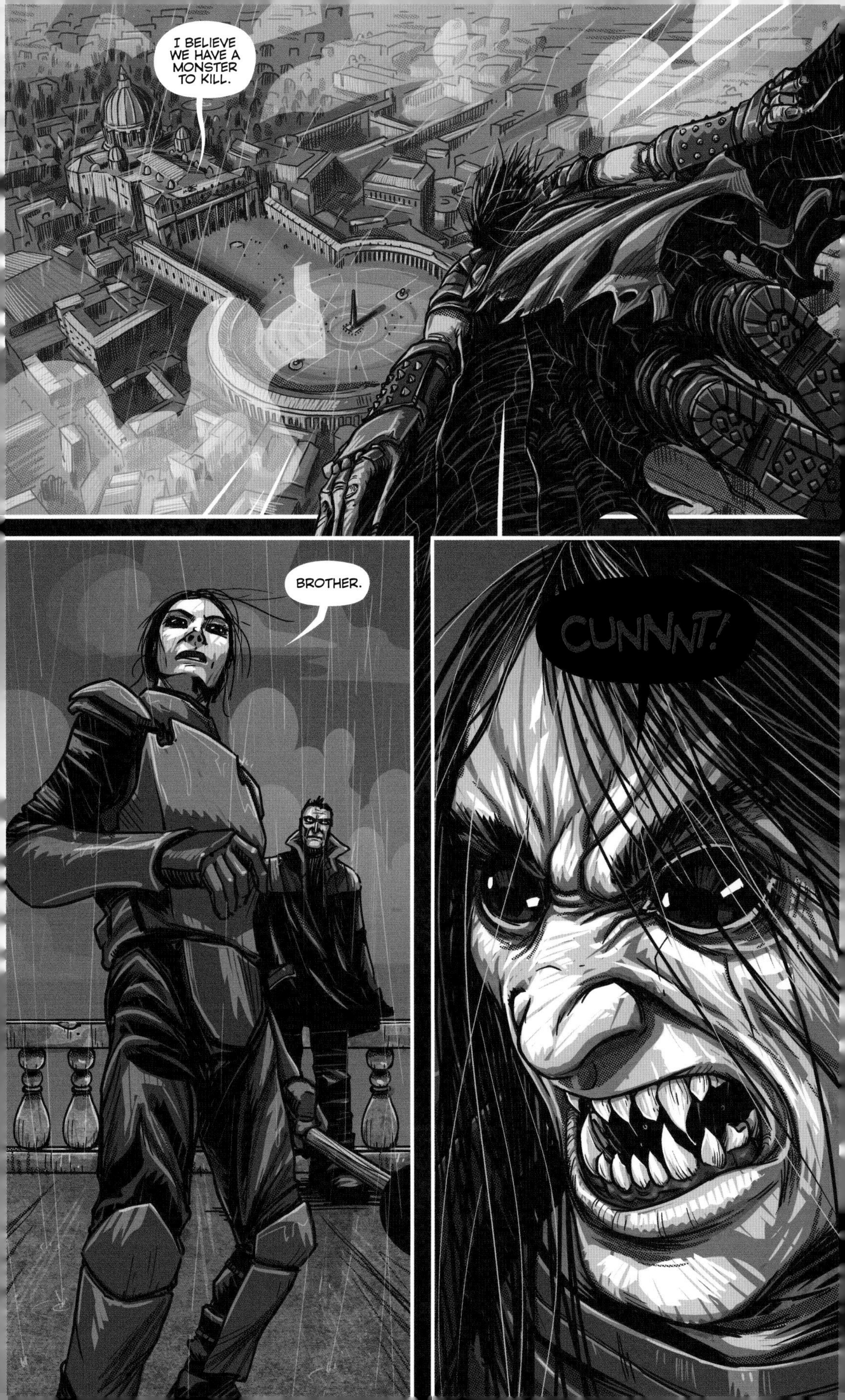
I BELIEVE WE HAVE A MONSTER TO KILL.
BROTHER.
CUNNNT!

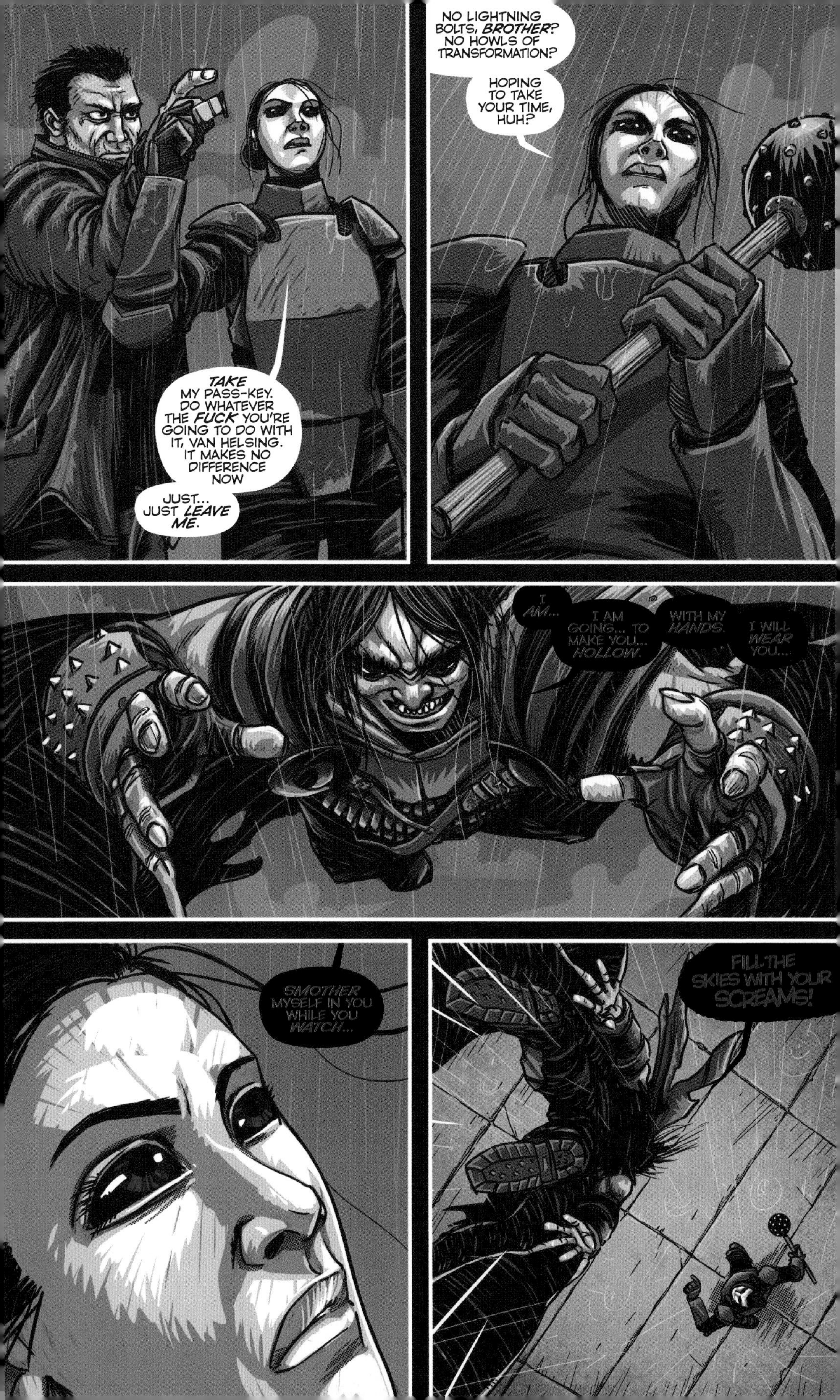
TAKE MY PASS-KEY. DO WHATEVER THE FUCK YOU'RE GOING TO DO WITH IT, VAN HELSING. IT MAKES NO DIFFERENCE NOW
JUST... JUST LEAVE ME.
NO LIGHTNING BOLTS, BROTHER? NO HOWLS OF TRANSFORMATION?
HOPING TO TAKE YOUR TIME, HUH?
I AM...
I AM GOING... TO MAKE YOU... HOLLOW.
WITH MY HANDS.
I WILL WEAR YOU...
SMOTHER MYSELF IN YOU WHILE YOU WATCH...
FILL THE SKIES WITH YOUR SCREAMS!

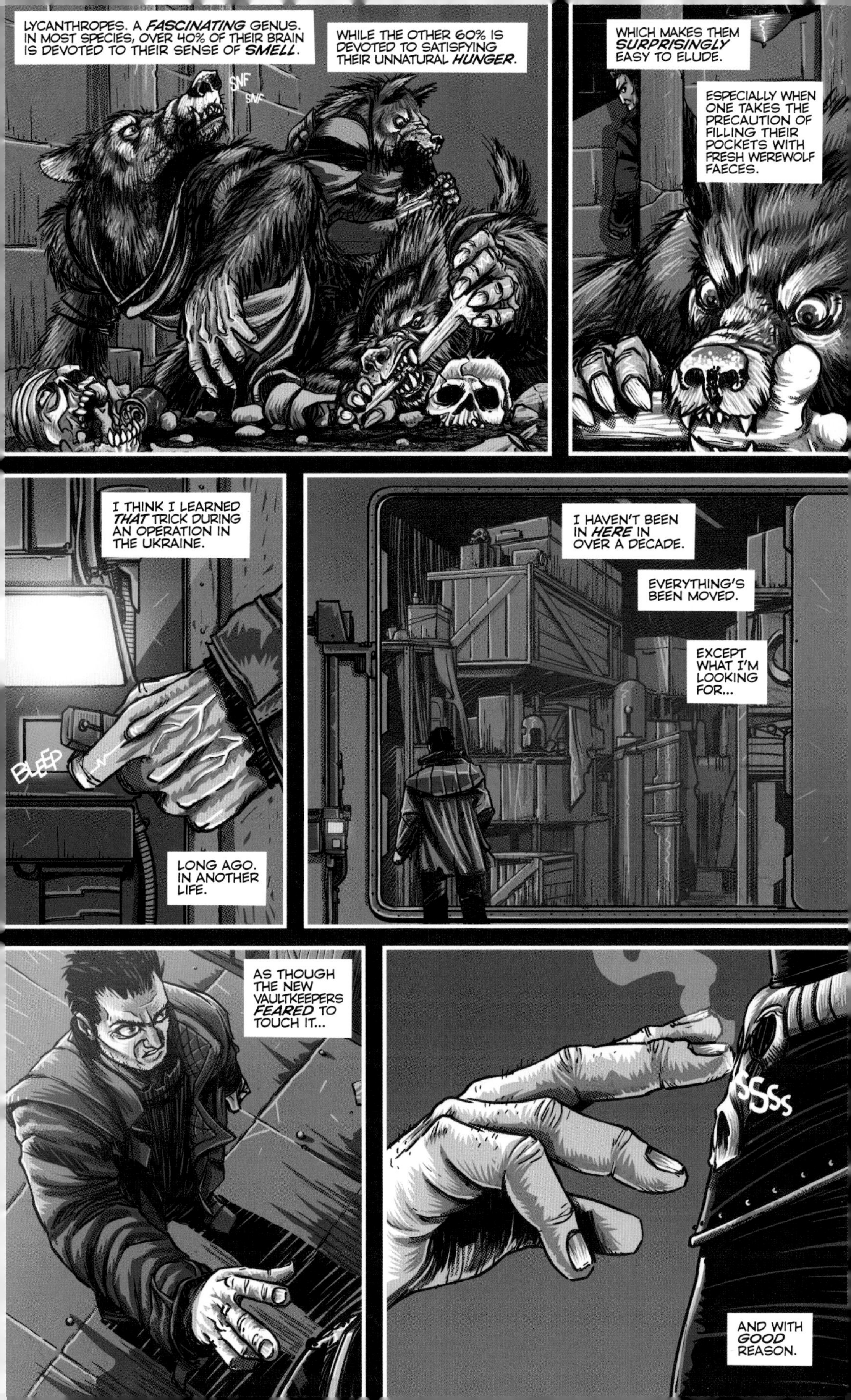
LYCANTHROPES. A *FASCINATING* GENUS. IN MOST SPECIES, OVER 40% OF THEIR BRAIN IS DEVOTED TO THEIR SENSE OF *SMELL*.
SNF
SNF
WHILE THE OTHER 60% IS DEVOTED TO SATISFYING THEIR UNNATURAL *HUNGER*.
WHICH MAKES THEM *SURPRISINGLY* EASY TO ELUDE.
ESPECIALLY WHEN ONE TAKES THE PRECAUTION OF FILLING THEIR POCKETS WITH FRESH WEREWOLF FAECES.
I THINK I LEARNED *THAT* TRICK DURING AN OPERATION IN THE UKRAINE.
BLEEP
LONG AGO. IN ANOTHER LIFE.
I HAVEN'T BEEN IN *HERE* IN OVER A DECADE.
EVERYTHING'S BEEN MOVED.
EXCEPT WHAT I'M LOOKING FOR...
AS THOUGH THE NEW VAULTKEEPERS *FEARED* TO TOUCH IT...
SSSS
AND WITH *GOOD* REASON.

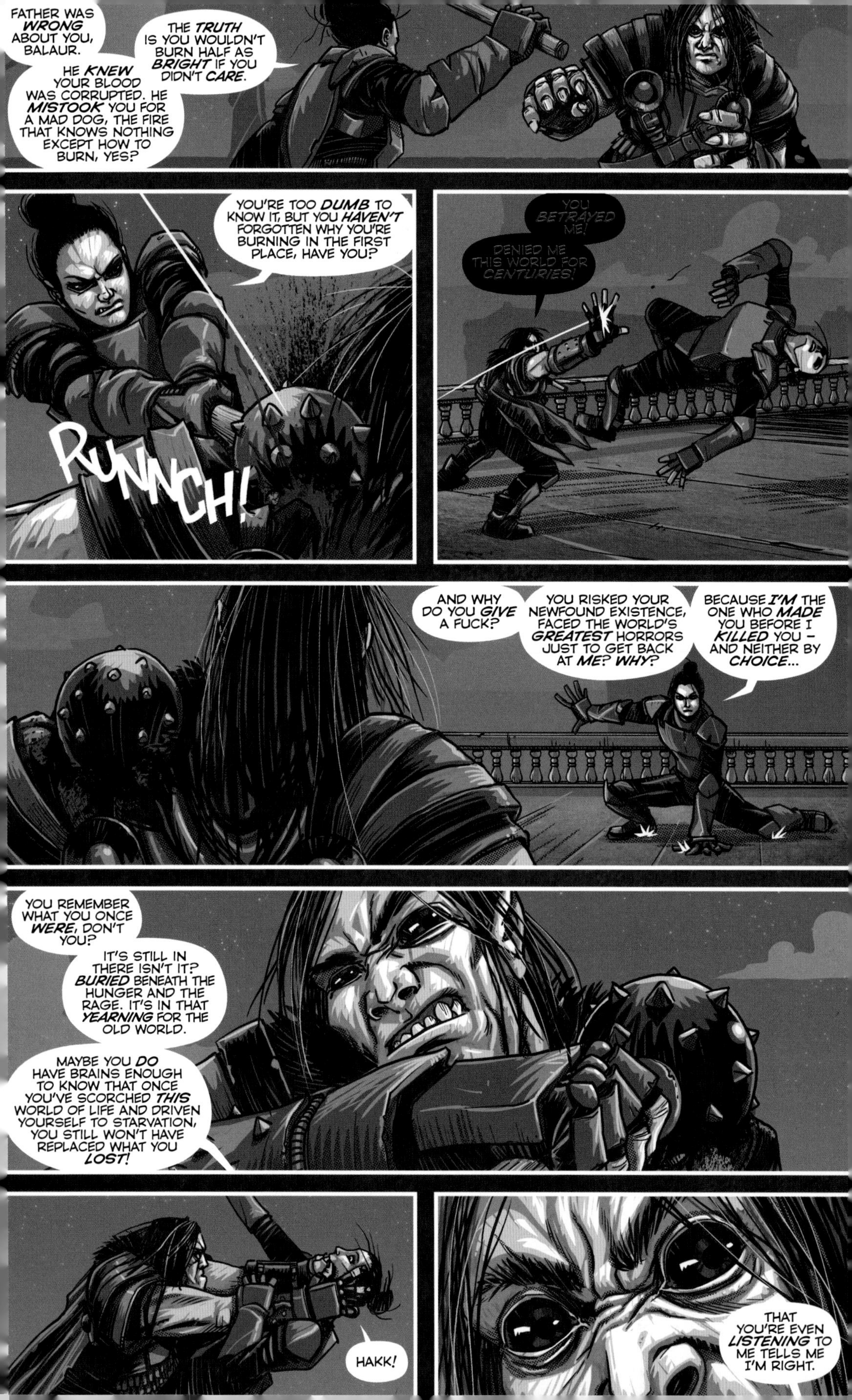
FATHER WAS WRONG ABOUT YOU, BALAUR.
HE KNEW YOUR BLOOD WAS CORRUPTED. HE MISTOOK YOU FOR A MAD DOG, THE FIRE THAT KNOWS NOTHING EXCEPT HOW TO BURN, YES?
THE TRUTH IS YOU WOULDN'T BURN HALF AS BRIGHT IF YOU DIDN'T CARE.
YOU'RE TOO DUMB TO KNOW IT, BUT YOU HAVEN'T FORGOTTEN WHY YOU'RE BURNING IN THE FIRST PLACE, HAVE YOU?
RUNNCH!
YOU BETRAYED ME!
DENIED ME THIS WORLD FOR CENTURIES!
AND WHY DO YOU GIVE A FUCK?
YOU RISKED YOUR NEWFOUND EXISTENCE, FACED THE WORLD'S GREATEST HORRORS JUST TO GET BACK AT ME? WHY?
BECAUSE I'M THE ONE WHO MADE YOU BEFORE I KILLED YOU – AND NEITHER BY CHOICE...
YOU REMEMBER WHAT YOU ONCE WERE, DON'T YOU?
IT'S STILL IN THERE ISN'T IT? BURIED BENEATH THE HUNGER AND THE RAGE. IT'S IN THAT YEARNING FOR THE OLD WORLD.
MAYBE YOU DO HAVE BRAINS ENOUGH TO KNOW THAT ONCE YOU'VE SCORCHED THIS WORLD OF LIFE AND DRIVEN YOURSELF TO STARVATION, YOU STILL WON'T HAVE REPLACED WHAT YOU LOST!
HAKK!
THAT YOU'RE EVEN LISTENING TO ME TELLS ME I'M RIGHT.

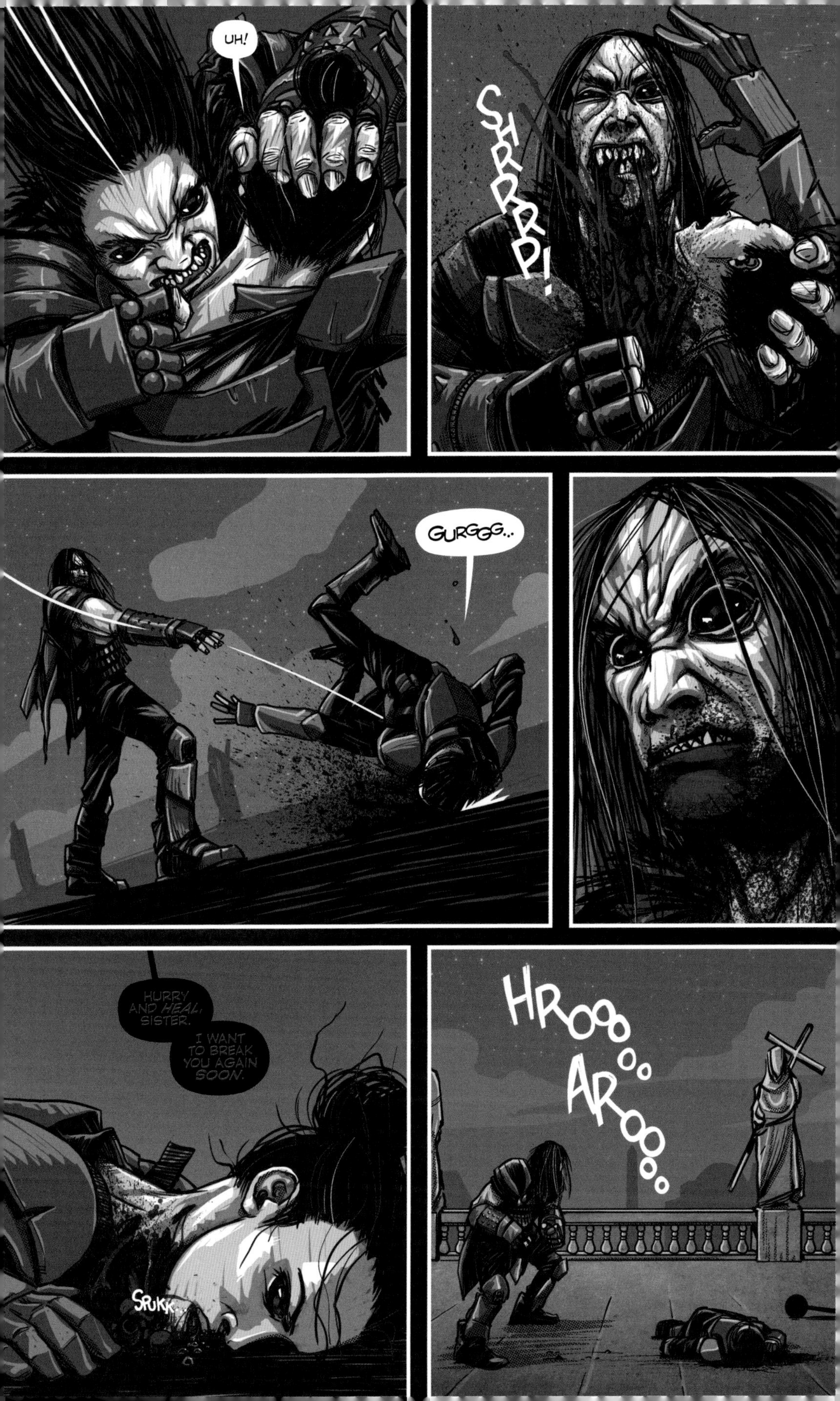
UH!
SHRRRP!
GURGGG..
HURRY AND HEAL, SISTER.
I WANT TO BREAK YOU AGAIN SOON.
SPUKK...
HROOO... AROOO...

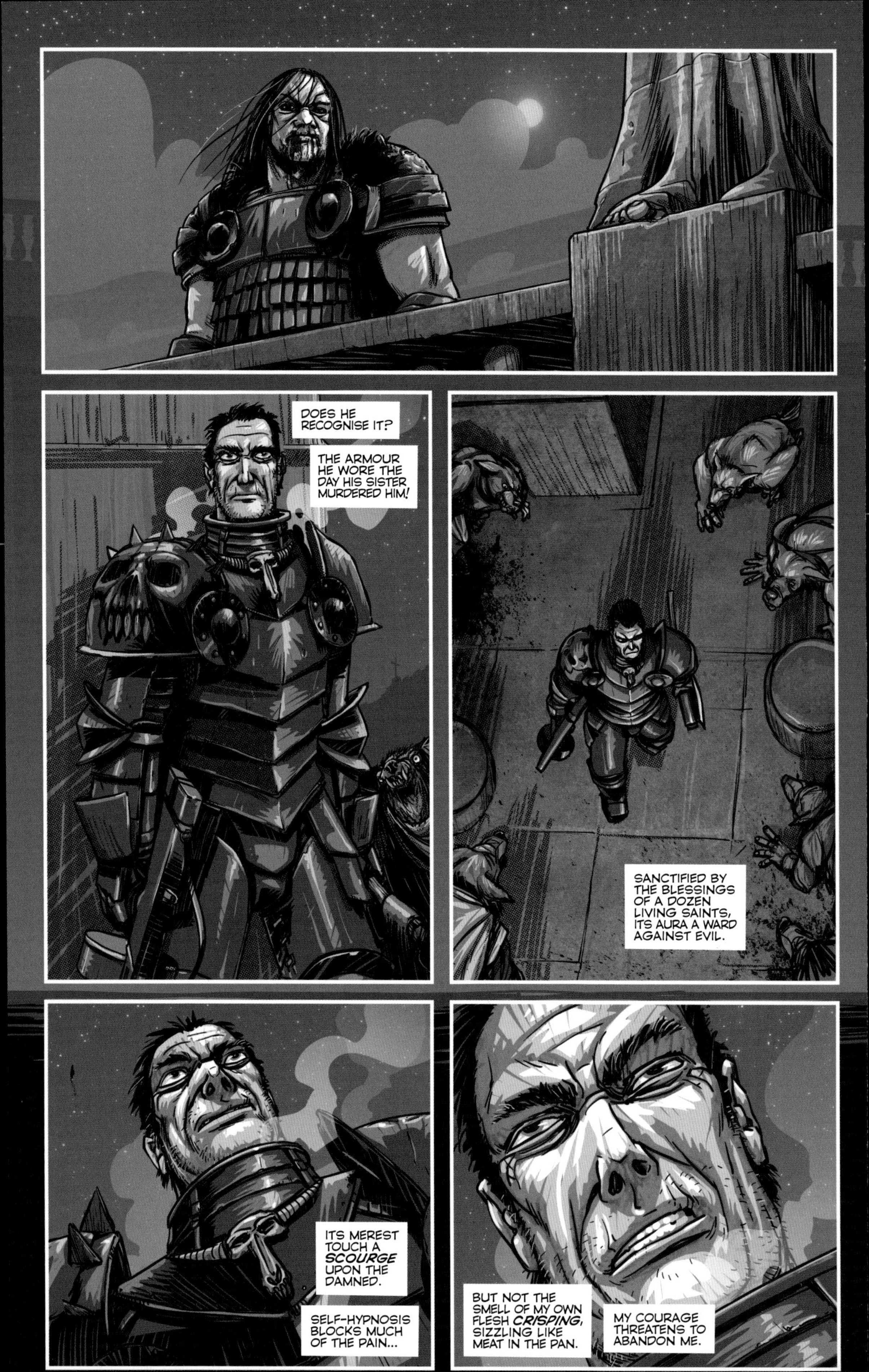
DOES HE RECOGNISE IT?
THE ARMOUR HE WORE THE DAY HIS SISTER MURDERED HIM!
SANCTIFIED BY THE BLESSINGS OF A DOZEN LIVING SAINTS, ITS AURA A WARD AGAINST EVIL.
ITS MEREST TOUCH A SCOURGE UPON THE DAMNED.
SELF-HYPNOSIS BLOCKS MUCH OF THE PAIN...
BUT NOT THE SMELL OF MY OWN FLESH CRISPING, SIZZLING LIKE MEAT IN THE PAN.
MY COURAGE THREATENS TO ABANDON ME.

AND FOR
THE FIRST
TIME IN
MY LIFE...

I FACE
THE DEVIL
ALONE.

FWOOOOSSH!

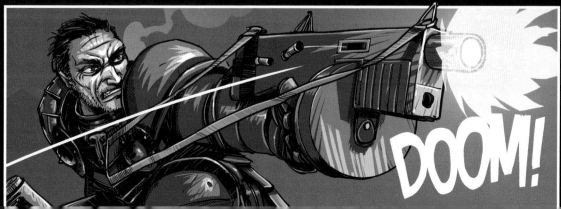

DOOM!

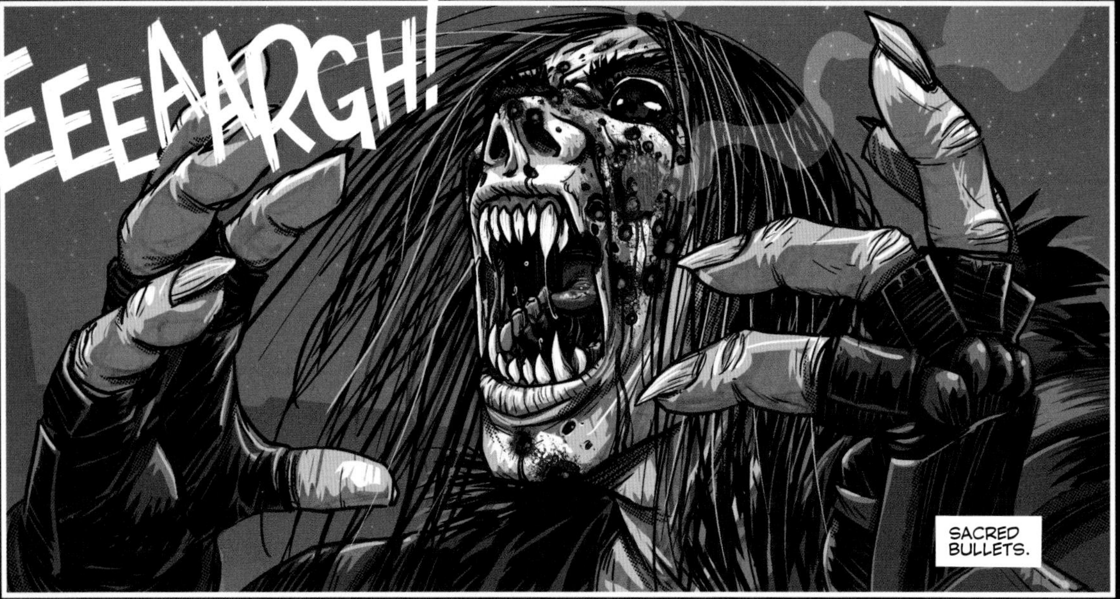
EEEAARGH!
SACRED BULLETS.

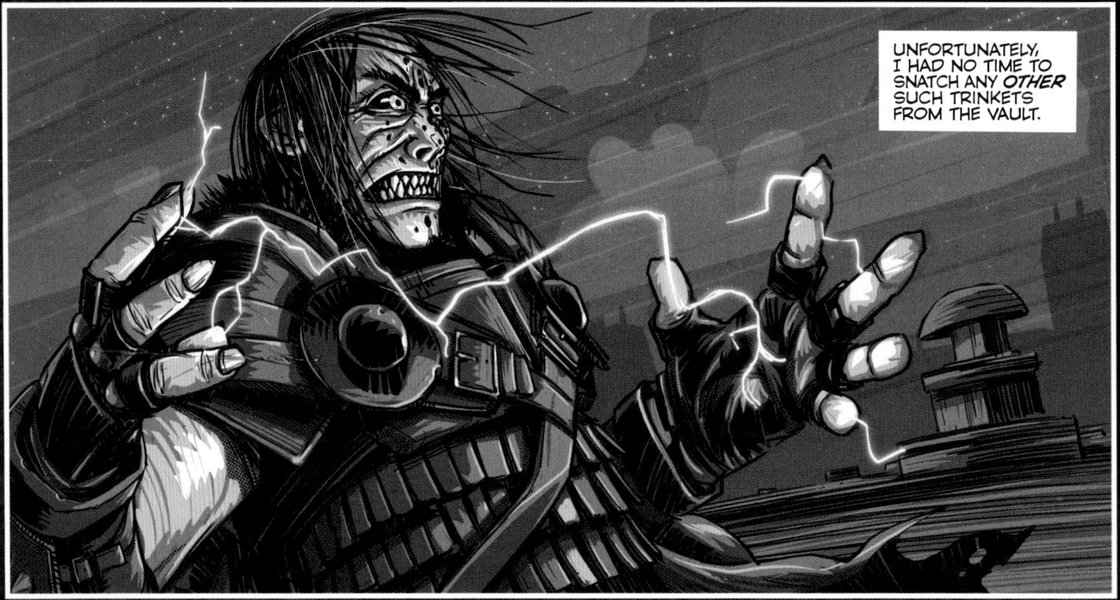
UNFORTUNATELY, I HAD NO TIME TO SNATCH ANY *OTHER* SUCH TRINKETS FROM THE VAULT.

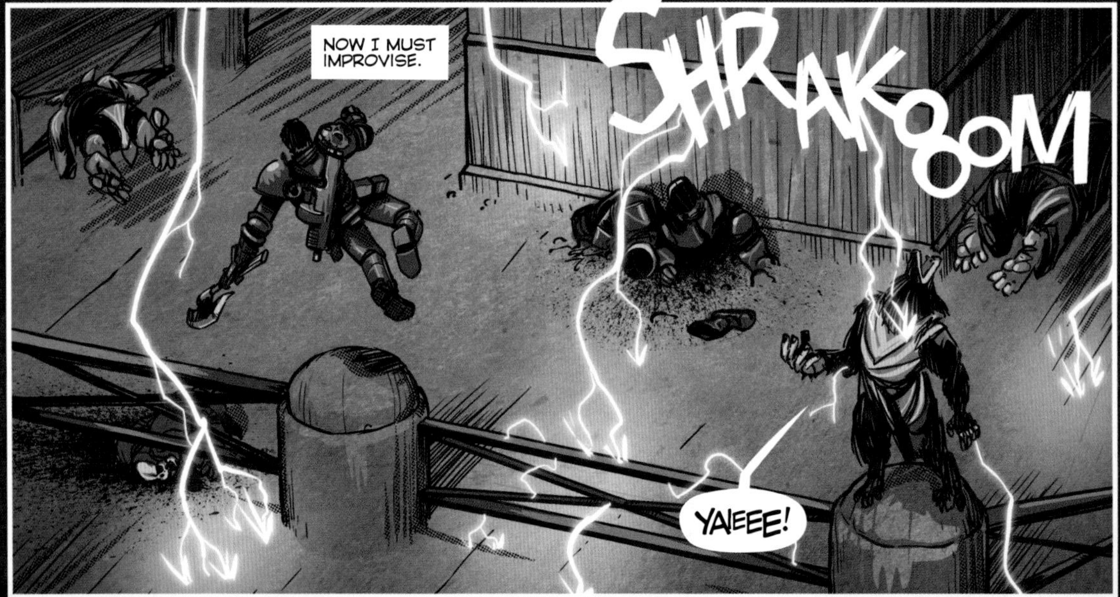
NOW I MUST IMPROVISE.
SHRAKBOOM
YAIEEE!

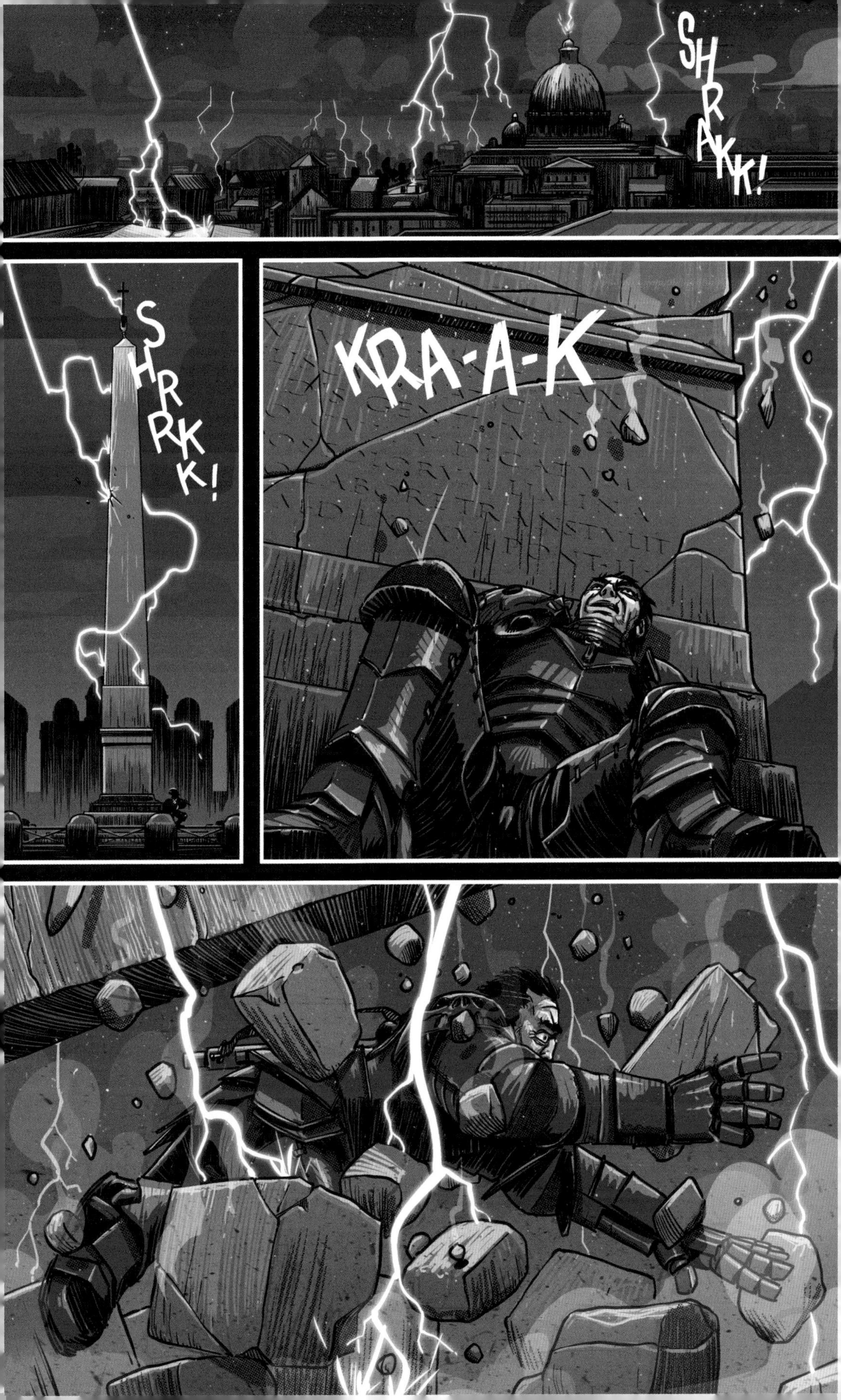
SHRAKKK!
SHRRKK!
KRA-A-K

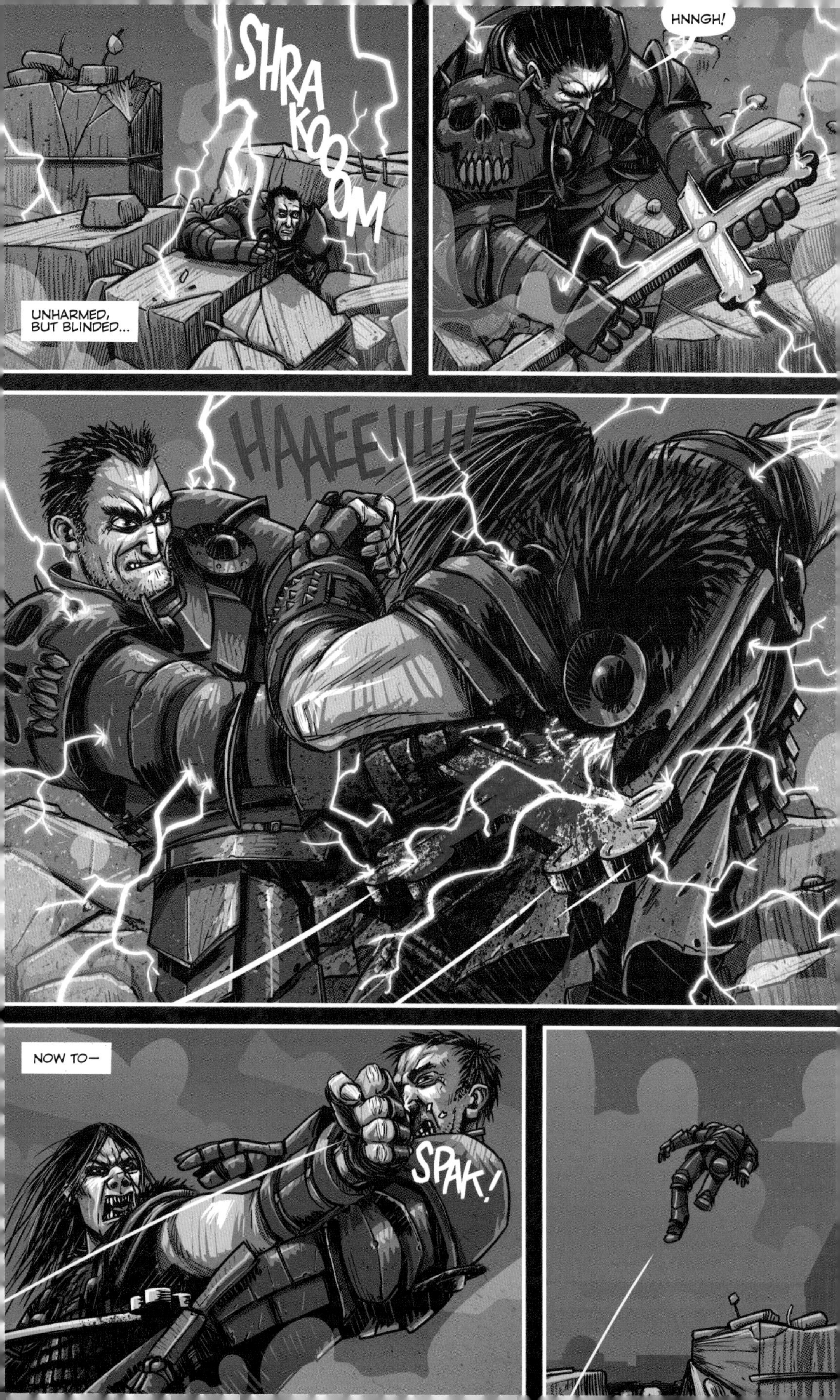
SHRAKOOOOM
UNHARMED, BUT BLINDED...
HNNGH!
HAAEE!!!!!
NOW TO—
SPAK!

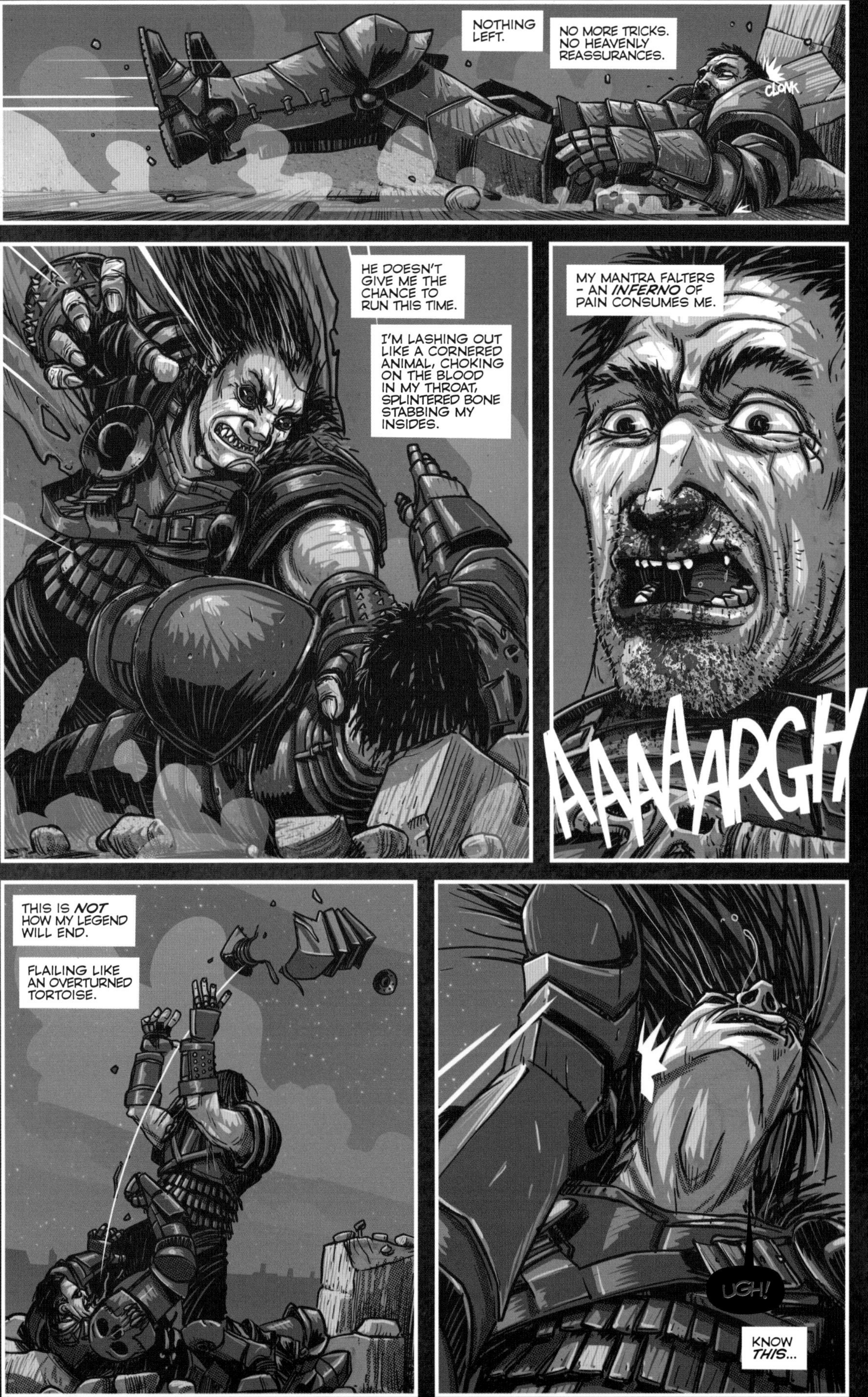
NOTHING LEFT.
NO MORE TRICKS. NO HEAVENLY REASSURANCES.
CLONK
HE DOESN'T GIVE ME THE CHANCE TO RUN THIS TIME.
I'M LASHING OUT LIKE A CORNERED ANIMAL, CHOKING ON THE BLOOD IN MY THROAT, SPLINTERED BONE STABBING MY INSIDES.
MY MANTRA FALTERS - AN INFERNO OF PAIN CONSUMES ME.
AAAAARGH
THIS IS NOT HOW MY LEGEND WILL END.
FLAILING LIKE AN OVERTURNED TORTOISE.
UGH!
KNOW THIS...

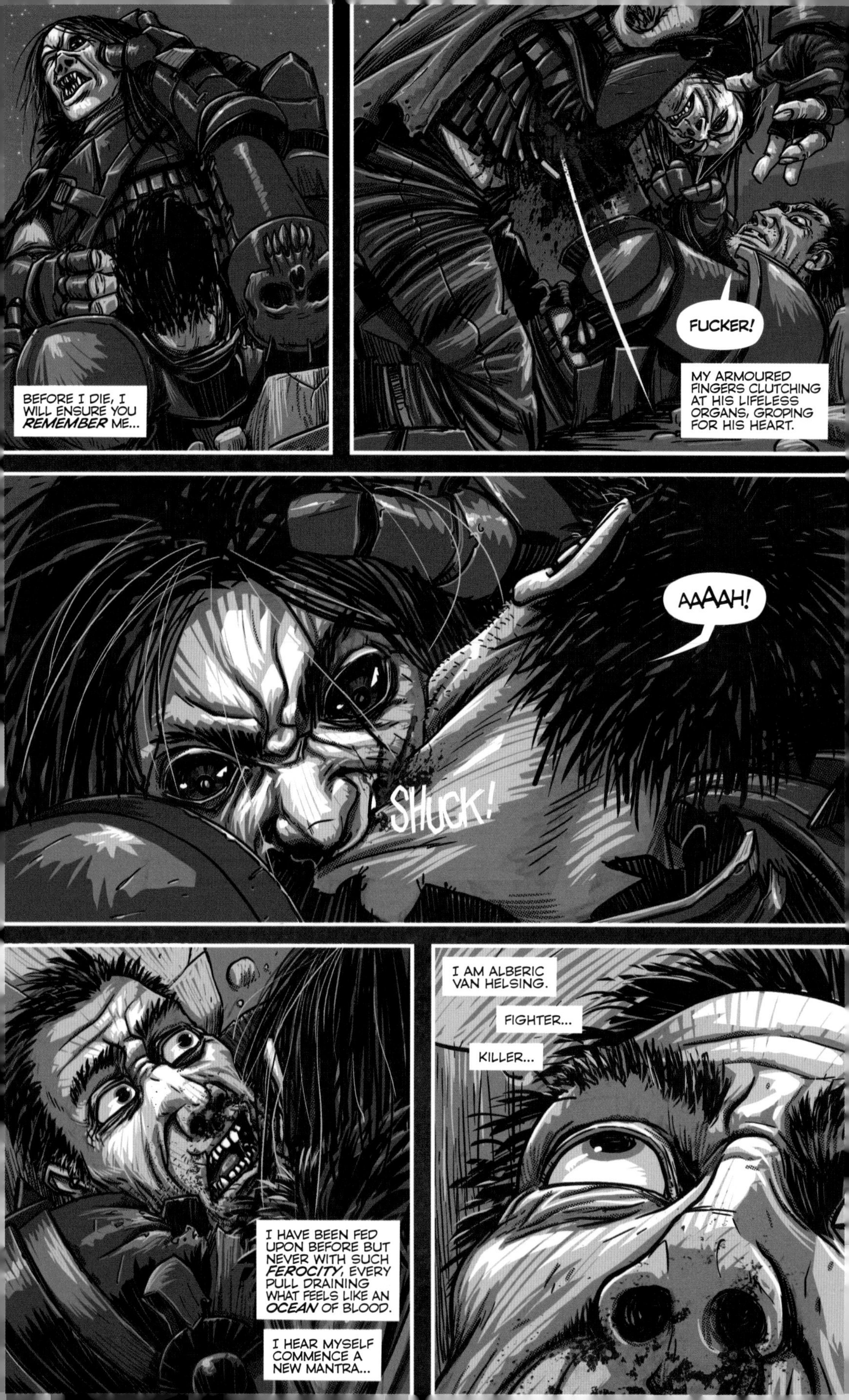

BEFORE I DIE, I WILL ENSURE YOU *REMEMBER* ME...
FUCKER!
MY ARMOURED FINGERS CLUTCHING AT HIS LIFELESS ORGANS, GROPING FOR HIS HEART.
AAAAH!
SHUCK!
I HAVE BEEN FED UPON BEFORE BUT NEVER WITH SUCH *FEROCITY*, EVERY PULL DRAINING WHAT FEELS LIKE AN *OCEAN* OF BLOOD.
I HEAR MYSELF COMMENCE A NEW MANTRA...
I AM ALBERIC VAN HELSING.
FIGHTER...
KILLER...

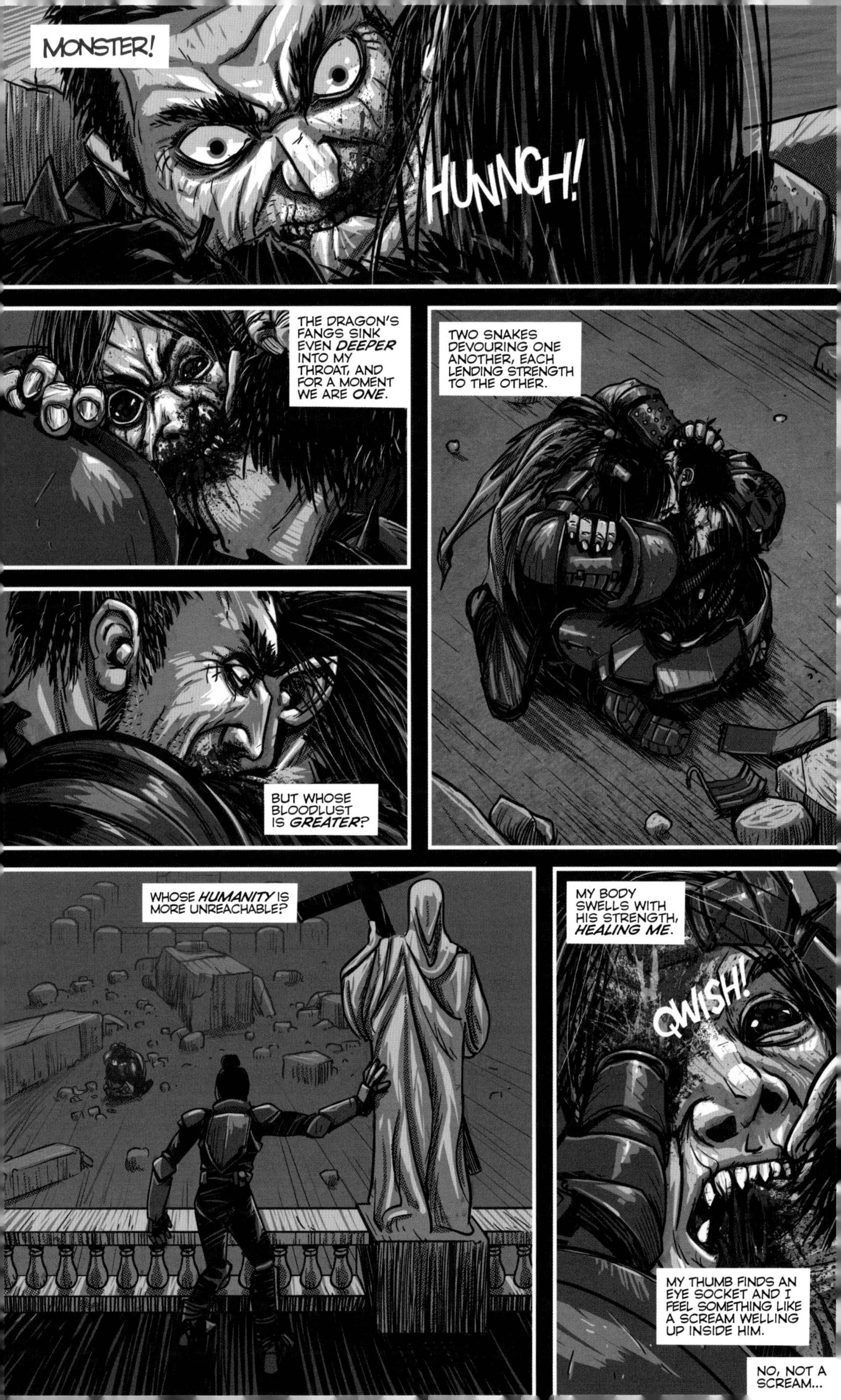

MONSTER!
HUNNCH!
THE DRAGON'S FANGS SINK EVEN *DEEPER* INTO MY THROAT, AND FOR A MOMENT WE ARE *ONE*.
BUT WHOSE BLOODLUST IS *GREATER*?
TWO SNAKES DEVOURING ONE ANOTHER, EACH LENDING STRENGTH TO THE OTHER.
WHOSE *HUMANITY* IS MORE UNREACHABLE?
MY BODY SWELLS WITH HIS STRENGTH, *HEALING ME*.
QWISH!
MY THUMB FINDS AN EYE SOCKET AND I FEEL SOMETHING LIKE A SCREAM WELLING UP INSIDE HIM.
NO, NOT A SCREAM...

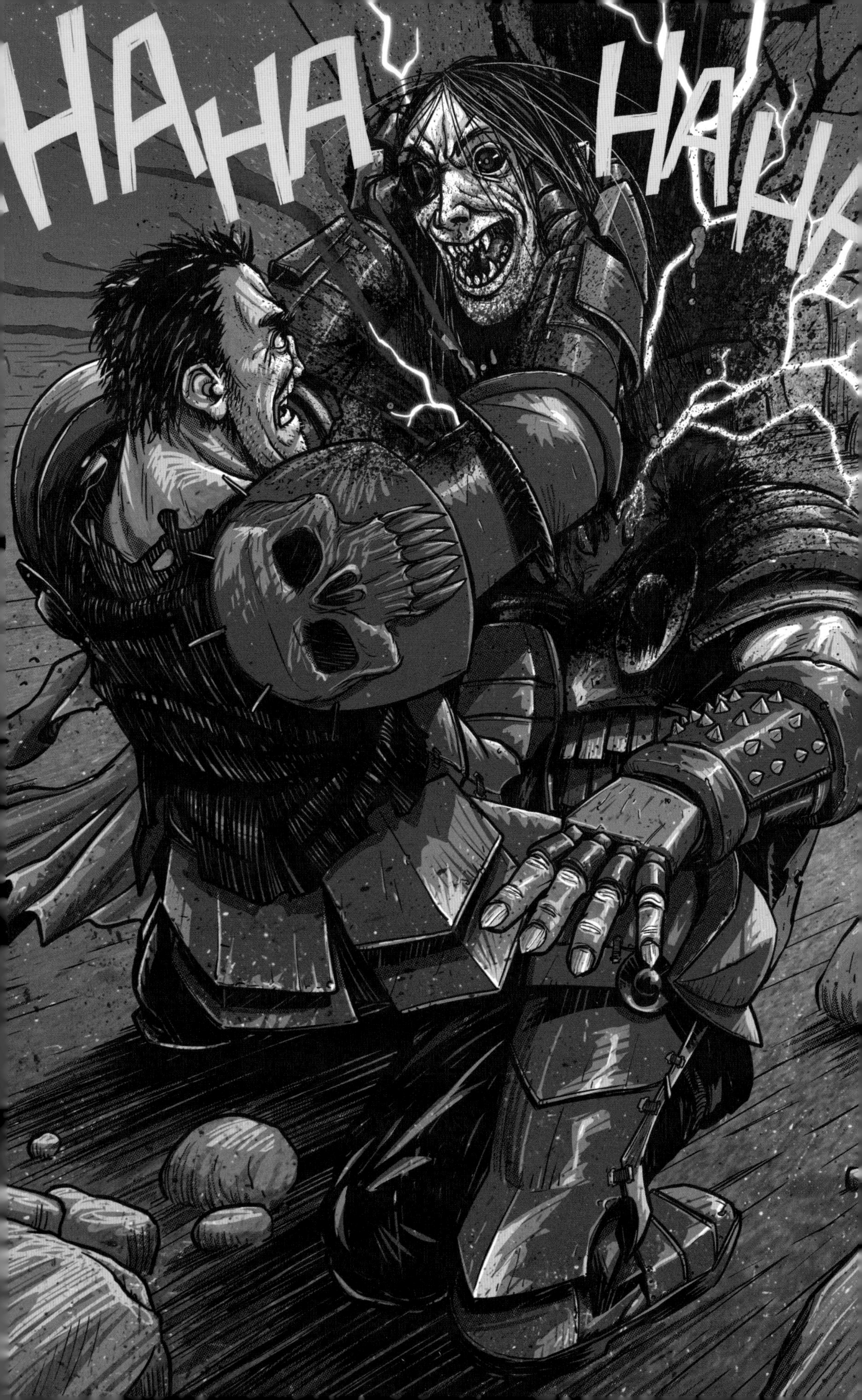
HAHA
HAH

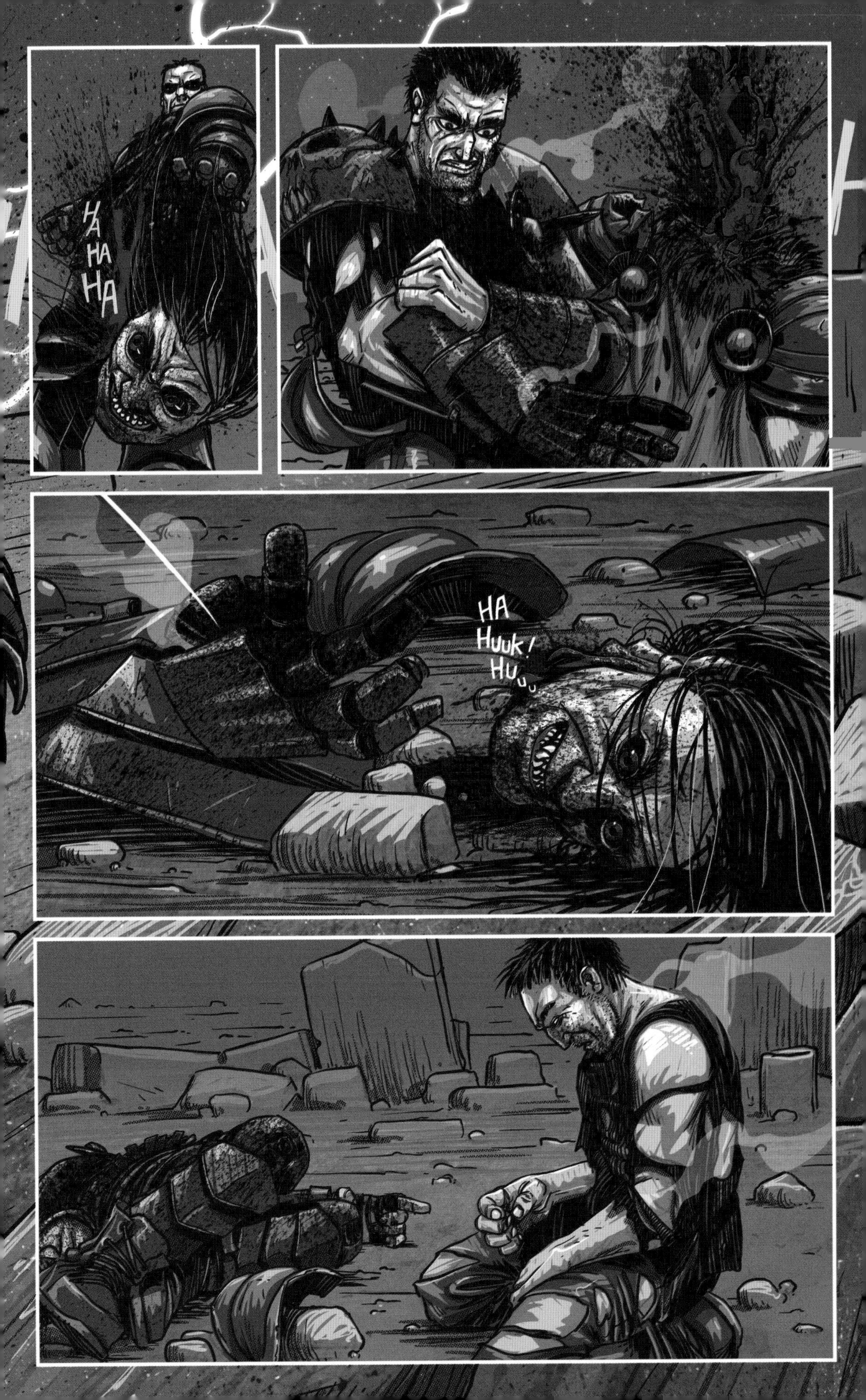
HA HA HA
HA
Huuk!
Huuu

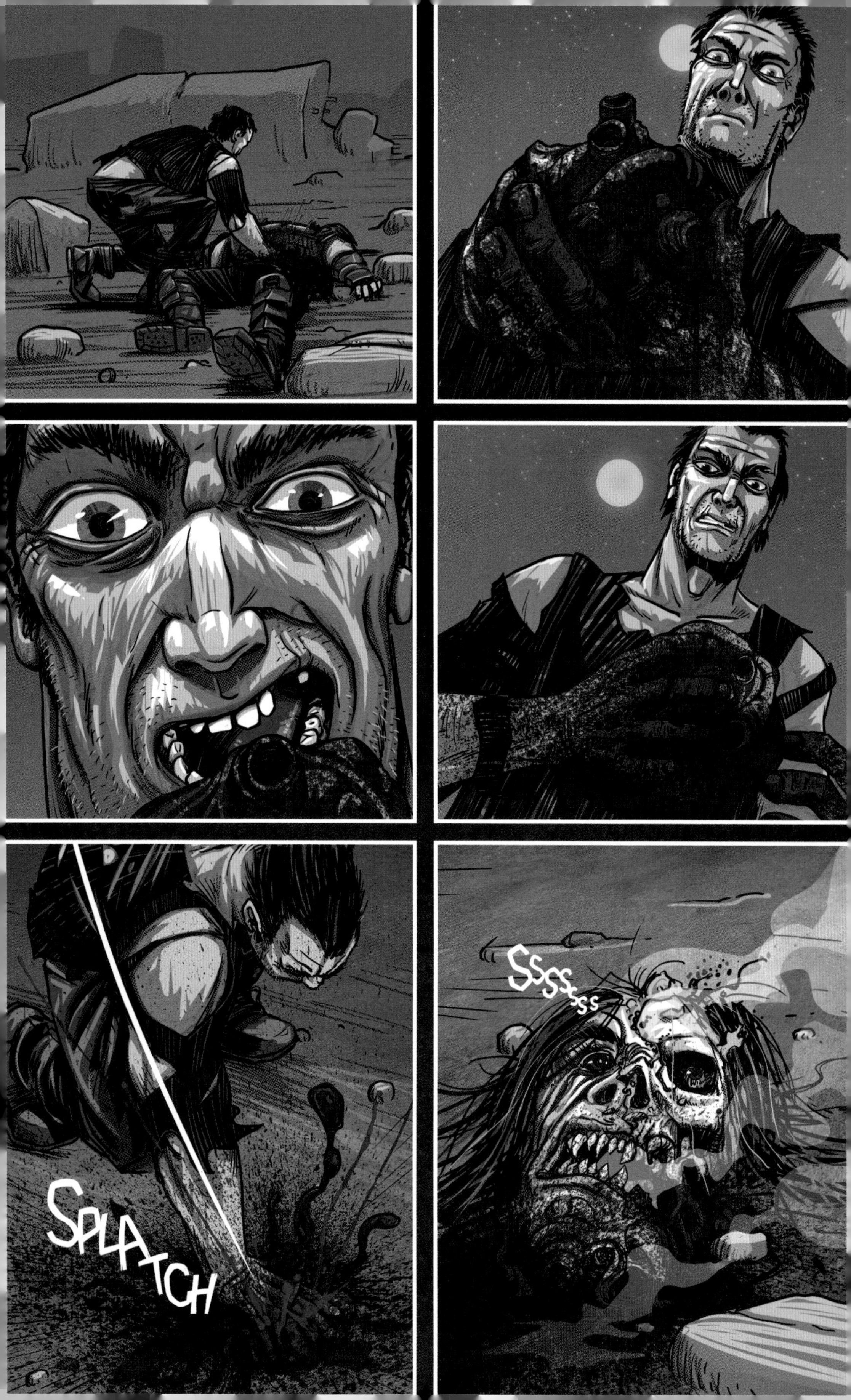
SPLATCH
SSSSsss

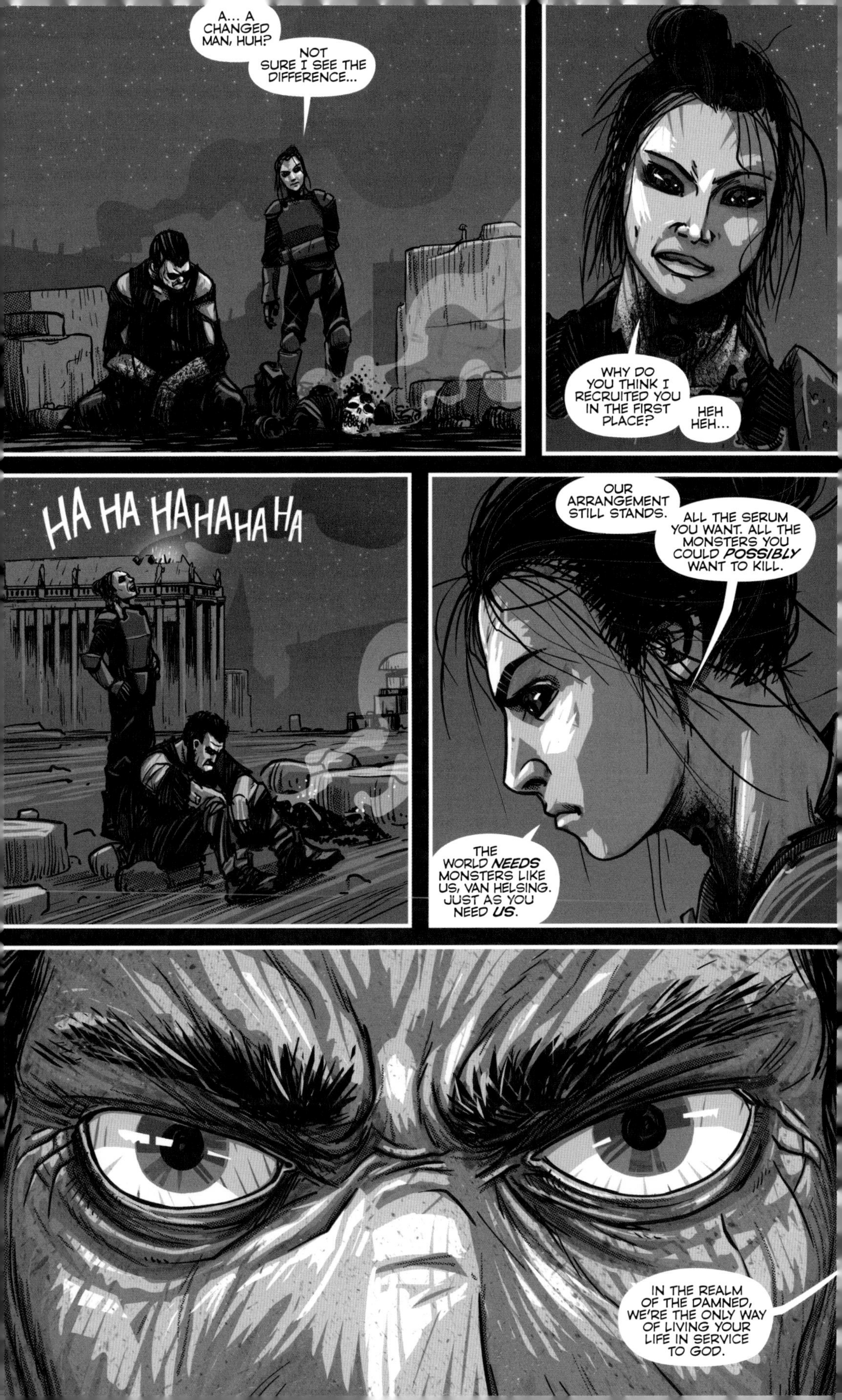
A... A CHANGED MAN, HUH?
NOT SURE I SEE THE DIFFERENCE...
WHY DO YOU THINK I RECRUITED YOU IN THE FIRST PLACE?
HEH HEH...
HA HA HAHAHAHA HA
OUR ARRANGEMENT STILL STANDS.
ALL THE SERUM YOU WANT. ALL THE MONSTERS YOU COULD *POSSIBLY* WANT TO KILL.
THE WORLD *NEEDS* MONSTERS LIKE US, VAN HELSING. JUST AS YOU NEED *US*.
IN THE REALM OF THE DAMNED, WE'RE THE ONLY WAY OF LIVING YOUR LIFE IN SERVICE TO GOD.

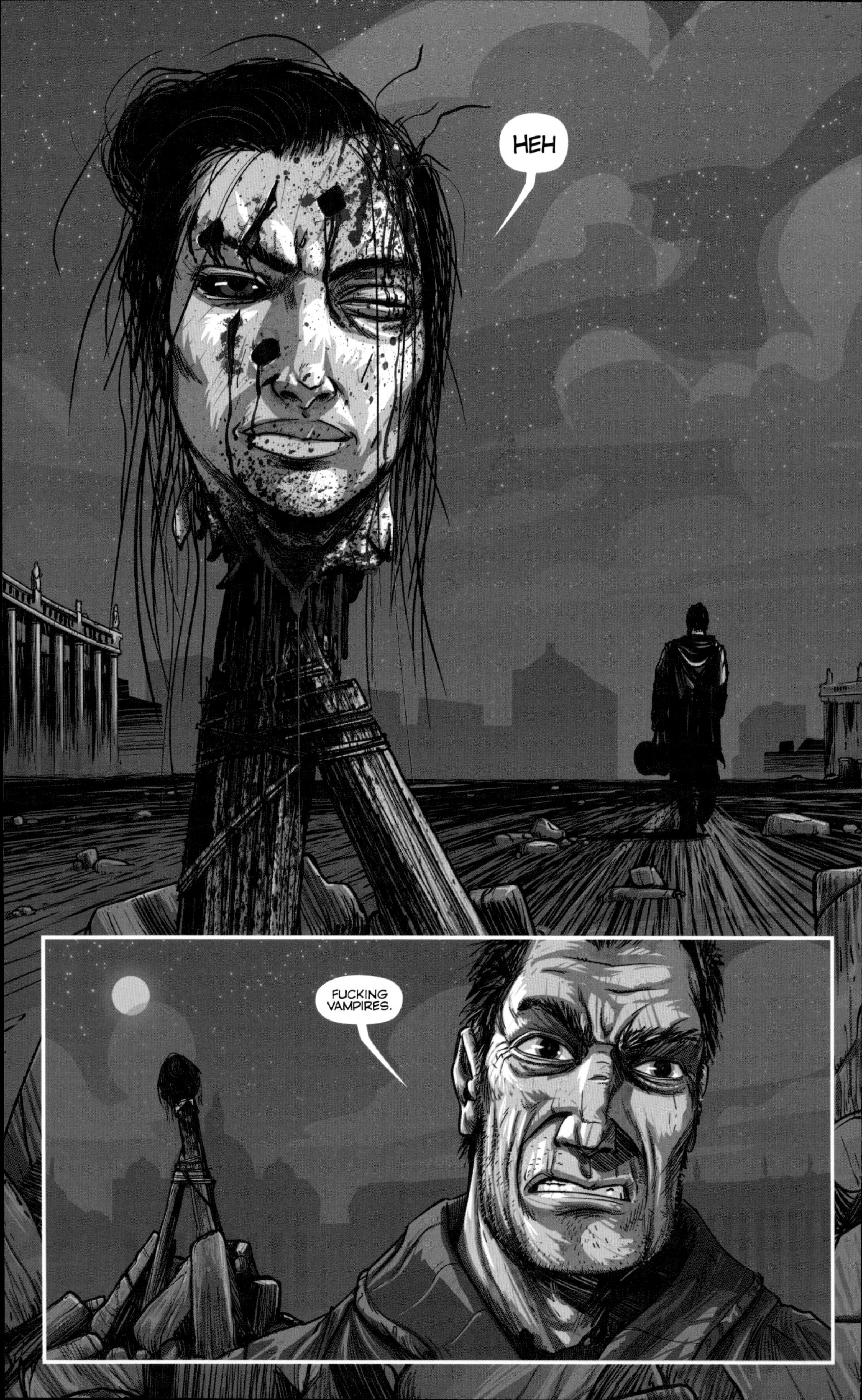
HEH
FUCKING VAMPIRES.

PYE'S SKETCHBOOK

COVER ART PROGRESSION

PENCILS

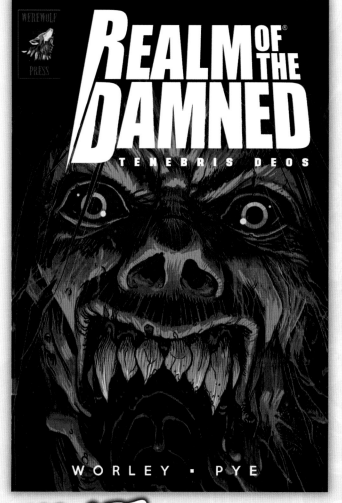

WEREWOLF PRESS

REALM OF® THE DAMNED

TENEBRIS DEOS

WORLEY • PYE

PYE'S SKETCHBOOK

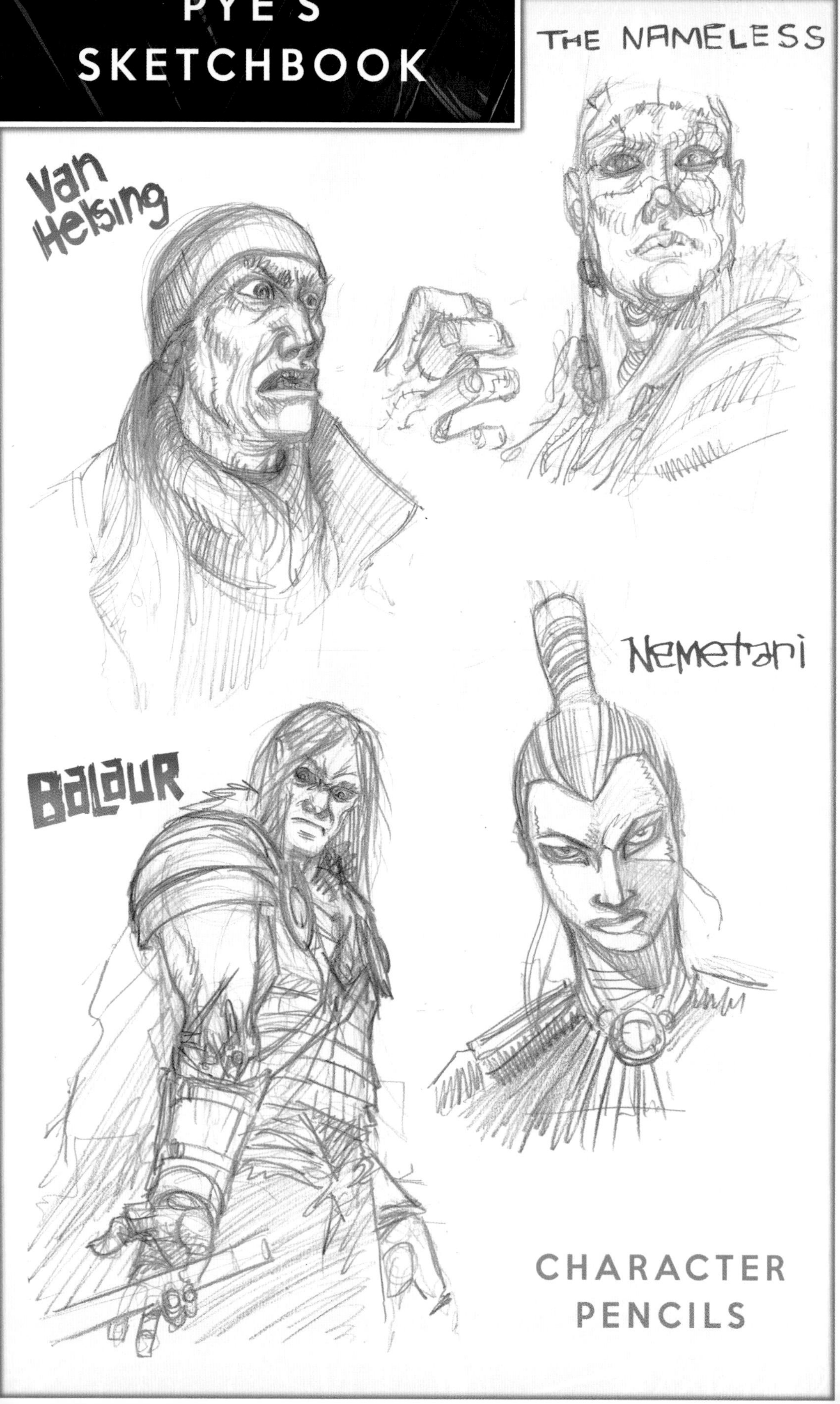

THE NAMELESS
Van Helsing
Nemetari
Balaur

CHARACTER PENCILS

PYE'S SKETCHBOOK

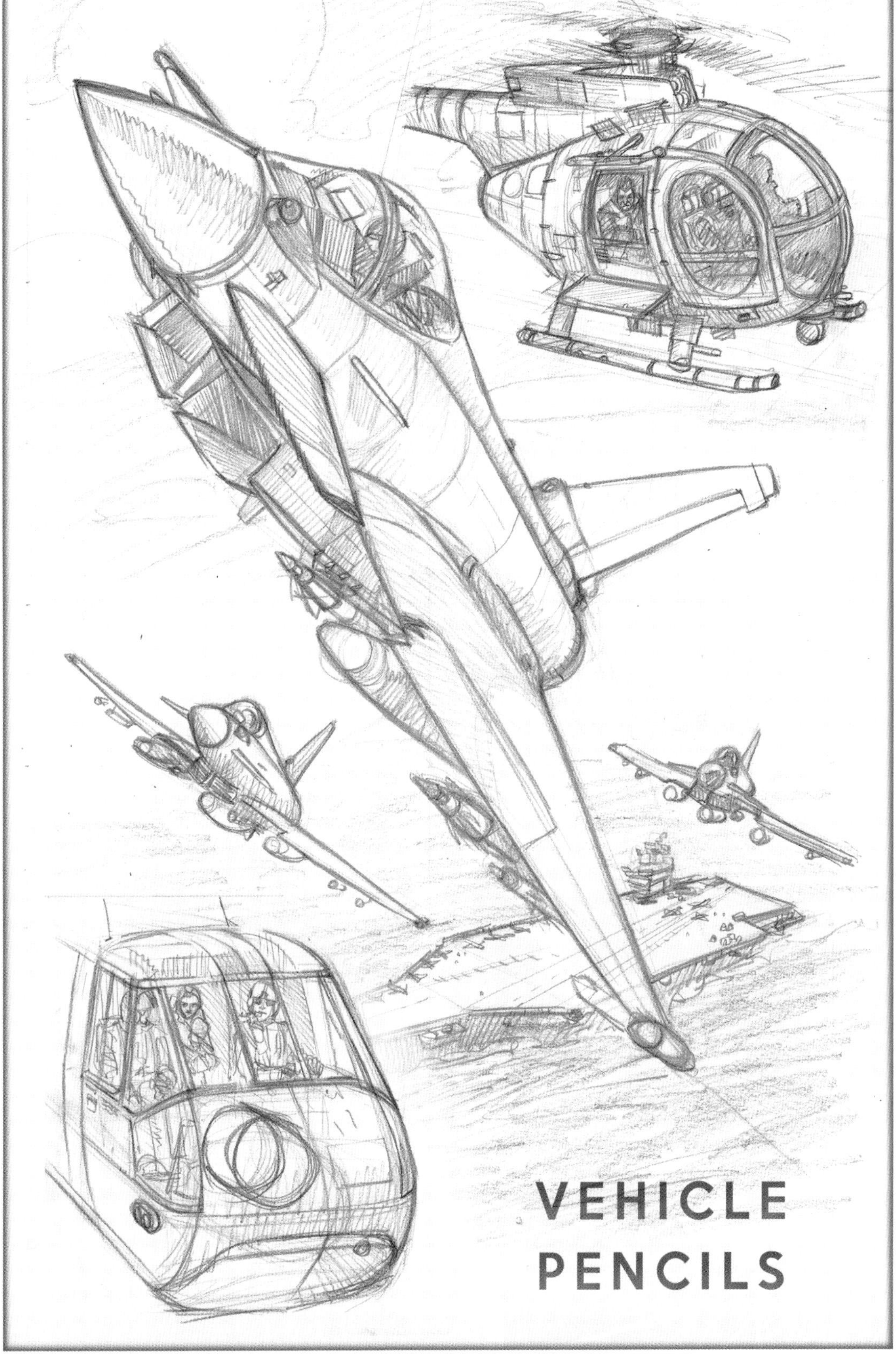

VEHICLE PENCILS

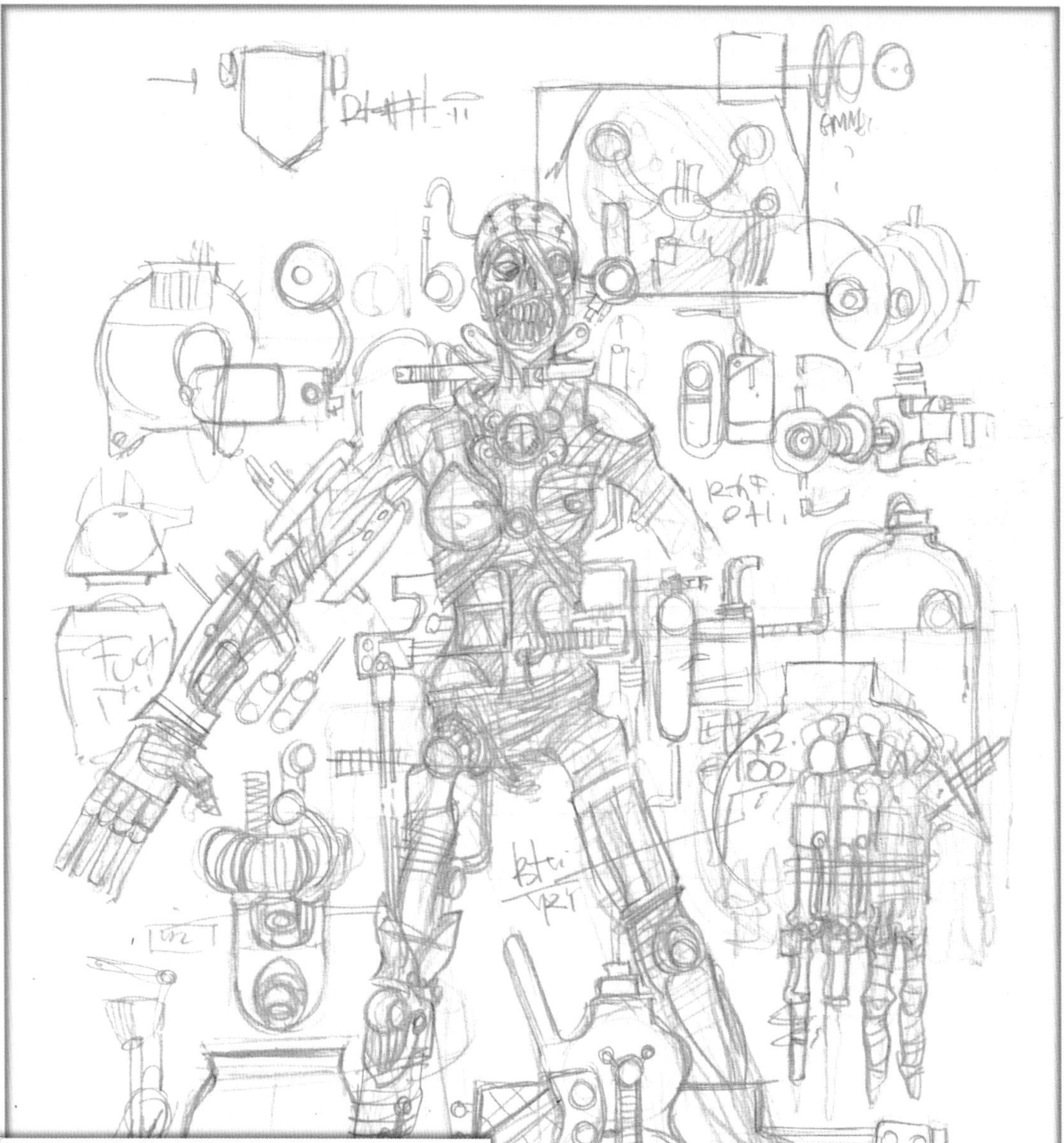

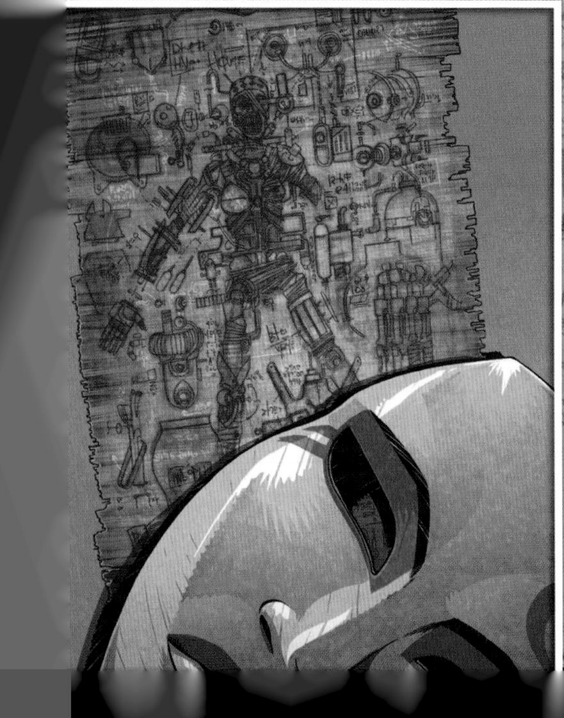

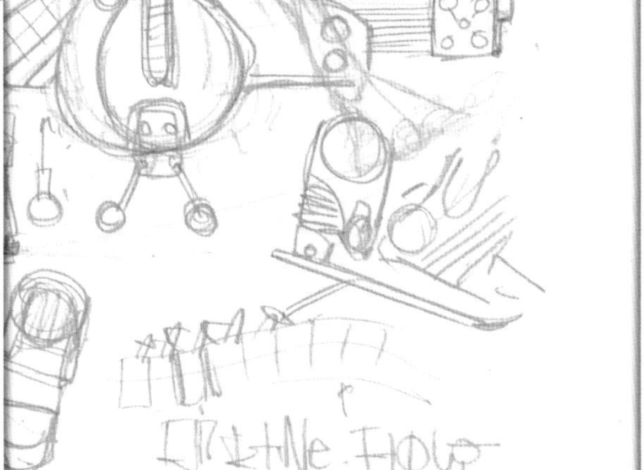

PYE'S SKETCHBOOK

PYE'S SKETCHBOOK

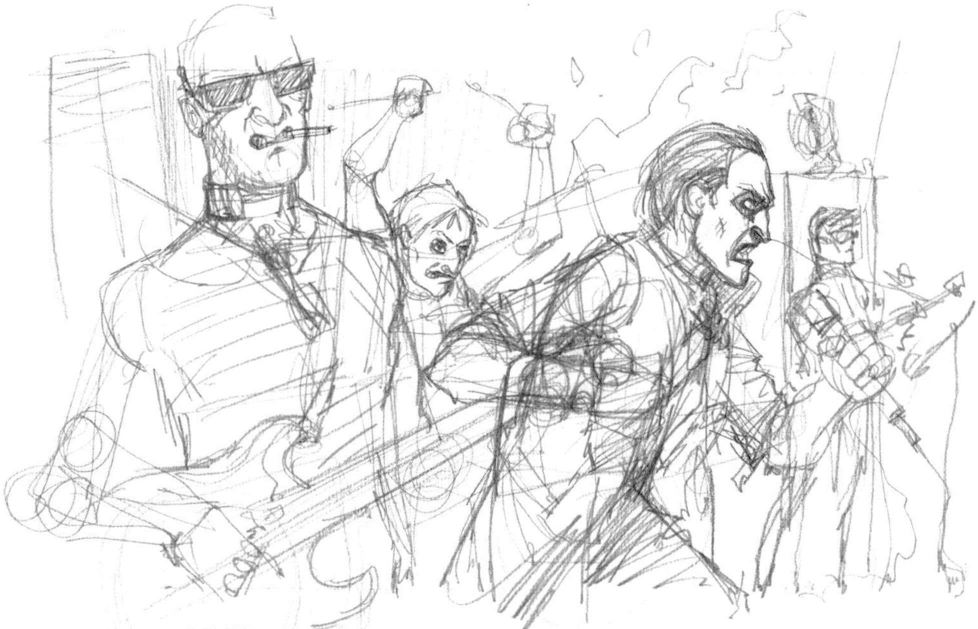

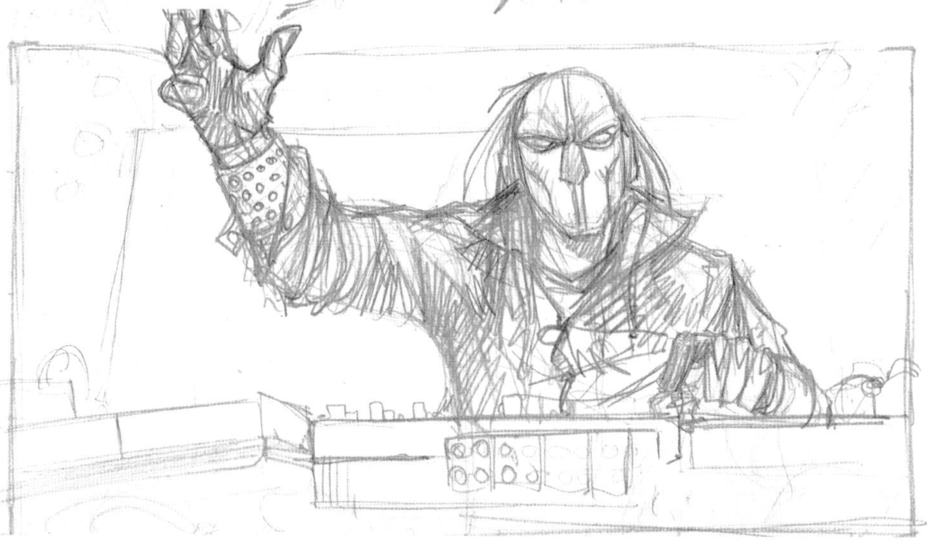

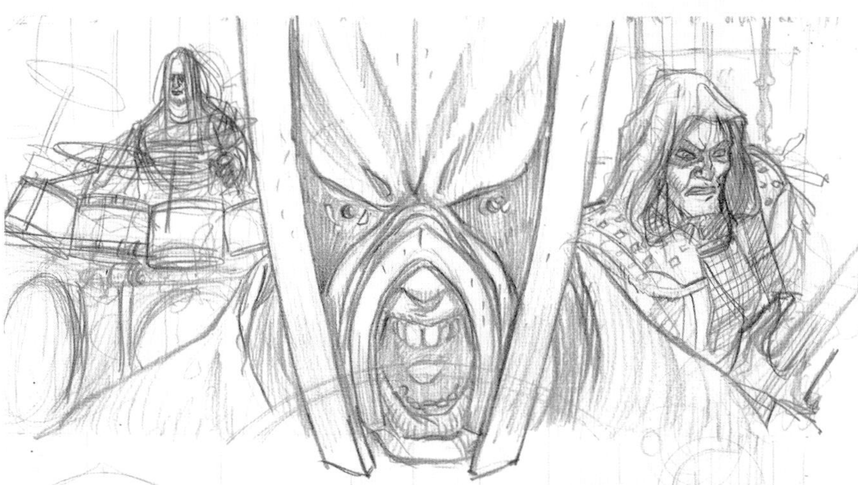

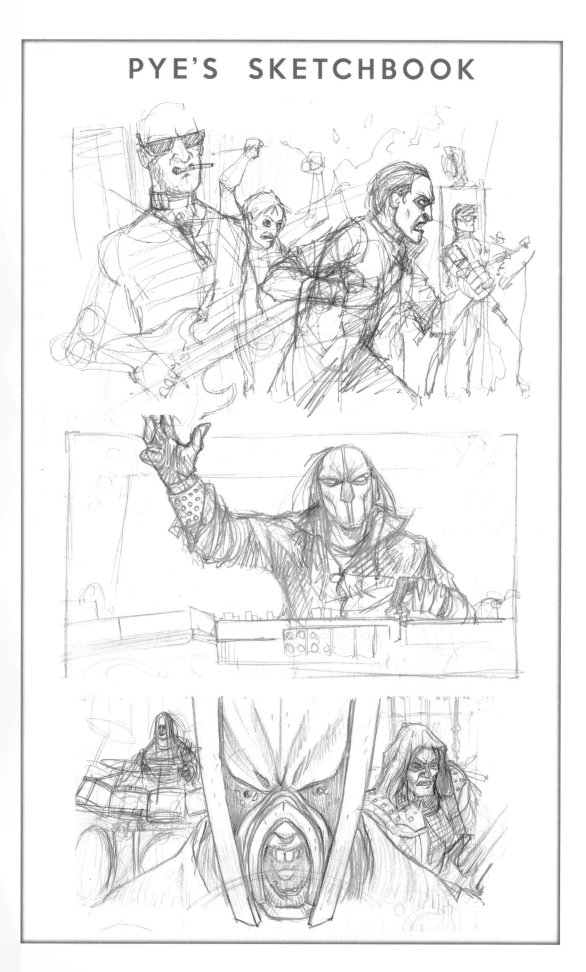

PYE'S SKETCHBOOK

BALAUR

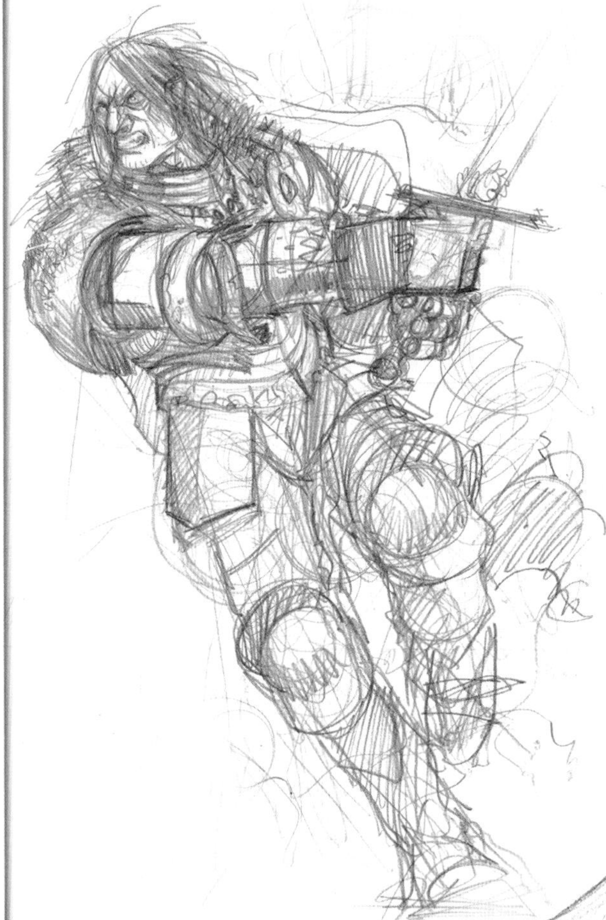

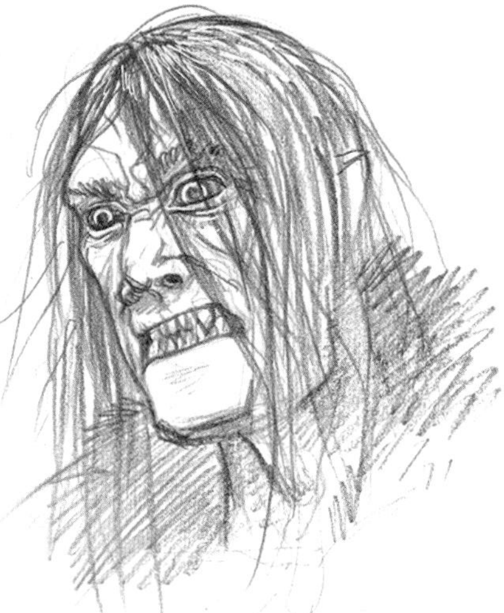

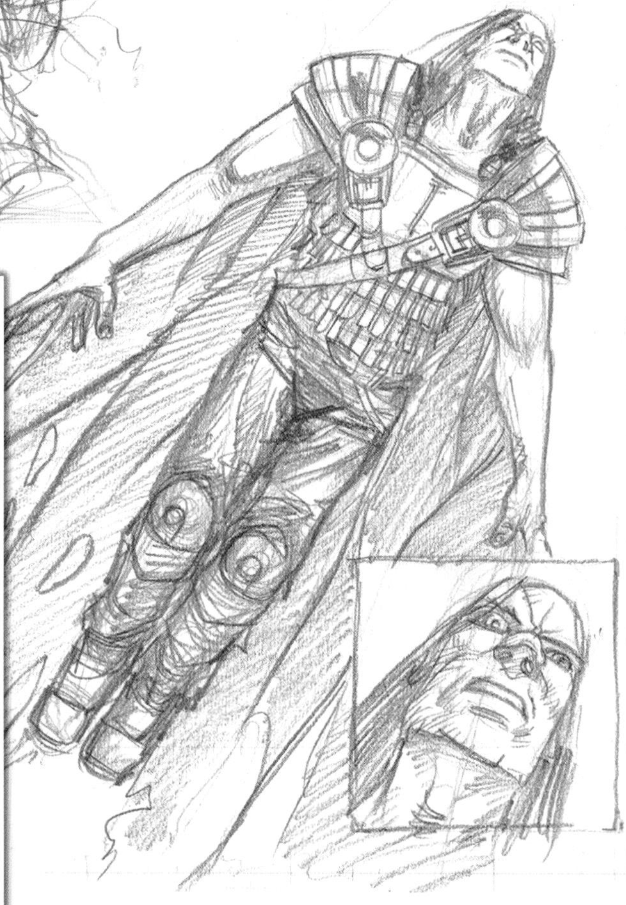

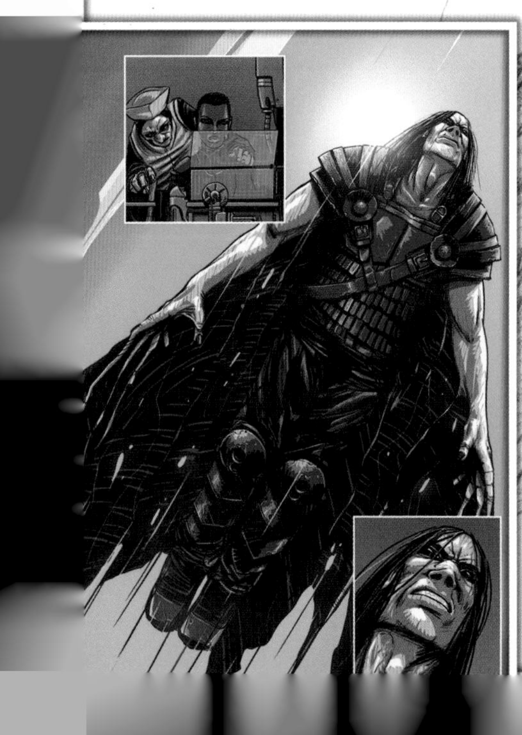

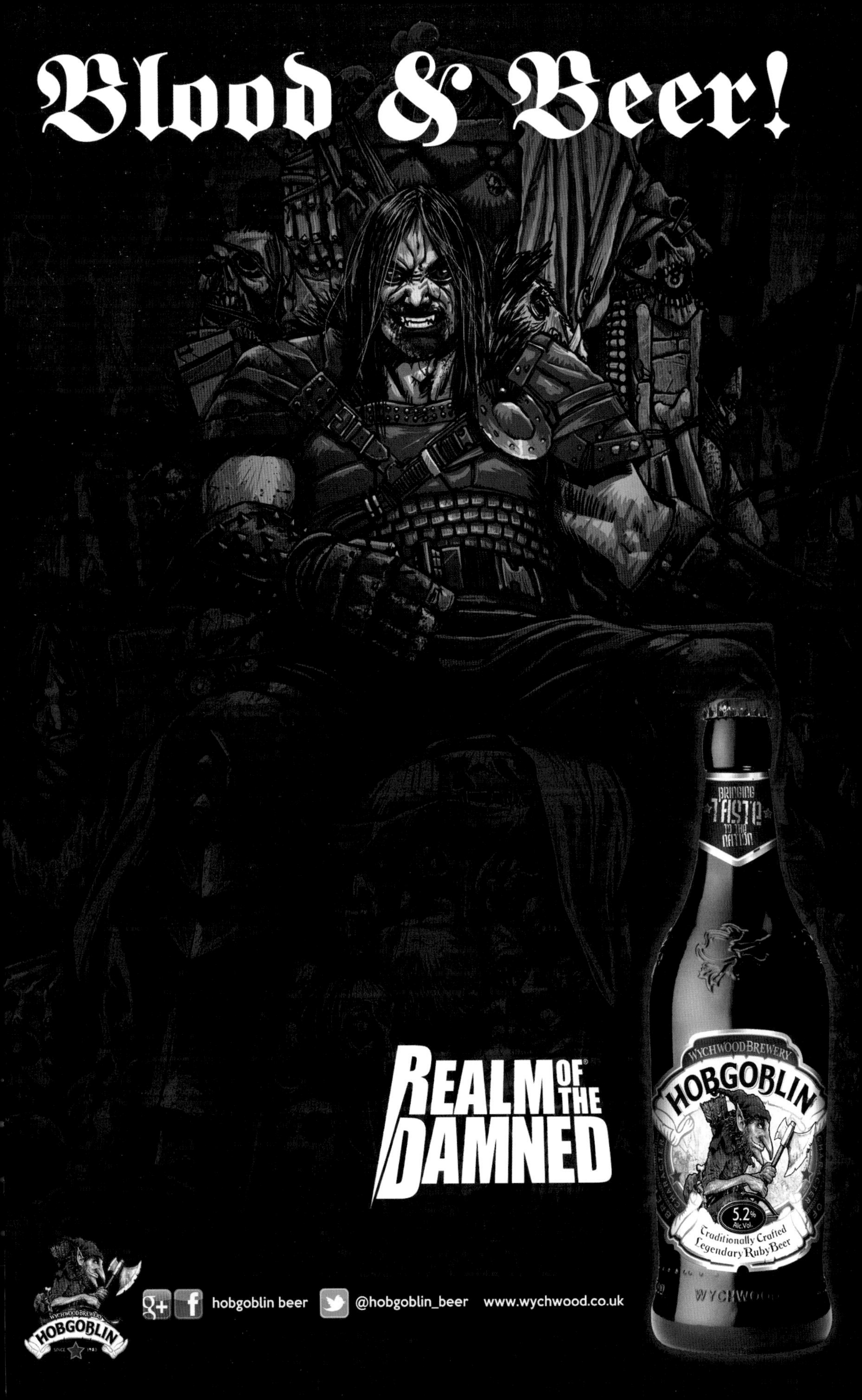

Blood & Beer!
REALM OF THE DAMNED
BRINGING TASTE TO THE NATION
WYCHWOOD BREWERY
HOBGOBLIN
5.2% Alc.Vol.
Traditionally Crafted Legendary Ruby Beer
hobgoblin beer
@hobgoblin_beer
www.wychwood.co.uk

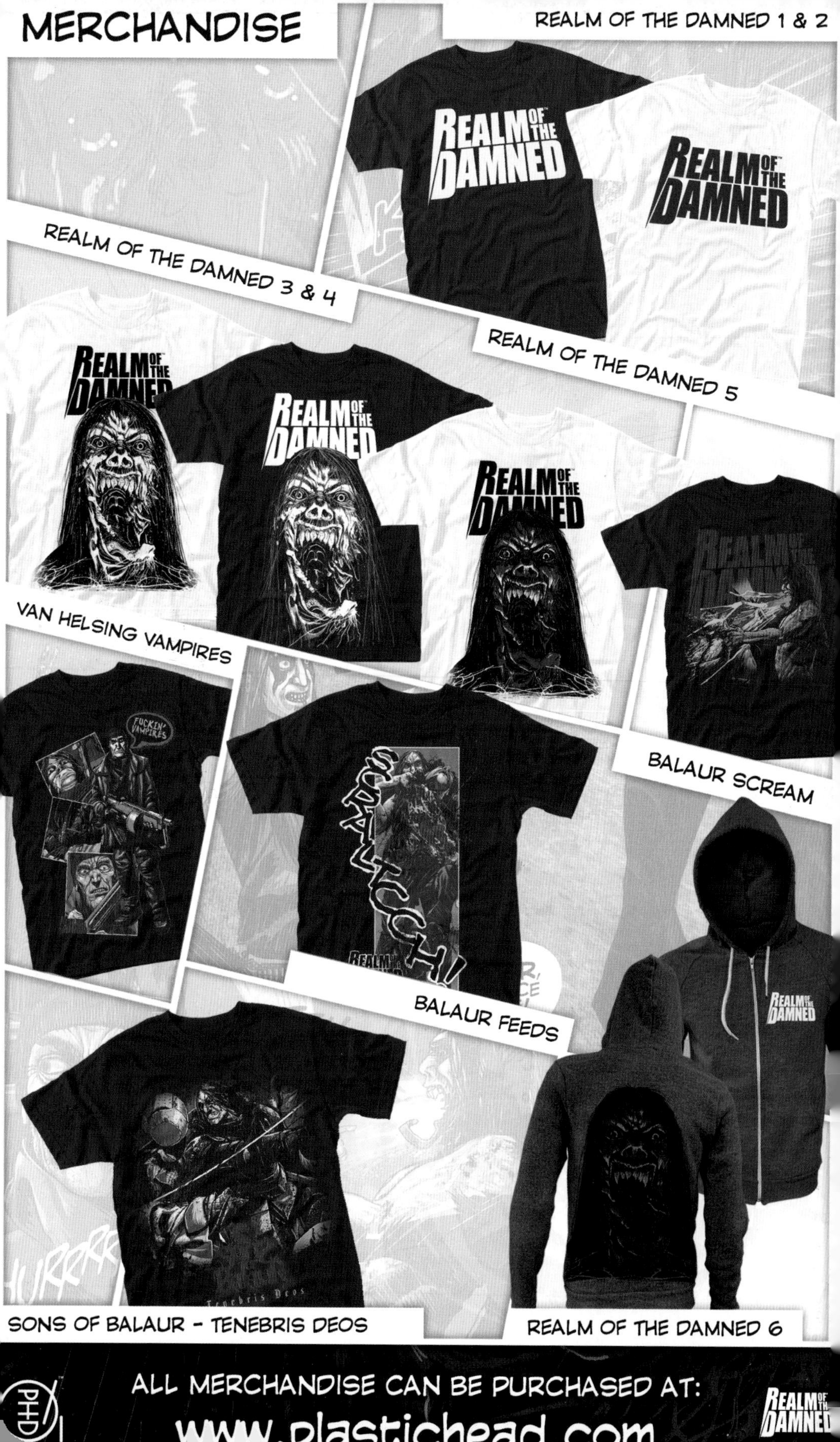
MERCHANDISE
REALM OF THE DAMNED 1 & 2
REALM OF THE DAMNED 3 & 4
REALM OF THE DAMNED 5
VAN HELSING VAMPIRES
FUCKIN' VAMPIRES
BALAUR SCREAM
BALAUR FEEDS
SONS OF BALAUR - TENEBRIS DEOS
Tenebris Deos
REALM OF THE DAMNED 6
ALL MERCHANDISE CAN BE PURCHASED AT:
www.plastichead.com
REALM OF THE DAMNED